MathFlare

Name: _______________________

Class: ___________

Teacher: _______________________

<u>Introduction</u>

As parents and educators, we recognize the pivotal role mathematics plays in shaping a child's academic journey and future success. Yet, the path to mathematical proficiency can often seem daunting, fraught with challenges and complexities. That's where the transformative power of MathFlare Workbooks shine through, illuminating the way forward with clarity, precision, and purpose.

Introducing MathFlare Workbooks – a beacon of guidance, a testament to excellence, and a catalyst for achievement. Crafted with meticulous care and expertise, MathFlare Workbooks stand as paragons of educational excellence, designed to nurture young minds, ignite a passion for learning, and develop a deep-rooted understanding of mathematical concepts.

Picture this: your child eagerly delves into the pages of Mathflare Workbook, greeted by a step-by-step guide illuminated with vivid examples that demystify complex mathematical concepts. With each turn of the page, they embark on a journey of discovery, encountering thoughtfully curated practice questions that reinforce learning and hone problem-solving skills. And when they unveil the answers to those very questions, a sense of accomplishment blossoms within them – a tangible reward for their hard work and dedication.

But MathFlare Workbooks are more than just tools for learning; they are pathways to comprehension, fostering a deep-seated understanding of mathematical concepts through a sequential, logical flow. From fundamental principles to advanced problem-solving strategies, every chapter builds upon the last, ensuring a robust foundation upon which future knowledge can be constructed.

As parents, we yearn for nothing more than to see our children thrive, to witness the spark of inspiration ignited within them as they conquer academic challenges with confidence and poise. MathFlare Workbooks serve as partners in this noble endeavor, offering not just practice questions, but the keys to unlocking a world of opportunity.

And for teachers, MathFlare Workbooks stand as invaluable allies in the quest to cultivate mathematical proficiency in the classroom. With answers readily available, instructors can focus on guiding and nurturing their students, confident in the knowledge that MathFlare Workbooks provide a solid framework upon which to build.

In the pages of MathFlare Workbooks, we find not just the promise of academic excellence, but the seeds of a brighter tomorrow. So let us embrace the power of mathematics, let us champion the journey of learning, and let us pave the way for a generation of young minds poised to shape the world. With MathFlare Workbooks as our guide, the possibilities are infinite, and the future, bright.

Table of Contents

MathFlare
Grade 2
MATH WORKBOOK
Step by Step Guide and Essential Practice with Answers
Addition Subtraction
Multiplication
Place Value and Expanded Notations
Geometry
MathFlare Publishing

MathFlare
Grade 2-3
MATH WORKBOOK
Step by Step Guide and Essential Practice with Answers
Addition Subtraction
Multiplication and Division
Place Value and Expanded Notations
Geometry
MathFlare Publishing

MathFlare
Grade 3
MATH WORKBOOK
Step by Step Guide and Essential Practice with Answers
Multiplication and Division
Decimals
Place Value and Expanded Notations
Fractions and Geometry
MathFlare Publishing

MathFlare
Grade 1
MATH WORKBOOK
Step by Step Guide and Essential Practice with Answers
Counting and Numbers
Addition and Subtraction
Place Value and Expanded Notations
Understanding Time
MathFlare Publishing

MathFlare
Grade 1-2
MATH WORKBOOK
Step by Step Guide and Essential Practice with Answers
Counting and Numbers
Addition and Subtraction
Place Value and Expanded Notations
Understanding Time
MathFlare Publishing

MathFlare
Grade 3-4
MATH WORKBOOK
Step by Step Guide and Essential Practice with Answers
Addition Subtraction
Multiplication Division
Place Value and Expanded Notations
Fractions and Geometry
MathFlare Publishing

MathFlare
Grade 4
MATH WORKBOOK
Step by Step Guide and Essential Practice with Answers
Addition Subtraction
Multiplication Division
Place Value and Expanded Notations
Fractions and Geometry
MathFlare Publishing

MathFlare
Grade 4-5
MATH WORKBOOK
Step by Step Guide and Essential Practice with Answers
Multiplication Division
Place Value and Expanded Notations
Fractions and Geometry
Unit Conversion
MathFlare Publishing

MathFlare
Grade 5
MATH WORKBOOK
Step by Step Guide and Essential Practice with Answers
Multiplication Division
Place Value and Expanded Notation
Fractions and Geometry
Unit Conversion
MathFlare Publishing

MathFlare
Grade 5-6
MATH WORKBOOK
Step by Step Guide and Essential Practice with Answers
Multiplication Division
Place Value and Expanded Notation
Fractions and Geometry
Units and Statistics
MathFlare Publishing

MathFlare
Grade 6
MATH WORKBOOK
Step by Step Guide and Essential Practice with Answers
Integers and Statistics
Arithmetic and Pre-Algebra
Fractions and Geometry
Ratio and Percentage
MathFlare Publishing

MathFlare
Grade 6-7
MATH WORKBOOK
Step by Step Guide and Essential Practice with Answers
Arithmetic and Pre-Algebra
Ratio, Percent Proportion
Geometry
Statistics
MathFlare Publishing

MathFlare
Grade 7
MATH WORKBOOK
Step by Step Guide and Essential Practice with Answers
Pre-Algebra
Ratio, Percent Proportion
Geometry
Statistics
MathFlare Publishing

MathFlare
Grade 7-8
MATH WORKBOOK
Step by Step Guide and Essential Practice with Answers
Pre-Algebra
Ratio, Percent Proportion
Geometry and Cartesian Plane
Statistics
MathFlare Publishing

MathFlare
Grade 8-9
MATH WORKBOOK
Step by Step Guide and Essential Practice with Answers
Pre-Algebra
Ratio, Proportion and Percentage
Linear Equations
Geometry and Cartesian Plane
MathFlare Publishing

MathFlare
Grade 8
MATH WORKBOOK
Step by Step Guide and Essential Practice with Answers
Pre-Algebra
Percentage
Linear Equations
Geometry
MathFlare Publishing

Operations with Rational Numbers

Positive and negative integers are whole numbers that can represent quantities greater than zero and less than zero, respectively.

Positive Integers: Positive integers are whole numbers greater than zero. They are denoted by the numbers 1,2,3,4...

Negative Integers: Negative integers are whole numbers less than zero. They are denoted by placing a negative sign ("-") before the numbers, such as −1,−2,−3,−4,...

The positive integers are used to represent the number of objects, scores, etc. whereas the negative integers can be used to represent debt, losses, temperatures below freezing points, etc.

Let's solve some problems:

$$1. \quad 6 - (- 8) - 9$$

- Start by simplifying within the parentheses:

$$- (-8) \text{ becomes } 8.$$

- Rewrite the expression with the simplified part:

$$6 + 8 - 9.$$

- Now perform addition and subtraction from left to right:

$$6 + 8 = 14, \text{ then } 14 - 9 = 5$$

$$2. \quad (- 5) - (- 3) + 10$$

$$(-5) + 3 + 10$$

$$(-5) + 3 = - 2, \text{ then } - 2 + 10 = 8$$

Order of Operations (PEMDAS)

The order of operations, often remembered by the acronym PEMDAS, stands for:

- **Parentheses**: Perform operations inside parentheses first.
- **Exponents**: Evaluate exponents (powers and roots) next.
- **Multiplication and Division**: Perform multiplication and division from left to right.
- **Addition and Subtraction**: Perform addition and subtraction from left to right.

The order of operations helps to clarify which operations should be performed first in a mathematical expression to ensure consistent and accurate results.

- **Parentheses**: Evaluate expressions within parentheses first. If there are nested parentheses, start with the innermost ones and work your way out.

    1. Example: $2 \times (3 + 4) = 2 \times 7 = 14$

- **Exponents**: Evaluate expressions with exponents (powers and roots) next.

    1. Example: $2^3 + 4 = 8 + 4 = 12$

- **Multiplication and Division**: Perform multiplication and division from left to right.

    1. Example: $2 \times 3 + 4 = 6 + 4 = 10$

    2. Example: $6 \div 2 \times 3 = 3 \times 3 = 9$

- **Addition and Subtraction**: Perform addition and subtraction from left to right.

    1. Example: $2 + 3 \times 4 = 2 + 12 = 14$

    2. Example: $10 - 4 \div 2 = 10 - 2 = 8$

Combining and Distributing Terms

The distributive property is a fundamental concept in algebra that helps simplify expressions by distributing terms. Understanding the distributive property is essential for simplifying, factoring, expanding expressions and solving equations in algebra.

The distributive property states that for any numbers a, b, and c, the expression $a\times(b+c)$ is equal to $a\times b+a\times c$. In other words, we can distribute the term a across the terms inside the parentheses.

Combining and Distributing Terms:

1. **Combining Like Terms:** Combining like terms involves adding or subtracting terms that have the same variable and exponent.

2. **Distributing Terms:** Distributing terms involves multiplying a term outside parentheses by each term inside the parentheses.

Let's solve some examples:

1. **Combining Like Terms:** $-6m+6m$

    The terms $-6m$ and $6m$ cancel each other out, resulting in 0.

    $$-6m+6m=0$$

2. **Distributing Terms:** $-7(8x+7)-3(2-7x)$

    Distribute -7 and -3 across the terms inside the parentheses:

    $$-7\times 8x-7\times 7-3\times 2+3\times 7x$$

    $$-56x-49-6+21x$$

    Combine like terms:

$$-56x + 21x - 49 - 6$$

$$-35x - 55$$

3. **Combining and Distributing Terms:** $(1 + 6m) \times -5 - 3(3m + 2)$

   Distribute -5 and -3 across the terms inside the parentheses:

   $$-5 \times 1 - 5 \times 6m - 3 \times 3m - 3 \times 2$$

   $$-5 - 30m - 9m - 6$$

   Combine like terms:

   $$-5 - 36m - 6$$

   $$-36m - 11$$

Equations and Expressions

Solving One-Step Equations

Solving one-step equations involves finding the value of the variable that makes the equation true. In a one-step equation, there is only one operation (addition, subtraction, multiplication, or division) performed on the variable.

The goal is to isolate the variable on one side of the equation by performing inverse operations.

For example:

Given the equation $6 = -3z$, where we want to solve for z.

The given equation is already in the form of a one-step equation, with z being multiplied by -3.

To isolate z, we need to perform the inverse operation of multiplication, which is division.

Divide both sides by -3:

$$\frac{6}{-3} = \frac{-3z}{-3}$$

Simplify:

$$-2 = z$$

So, the solution to the equation is $z = -2$.

When we substitute the value of z = −2 back into the original equation, 6 = −3(-2), it simplifies to 6 = 6. This confirms that our solution is correct because it satisfies the original equation.

Solving Two-Step Equations

Solving two-step equations involves finding the value of the variable that makes the equation true. In a two-step equation, two operations (addition, subtraction, multiplication, or division) are performed on the variable.

The goal is to isolate the variable on one side of the equation by performing inverse operations in the reverse order of operations.

For example:

Given the equation 18 = (10 + b) − 2, where we want to solve for b.

To solve for b, we need to undo the operations that have been performed on b.

1. Undo the subtraction by adding 2 to both sides:

$$18 + 2 = (10 + b) - 2 + 2$$

$$20 = 10 + b$$

2. Undo the addition by subtracting 10 from both sides:

$$20 - 10 = 10 + b - 10$$

$$10 = b$$

So, the solution to the equation is b = 10

Let's substitute b = 10 back into the original equation to verify if it satisfies the equation:

Original equation:

$$18 = (10 + b) - 2:$$

Substitute b = 10:

$$18 = (10 + 10) - 2$$

simplify:

$$18 = 20 - 2$$

$$18 = 18$$

Since the equation simplifies to 18 =1 8, it confirms that our solution b = 10 is correct.

Solving Multi-Step Equations

Solving multi-step equations involves finding the value of the variable that makes the equation true. In a multi-step equation, multiple operations (addition, subtraction, multiplication, or division) are performed on the variable.

The goal is to isolate the variable on one side of the equation by performing inverse operations in the reverse order of operations.

Example:

Given the equation $-3m - m = -8$, where we want to solve for m.

To solve for m, we need to undo the operations that have been performed on m.

1. Combine like terms on the left side:

$$-3m - m = -4m$$

2. Substitute the combined term back into the equation:

$$-4m = -8$$

3. Undo the multiplication by dividing both sides by $-4-4$:

$$\frac{-4m}{-4} = \frac{-8}{-4}$$

$$m = 2$$

Let's substitute m = 2 back into the original equation to verify if it satisfies the equation:

Original equation:

$$-3m - m = -8$$

Substitute m = 2:

$$-3(2) - 2 = -8$$

simplify:

$$-6 - 2 = -8$$

$$-8 = -8$$

Since the equation simplifies to 8 = 8, it confirms that our solution m = 2 is correct.

Solving Equations (One Side)

Solving one-step equations involves performing a single operation to isolate the variable and find its value.

Let's solve an equation step by step: 16 + x = 31

1. **Identify the Goal:**

    The goal is to isolate the variable x on one side of the equation.

2. **Simplify the Equation**: Combine like terms on both sides of the equation, if necessary.

    The equation is already simplified.

3. **Undo Addition or Subtraction**: If there's addition or subtraction involving the variable, undo it by performing the opposite operation on both sides of the equation.

Since x is being added to 16, we'll undo this operation by subtracting 16 from both sides of the equation:

$$16 + x - 16 = 31 - 16$$

4. **Isolate the Variable**: Ensure that the variable is alone on one side of the equation.

$$x = 15$$

5. **Check Your Solution**: Substitute the value of x back into the original equation to verify that it satisfies the equation.

$$16 + 15 = 31$$

$$31 = 31$$

The equation is balanced.

Equations (Two Sides)

A two-sided equation is an equation where both sides have expressions with variables and constants. The goal when solving a two-sided equation is to find the value of the variable that makes both sides equal.

For example: Let's solve an equation:

$$9 + 8x + 8 = 64 + x + 2$$

- **Combine Like Terms**: Simplify each side of the equation by combining like terms (terms with the same variable or constants).

$$9 + 8x + 8 = 64 + x + 2$$
$$17 + 8x = 66 + x$$

- **Isolate the Variable**: Use inverse operations to isolate the variable on one side of the equation.

subtract x from both sides:

$$17 + 8x - x = 66 + x - x$$

$$17 + 7x = 66$$

subtracting 17 from both sides:

$$17 - 17 + 7x = 66 - 17$$

$$7x = 49$$

divide both sides by 7:

$$\frac{7x}{7} = \frac{49}{7} = x = 7$$

- **Check Solution:** Once you find the solution, substitute it back into the original equation to ensure it makes the equation true.

Substitute $x = 7$ back into the original equation:

$$9 + 8(7) + 8 = 64 + 7 + 2$$

$$9 + 56 + 8 = 64 + 7 + 2$$

$$73 = 73$$

Simplifying expressions

It involves combining like terms and performing operations to make the expression easier to understand and work with.

Let's simplify the expression:

$$2x - 2x + 8 + 4$$

- **Combine like terms:** First, we look for terms with the same variable and exponent. In this expression, $2x$ and $-2x$ are like terms, so they can be combined:

$$2x - 2x = 0$$

- **Substitute the simplified terms:** After combining the like terms, the expression becomes:

$$0 + 8 + 4$$

- **Combine the remaining terms:** Now, we add the constants together:

$$8 + 4 = 12$$

Let's solve another problem:

$$-7m - 3 - 3 - 6m$$

combine like terms

$$-7m - 6m - 3 - 3$$

$$13m - 6$$

<u>Evaluate Expressions</u>

Evaluating expressions involves substituting given values for variables in an expression and then performing the indicated operations to find the result.

For example: Let's evaluate $4x - 10$, when $x = 3$:

Step 1: Substitute the given value for the variable:

Replace every occurrence of x in the expression $4x - 10$ with the given value, which is 3:

$$= 4(3) - 10$$

Step 2: Perform the operations:

Perform the indicated operations according to the order of operations (PEMDAS - Parentheses, Exponents, Multiplication and Division, Addition and Subtraction):

$$= 4 \times 3 - 10$$

Step 3: Simplify:

Calculate the result:

$$12 - 10 = 2$$

Solving Inequalities

Inequalities are mathematical expressions that compare the relative sizes of two values. They are used to express relationships where one quantity is:

- "$<$" (less than),
- "$>$" (greater than),
- "$<=$" (less than or equal to),
- "$>=$" (greater than or equal to),
- and "$\neq$" (not equal to) another quantity.

For example:

$$y + -10 \leq -8$$

To isolate y, we need to get rid of the constant term -10. Since -10 is being subtracted from y, we can undo this operation by adding 10 to both sides of the inequality:

$$y - 10 + 10 \leq -8 + 10$$

$$y \leq 2$$

To check the solution:

$$2 - 10 \leq -8$$

$$-8 = -8$$

The inequality is true when $y = 2$

Linear Equation

A linear equation is an algebraic equation that represents a straight line when graphed on a coordinate plane. It consists of variables raised to the power of 1 (i.e., no exponents higher than 1) and constant coefficients.

The general form of a linear equation in one variable x is:

$$ax + b = 0$$

Where a and b are constants, and x is the variable.

Let's solve the linear equation:

$$-2x + 9 = 5$$

- **Isolate the variable term:** We want to isolate the term containing x on one side of the equation. To do this, we'll move the constant term to the other side. Subtract 9 from both sides:

$$-2x + 9 - 9 = 5 - 9$$

$$-2x = -4$$

- **Divide by the coefficient of the variable:** To solve for x, divide both sides by the coefficient of x, which is -2:

$$\frac{-2x}{-2} = \frac{-4}{-2}$$

$$x = 2$$

<u>Slop from Two Points</u>

The slope between two points on a Cartesian coordinate system is a measure of the steepness of the line connecting those points. It's calculated by finding the change in the y-coordinates divided by the change in the x-coordinates.

- The coordinates of the first point as $(x1, y1) = (2, -30)$.

- The coordinates of the second point as $(x2, y2) = (-5, 40)$.

The formula to calculate the slope (m) between two points:

$$\frac{y2 - y1}{x2 - x1}$$

$$= \frac{40 - (-30)}{-5 - 2} = \frac{70}{-7}$$

$$\text{Slope} = -10$$

Graphing Linear Equation

Graphing a linear equation involves plotting the points that satisfy the equation on a coordinate plane and connecting them to form a straight line. Linear equations are equations of the form $y = mx + b$, where m represents the slope of the line, and b represents the y-intercept, the point where the line intersects the y-axis.

To graph a linear equation:

1. Identify the slope (m) and y-intercept (b) from the equation.

2. Plot the y-intercept $(0,b)$) as a point on the y-axis.

3. Use the slope to find additional points on the line. The slope represents the change in y for every unit change in x.

4. Connect the points to form a straight line.

For example, to graph the equation:

$$y = \frac{9}{4}x - 8$$

1. **Identify the slope and y-intercept:** The slope is $\frac{9}{4}$, and the y-intercept is −8.

2. **Plot the y-intercept:** Plot the point $(0,-8)$.

3. **Use the slope to plot additional points:** the slop is $\frac{9}{4}$ to find another point. we will move up 9 units and 4 units to the right from the y-intercept to find another point.

4. **Draw the line:** Once we have at least two points, we can draw a straight line.

We can continue this process to plot more points and extend the line further if needed.

$$y = \frac{9}{4}x - 8$$

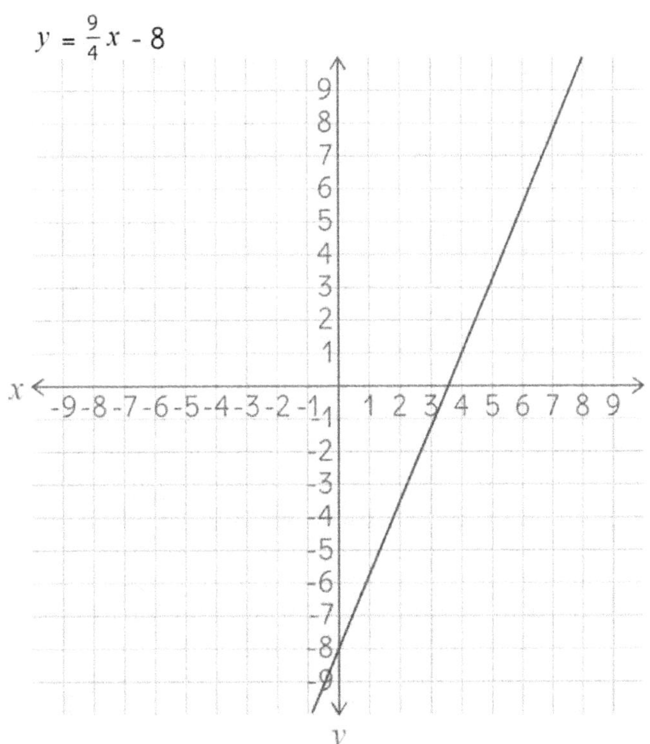

System of Equations

A system of equations is a collection of two or more equations involving the same set of variables. The solution to a system of equations is the set of values for the variables that satisfy all the equations simultaneously.

Solving by Elimination:

To solve a system of equations by elimination, we manipulate the equations to eliminate one of the variables.

Given the system:

$$4x + 5y = 6$$

$$10x + 6y = 8$$

Step 1: Multiply each equation by a constant such that the coefficients of one of the variables become equal or multiples of each other.

Let's try to eliminate the variable x.

- Multiply the first equation by 5 and the second equation by -2:

$$20x + 25y = 30$$

$$-20x - 12y = -16$$

Step 2: Add the two equations together to eliminate the variable x.

$$(20x - 20x) + (25y - 12y) = 30 - 16$$

$$13y = 14$$

Step 3: Solve for y:

$$y = \frac{14}{13} = 1.077$$

Step 4: Substitute the value of y into one of the original equations to solve for x. Let's use the first equation:

$$4x + 5\left(\frac{14}{13}\right) = 6$$

$$4x + \frac{70}{13} = 6$$

$$4x = 6 - \frac{70}{13}$$

$$4x = \frac{78 - 70}{13}$$

$$4x = \frac{8}{13}$$

$$x = \frac{2}{13} = 0.154$$

the solution to the system of equations is x =0.154 and y = 1.077.

Polynomials

A polynomial is an algebraic expression consisting of one or more terms, where each term is a constant, a variable, or a product of constants and variables raised to whole number exponents.

Examples of polynomials include:

- $(7v^2 + 2v^4) + (8v^2 + 4v^4)$
- $(2v + 4v^2 + 2) - (5v - 4v^4 - 6v^2)$
- $(7x - 5y)(2x - 6y)$
- $(6x^2 + 4xy + 6y^2)(8x^2 + 3xy + 3y^2)$
- $\dfrac{2x^3 + 8x^2 + 2x}{2x^2}$

Operations on Polynomials

Addition of Polynomials:

- To add polynomials, simply combine like terms.
- Like terms are terms that have the same variable(s) raised to the same power(s).
- For example, to add $3x^2 + 2x$ and $5x^2 - 7x$, group the like terms: $3x^2 + 5x^2$ and $2x - 7x$, then add each group separately.

Subtraction of Polynomials:

- To subtract polynomials, distribute the negative sign and then add.
- For example, to subtract $x^2 - 2x$ from $4x^2 + 3x$, distribute the negative sign to each term in the second polynomial: $-(x^2 - 2x)$, then add each term separately.

<u>Multiplication of Polynomials:</u>

- To multiply polynomials, use the distributive property and then combine like terms.

- For example, to multiply $(x + 2)(3x - 4)$, distribute each term in the first polynomial to each term in the second polynomial, then combine like terms.

<u>Division of Polynomials:</u>

- Division of polynomials involves dividing one polynomial by another. It can be done using long division or synthetic division.

Let's solve the expression:

$$(7x^2 - 7x) - (x - 2x^2)$$

Step 1: Distribute the Negative Sign:

Distribute the negative sign in the second polynomial:

$$(7x^2 - 7x) - x + 2x^2$$

Step 2: Combine Like Terms:

$$(7x^2 + 2x^2) + (- 7x - x)$$

Step 3: Perform addition and subtraction of coefficients:

$$9x^2 - 8x$$

Let's perform the multiplication of polynomials:

$$(5u + 2v)(8u^2 - uv - 3v^2)$$

We can distribute each term in the first polynomial $(5u+2v)$ to every term in the second polynomial $(8u^2 - uv - 3v^2)$.

1. Multiply $5u$ by each term in the second polynomial:

$$5u \cdot 8u^2 = 40u^3$$

$$5u \cdot (-uv) = -5u^2v$$

$$5u \cdot (-3v^2) = -15uv^2$$

2. Multiply $2v$ by each term in the second polynomial:

$$2v \cdot 8u^2 = 16u^2v$$

$$2v \cdot (-uv) = -2uv^2$$

$$2v \cdot (-3v^2) = -6v^3$$

Combine the like terms:

$$40u^3 - 5u^2v - 15uv^2 + 16u^2v - 2uv^2 - 6v^3$$

Combine the like terms involving u and v.

$$40u^3 + (16u^2v - 5u^2v) + (-15uv^2 - 2uv^2) - 6v^3$$

$$40u^3 + 11u^2v - 17uv^2 - 6v^3$$

Quadratic Equations

A quadratic equation is a polynomial equation of the second degree, meaning it can be written in the form:

$$ax^2 + bx + c = 0$$

where a, b, and c are constants, and x is the variable being solved for. The solutions to a quadratic equation are the values of x that make the equation true.

Now, let's solve the quadratic equation $11x^2 - 1 = 0$ and understand it step by step using quadratic formula.

1. **Identify the coefficients:**

   In the equation $11x^2 - 1 = 0$,

   $$a=11, b=0, \text{ and } c=-1.$$

2. **Apply the quadratic formula:**

   The quadratic formula states that for an equation $ax^2 + bx + c = 0$, the solutions for x are given by:

   $$x = \frac{-b \pm \sqrt{b^2 - 4ac}}{2a}$$

   Plugging in the values a=11, b=0, and c=−1 into the quadratic formula, we get:

   $$x = \frac{-0 \pm \sqrt{0 - 4(11)(-1)}}{2(11)}$$

3. Simplify inside the square root:

$$0^2 - 4(11)(-1) = 0 - (-44) = 44$$

4. Plug in the simplified values:

$$x = \frac{\pm \sqrt{44}}{22}$$

5. Simplify the square root:

Since 44 is not a perfect square, we can write it as $\sqrt[2]{11}$

$$x = \frac{\pm \sqrt[2]{11}}{22}$$

6. Simplify further if possible:

We can simplify $\sqrt[2]{11}$ to $\sqrt{11}$ by canceling out the common factor:

$$x = \frac{\pm \sqrt{11}}{11}$$

7. Final solution:

So, the solutions to the equation are:

$$x = \frac{\sqrt{11}}{11} \text{ and } x = \frac{-\sqrt{11}}{11}$$

or

$$(x = 0.302, \text{ and } x = -0.302)$$

These are the roots of the quadratic equation. They represent the points where the graph of the quadratic equation intersects the x-axis.

Let's solve another equation:

$$-4p^2 + 6p - 6 = 0$$

$$p = \frac{-b \pm \sqrt{b^2 - 4ac}}{2a}$$

where $a = -4$, $b = 6$, and $c = -6$.

Let's plug these values into the quadratic formula:

$$p = \frac{-6 \pm \sqrt{6^2 - 4(-4)(-6)}}{2(-4)}$$

First, let's simplify inside the square root:

$$6^2 - 4(-4)(-6)$$

$$= 36 - 96 = -60$$

So, we have:

$$p = \frac{-6 \pm \sqrt{-60}}{-8}$$

We can simplify the square root of −60 by factoring out −1:

$$\sqrt{-60}$$

$$= \sqrt{-1 \times 60}$$

$$= \sqrt{-1} \times \sqrt{60}$$

$$= i\sqrt{60}$$

So, we have:

$$p = \frac{-6 \pm i\sqrt{60}}{-8}$$

Simplify:

$$\sqrt{60} \text{ to } \sqrt{4 \times 15} = 2\sqrt{15}$$

$$p = \frac{-6 \pm i \times 2\sqrt{15}}{-8}$$

Now, divide both the numerator and denominator by −2 to simplify:

$$p = \frac{3 \pm i\sqrt{15}}{4}$$

So, the solutions to the equation are:

$$p = \frac{3 + i\sqrt{15}}{4} \text{ and } p = \frac{3 - i\sqrt{15}}{4}$$

This equation $-4p^2 + 6p - 6 = 0$ has no real solutions.

When a quadratic equation has no real solutions, it means that the solutions are not real numbers, but rather complex numbers. In this case, the solutions involve the imaginary unit i because the discriminant ($b^2 - 4ac$) is negative, which results in taking the square root of a negative number when applying the quadratic formula.

In mathematics, such equations are said to have "no real roots" or "no real solutions." They are also sometimes referred to as having "complex roots" or "complex solutions." Complex numbers include a real part and an imaginary part, and they are often written in the form $a + bi$, where a and b are real numbers and i is the imaginary unit, defined as $i = \sqrt{-1}$.

Let's solve another equation:

$$12x^2 + 6x - 2 = 0$$

$$x = \frac{-b \pm \sqrt{b^2 - 4ac}}{2a}$$

where $a = 12$, $b = 6$, and $c = -2$.

Let's plug these values into the quadratic formula:

$$x = \frac{-6 \pm \sqrt{6^2 - 4(12)(-2)}}{2(12)}$$

First, let's simplify inside the square root:

$$6^2 - 4(12)(-2)$$

$$= 36 - (-96)$$

$$= 36 + 96$$

$$= 132$$

So, we have:

$$X = \frac{-6 \pm \sqrt{132}}{24}$$

Now, let's simplify the square root of 132:

$$X = \frac{-6 \pm \sqrt{4 \times 33}}{24}$$

$$X = \frac{-6 \pm 2\sqrt{33}}{24}$$

$$X = \frac{-6 \pm \sqrt{33}}{12}$$

So, the solutions to the equation are:

$$X = \frac{-6 + \sqrt{33}}{12} \text{ and } X = \frac{-6 - \sqrt{33}}{12}$$

or (x = 0.229, and x = -0.729)

Let's solve a quadratic equation where the right side is a number, instead of 0.

$$-8n^2 + 6n + 30 = 7$$

To solve the equation, we first need to bring all terms to one side to set the equation equal to zero:

$$-8n^2 + 6n + 30 - 7 = 0$$

Simplify:

$$-8n^2 + 6n + 23 = 0$$

Now, to solve for n, we can use the quadratic formula:

$$n = \frac{-b \pm \sqrt{b^2 - 4ac}}{2a}$$

where $a = -8$, $b = 6$, and $c = 23$.

Plugging these values into the formula, we get:

$$n = \frac{-6 \pm \sqrt{6^2 - 4(-8)(23)}}{2(-8)}$$

$$n = \frac{-6 \pm \sqrt{36 + 736}}{-16}$$

$$n = \frac{-6 \pm \sqrt{772}}{-16}$$

Now, let's simplify the square root of 772. We can factor out 4:

$$\sqrt{772} = \sqrt{4 \times 193} = 2\sqrt{193}$$

So, our equation becomes:

$$n = \frac{-6 \pm 2\sqrt{193}}{-8}$$

So, the solutions to the equation are:

$$n = \frac{-3 + \sqrt{193}}{-8} \text{ and } n = \frac{-3 - \sqrt{193}}{-8}$$

or

$$(n = -1.362, \text{ and } n = 2.112)$$

Exponents and Scientific Notations

<u>Exponents</u>

An exponent tells us how many times a number (called the base) is multiplied by itself. It is written as a superscript to the right of the base number. For example, in 2^3, 2 is the base and 3 is the exponent.

Rules:

1. **Product Rule**: When multiplying powers with the same base, add the exponents.

$$a^m \times a^n = a^{m+n}$$

For example:

$$2^3 = 2 \times 2 \times 2 = 8$$

$$3^2 \times 3^4 = 3^{2+4} = 3^6 = 3 \times 3 \times 3 \times 3 \times 3 \times 3 = 729$$

2. **Quotient Rule**: When dividing powers with the same base, subtract the exponents.

$$a^m \div a^n = a^{m-n}$$

For example:

$$5^3 \div 5^2 = 5^{3-2} = 5^1 = 5$$

3. **Power of a Power Rule**: When raising a power to another power, multiply the exponents.

$$(a^m)^n = a^{mn}$$

For example:

$$(2^2)^3 = 2^{2\times3} = 2^6 = 64$$

4. **Power of a Product Rule**: When raising a product to a power, distribute the power to each factor.

$$(ab)^n = a^n \times b^n$$

For example:

$$(2\times3)^2 = 2^2 \times 3^2 = 4 \times 9 = 36$$

5. **Power of a Quotient Rule**: When raising a quotient to a power, distribute the power to the numerator and denominator separately.

$$\left(\frac{a}{b}\right)^n = \frac{a^n}{b^n}$$

For example:

$$\left(\frac{4}{2}\right)^3 = \frac{4^3}{2^3} = \frac{64}{8} = 8$$

6. **Zero Exponent Rule**: Any nonzero number raised to the power of zero equals 11.

$$a^0 = 1$$

For example:

$$7^0 = 1$$

7. **Negative Exponent Rule**: A negative exponent means the reciprocal of the base raised to the positive exponent.

$$a^{-n} = \frac{1}{a^n}$$

For example:

$$2^{-3} = \frac{1}{2^3} = \frac{1}{8}$$

To evaluate expressions with exponents, we can use:

- **Repeated Multiplication**: Perform the multiplication indicated by the exponent.

- **Using the Rules of Exponents**: Apply the appropriate rule to simplify expressions involving exponents.

Scientific Notations

Scientific notation is a way to express very large or very small numbers in a concise and convenient manner. It involves writing a number as the product of a coefficient (a number between 1 and 10) and a power of 10.

This allows us to represent numbers with many zeros or decimal places more efficiently, making them easier to work with in calculations and comparisons.

$a \times 10^n$

where a is the coefficient (a number between 1 and 10) and n is the exponent, which indicates the power of 10.

For example:

Let's take the number 45,000 and express it in scientific notation.

To express 45,000 in scientific notation, we need to move the decimal point to the right until there is only one non-zero digit to its left.

1. Count the number of places we moved the decimal point. Since we moved it 4 places to the left, the exponent n will be -4.

2. The coefficient a is the number we obtain after moving the decimal point. In this case, it is 4.5.

3. Therefore, 45,000 in scientific notation is:

$$4.5 \times 10^4$$

To convert 4.5×10^4 back into standard notation, we need to multiply the coefficient 4.5 by 10 raised to the power of 4.

$$4.5 \times 10^4 = 4.5 \times (10 \times 10 \times 10 \times 10)$$

$$= 4.5 \times 10000$$

$$= 45000$$

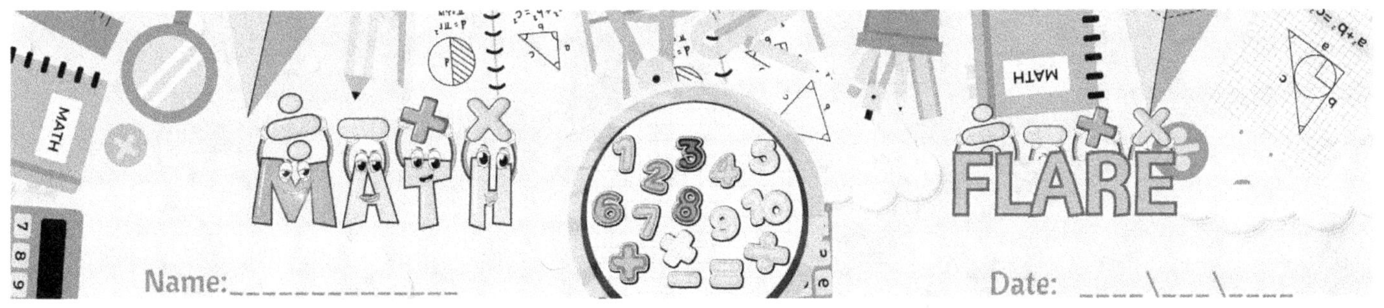

Rational Numbers: Operations

Evaluate Expressions.

1. $6 - 5 - (-8) =$

2. $10 - (-5) - 10 =$

3. $(-4) + 4 - (-8) =$

4. $2 - (-6) - (-3) =$

5. $(1)(-7)(8) =$

6. $6 \div 10 =$

7. $(2)(2)(2) =$

8. $(-7)(-7) =$

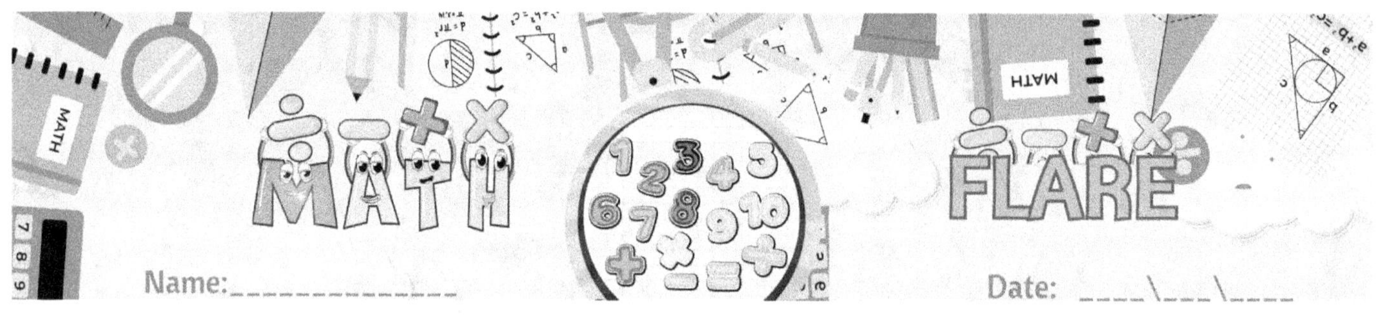

9. $(-3) - 3 - (-5) =$

10. $10 + 2 - (-2) =$

11. $-4 \div -1 =$

12. $2 + 3 - (-7) =$

13. $(-10) + 10 - (-2) =$

14. $(-5) + 9 - (-7) =$

15. $5 + 8 - (-6) =$

16. $(-6) + 3 - (-9) =$

17. $6 - 1 - (-10) =$

18. $(-1)(4) =$

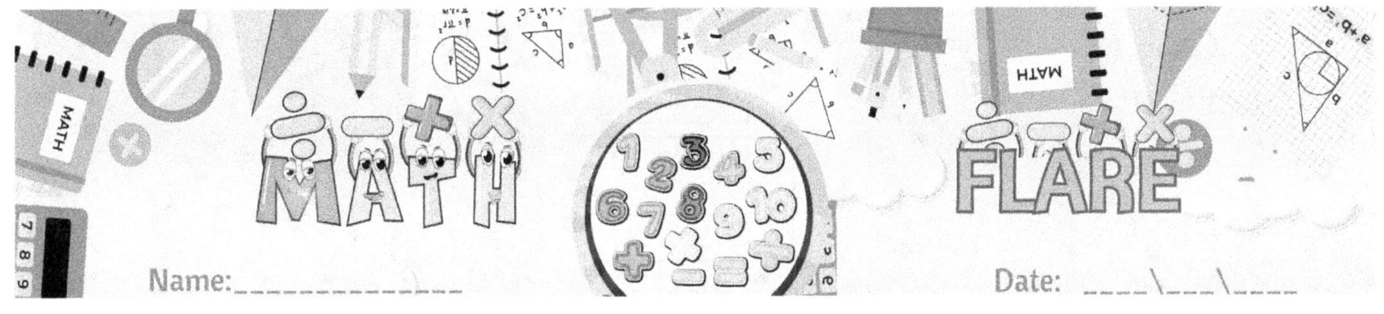

19. $5 + (-3) - (-6) =$

20. $10 + (-4) + 9 =$

21. $(-2) - 5 - (-6) =$

22. $(-5) + 9 + 2 =$

23. $1 \div 7 =$

24. $-(-10)(-3)(-6) =$

25. $(-2) + 8 - 7 =$

26. $(-2) + (-1) + 6 =$

27. $(-8)(-5)(2) =$

28. $2 - (-1) - 5 =$

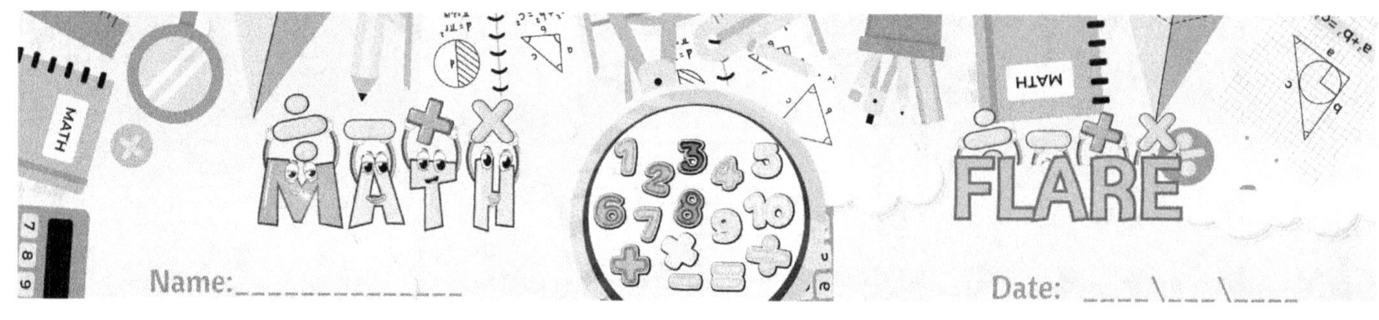

29. $9 + (-9) - 2 =$

30. $(-1)(-10) =$

31. $7 - 10 - (-7) =$

32. $8 + (-6) + (-1) =$

33. $-(-10)(-10)(-4) =$

34. $(2)(-6)(6) =$

35. $5 - 10 - (-3) =$

36. $(6)(10)(10) =$

37. $(-3) - 5 + (-3) =$

38. $(-4)(7)(9) =$

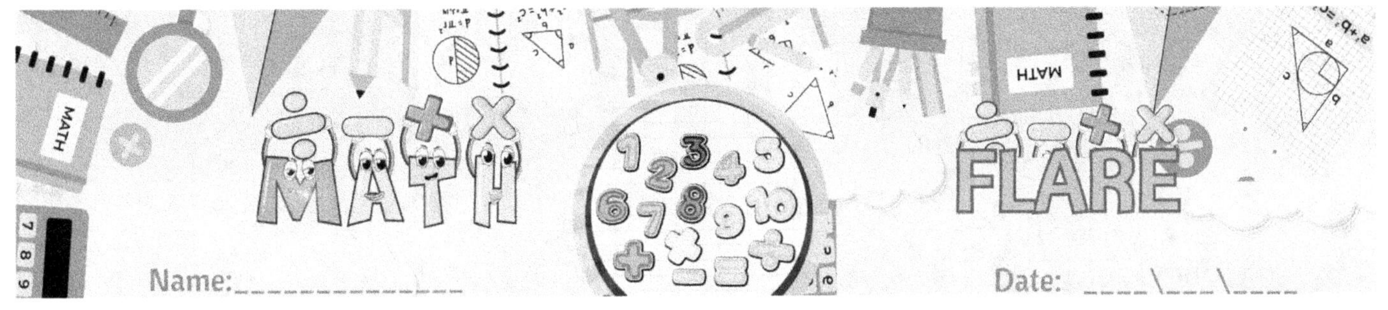

39. $6 - (-3) - 8 =$

40. $(2)(1) =$

41. $7 + (-6) + 7 =$

42. $2 + (-2) - 1 =$

43. $(-1)(-7) =$

44. $(-9)(6) =$

45. $(-7) - 7 + (-2) =$

46. $8 + (-5) + 2 =$

47. $9 - (-7) - (-3) =$

48. $-(-8)(10) =$

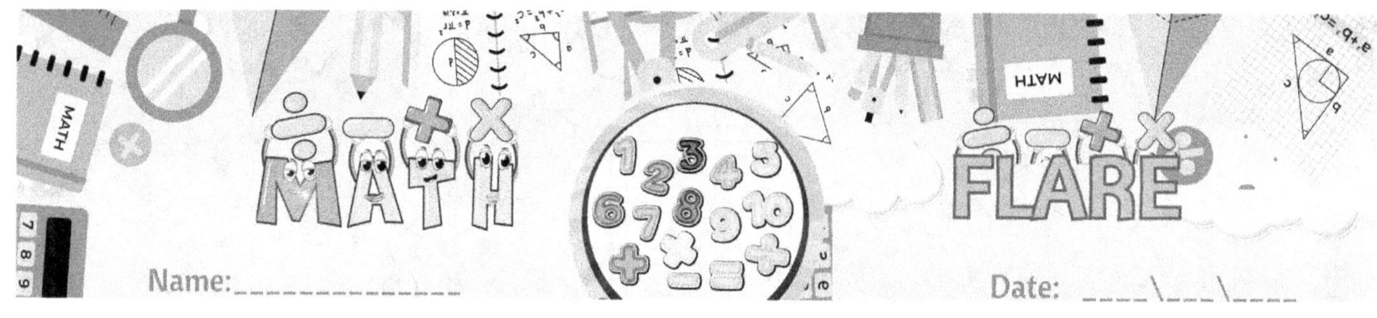

49. $(9)(10) =$

50. $10 - (-6) - (-7) =$

51. $(3)(3) =$

52. $(-8) + (-3) + 4 =$

53. $(-4)(-9)(-10) =$

54. $(-7)(6) =$

55. $9 - 4 - (-4) =$

56. $-10 \div 3 =$

57. $10 - (-2) - 5 =$

58. $6 + (-9) + 1 =$

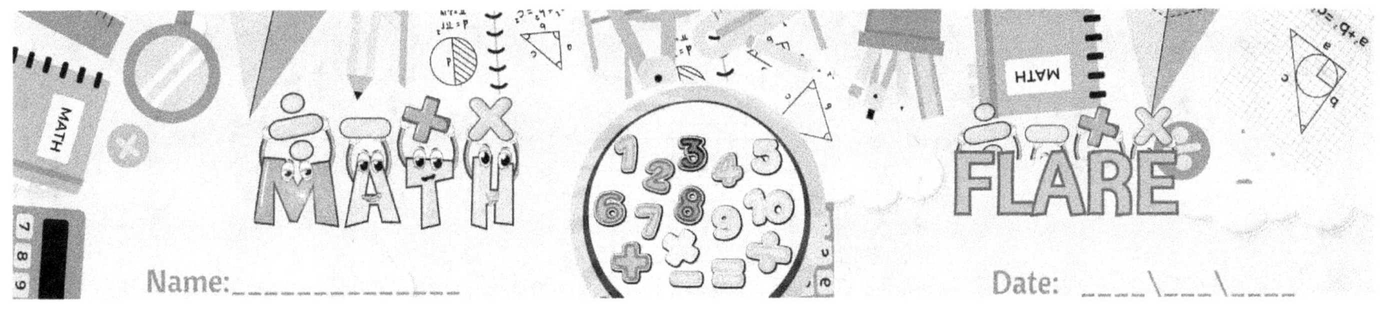

59. $(-7)(-3)(-8) =$

60. $(-7)(6)(6) =$

61. $4 - (-1) - (-9) =$

62. $-(-7)(8) =$

63. $7 + (-5) + (-8) =$

64. $(-8)(-9) =$

65. $-7 \div -3 =$

66. $(-3)(9)(3) =$

67. $-(-2)(-9) =$

68. $3 + (-6) + 4 =$

69. $(-3) - 6 - (-10) =$

70. $(8)(5)(4) =$

71. $8 \div 7 =$

72. $7 - (-10) - (-1) =$

73. $6 - 9 - (-9) =$

74. $-(-5)(-9) =$

75. $9 + (-9 + 2) =$

76. $(-8)(-9)(-2) =$

77. $5 \div -2 =$

78. $(-5) + 2 + 3 =$

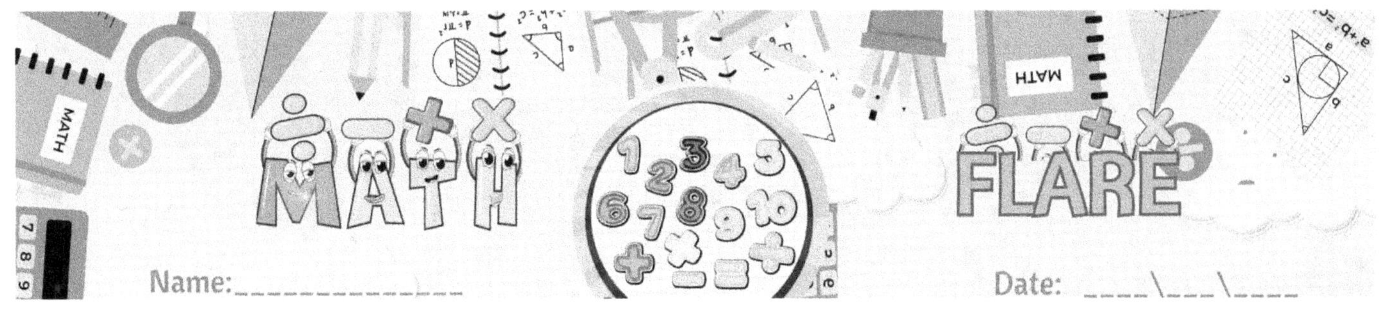

79. $-(-10)(9) =$

80. $(-6) - 4 + (-5) =$

81. $(2)(2)(-3) =$

82. $(-9) - 2 - (-1) =$

83. $2 - 5 - (-9) =$

84. $9 - 2 - (-9) =$

85. $8 \div -1 =$

86. $5 - (-5) - (-5) =$

87. $(-4) - 3 + 1 =$

88. $2 + (-8) + 5 =$

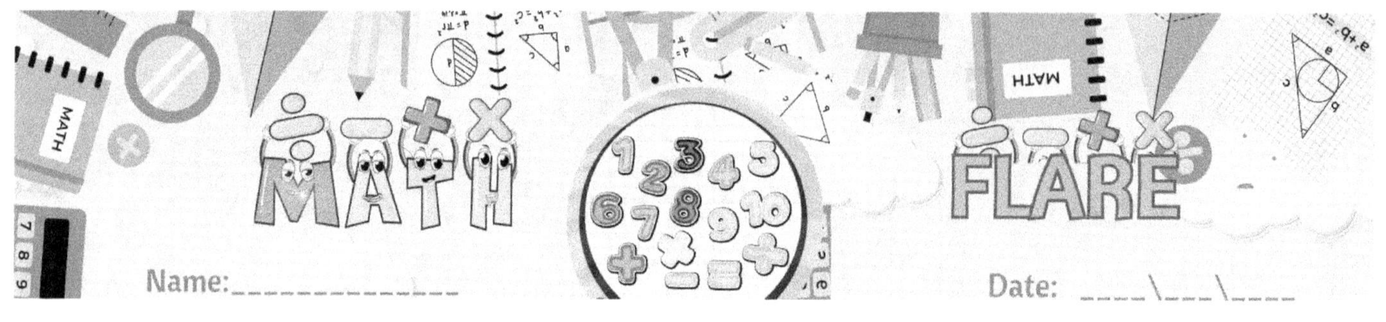

89. $(2)(2)(-9) =$

90. $(-4) - 4 - (-1) =$

91. $-(-8)(-8) =$

92. $(1)(6)(-6) =$

93. $-5 \div -7 =$

94. $7 + (-6) - 8 =$

95. $8 + 7 - (-7) =$

96. $(-10)(-1)(-1) =$

97. $(-7) - 4 - (-4) =$

98. $8 + (-9 + 6) =$

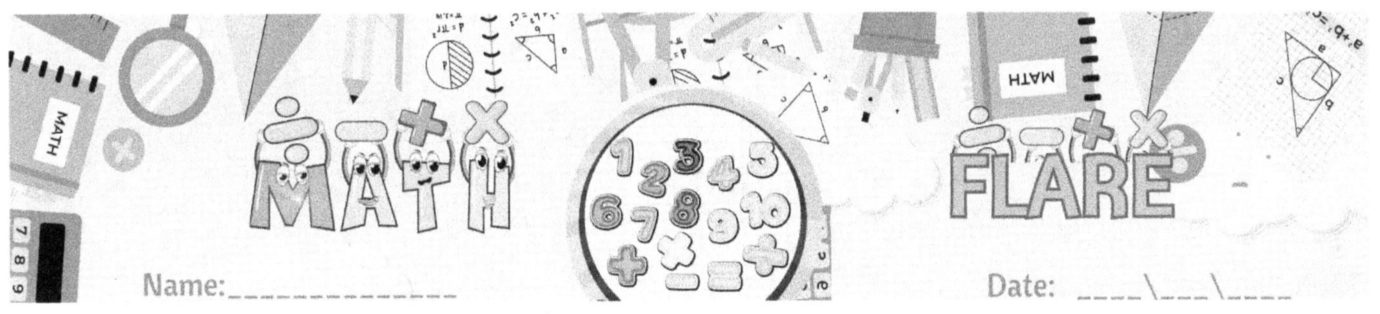

Order of Operations (PEMDAS)

1. $6 + 10 + 6 + 5 =$

2. $5(6 + 10) =$

3. $(10 + 3)(1 + 7) =$

4. $5 + 1 + 3 + 8 =$

5. $(10 \times 5) - (10 + 9) =$

6. $3(4 + 7) =$

7. $10 \times (5 + 2) =$

8. $4 \times 8 \times 7 =$

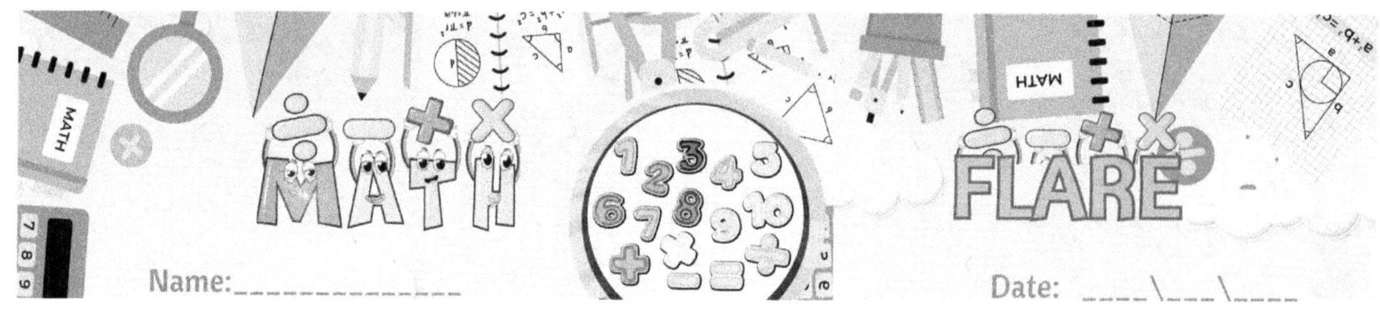

9. $(1^2) \times (7^2) + 6 =$

10. $6 + 3^2 + 7 + 2^2 =$

11. $6 + 6^2 + 1 + 6^2 =$

12. $2 + 1 + 1 =$

13. $9 + 3 + 4 =$

14. $(1^2) \times (1^2) + 4 =$

15. $(10 + 7)(5 + 6) =$

16. $(6 \times 10) - (1 + 9) =$

17. $(10 \times 1) - (4 + 2) =$

18. $8 + 3 - 9 + 7 =$

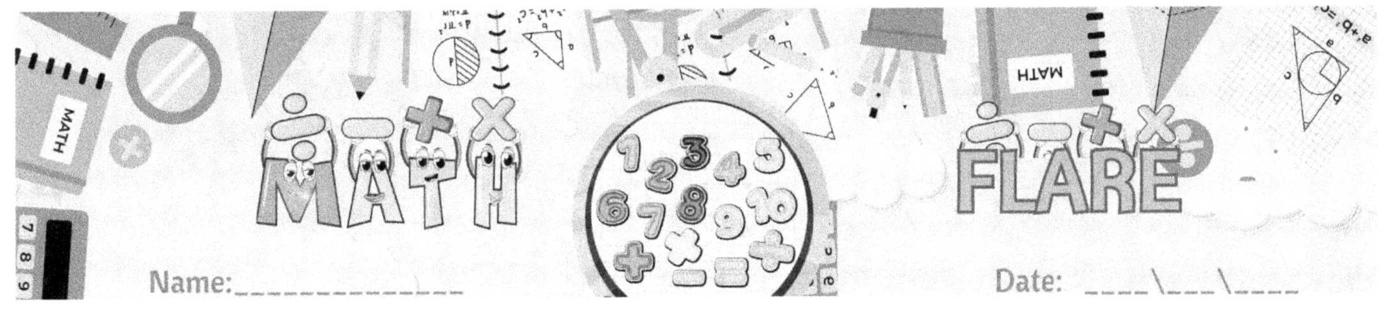

19. $6 \times 1 =$

20. $(3 + 5)(1 + 3) =$

21. $5 + 5 + 4 + 8 =$

22. $(2^2) \times (4^2) + 8 =$

23. $8(1 + 2) =$

24. $4 + 5^2 + 8 + 5^2 =$

25. $3 + 10 + 1 =$

26. $3 + 6^2 =$

27. $4 + 6 + 5 =$

28. $(7 + 5)^2 + (4 + 9)^2 =$

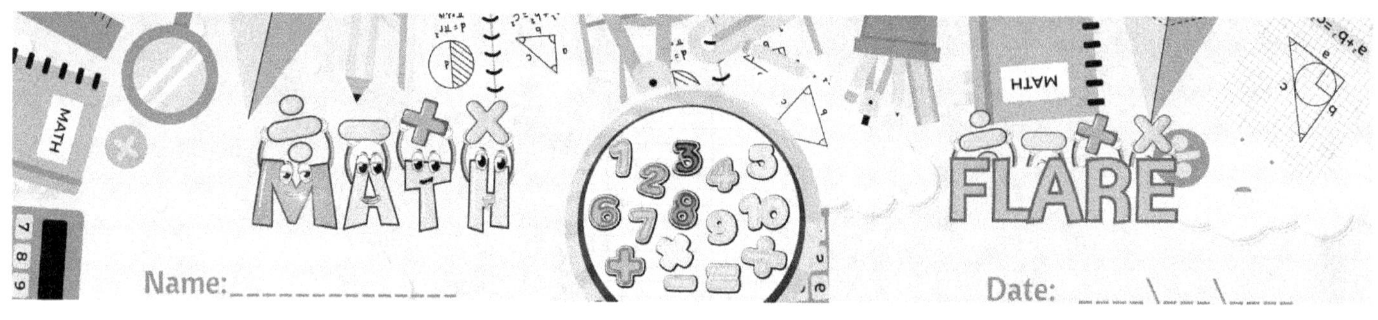

29. $(2 \times 3) - (7 + 4) =$

30. $8 + 6^2 =$

31. $(3^2) \times (7^2) + 3 =$

32. $(10 + 3) \div 8 =$

33. $8 + 8^2 =$

34. $(1 + 3) \div 1 =$

35. $(2 + 8) \times (3 + 6) =$

36. $5 + 5^2 =$

37. $6 + 1 + 1 =$

38. $(9 + 8)^2 + (8 + 10)^2 =$

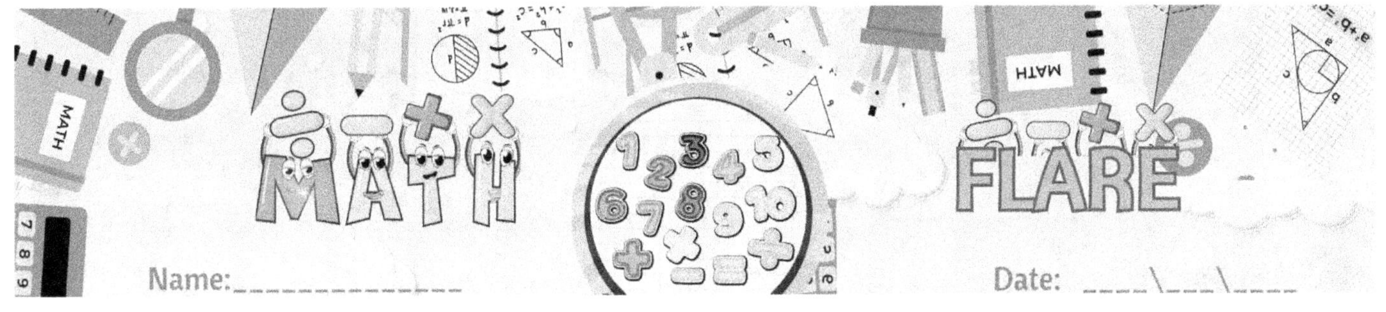

39. $(8 + 9)^2 + (4 + 4)^2 =$

40. $(2 \times 6) - (1 + 8) =$

41. $4(8 + 3) =$

42. $(1 + 2)^2 =$

43. $3 \times 7 \times 3 =$

44. $5 \times (9 + 3) =$

45. $4 + 5 - 5 + 8 =$

46. $1(3 + 8) =$

47. $8 + 1 + 4 + 8 =$

48. $7(5 + 10) =$

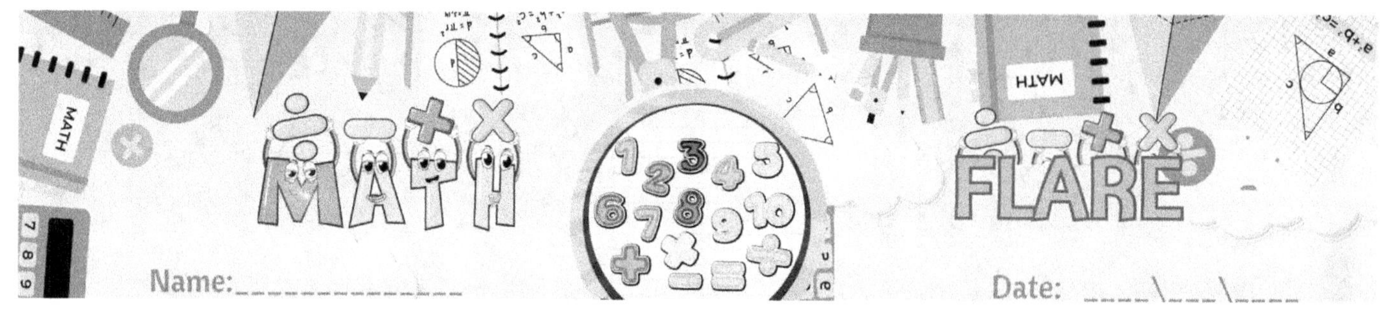

49. $3(3 + 5) =$

50. $(5 + 5) \div 6 =$

51. $6 + 2^2 + 3 + 9^2 =$

52. $(10 + 1)^2 + (5 + 3)^2 =$

53. $3 + 9 + 9 =$

54. $6 + 1^2 =$

55. $(6 + 4)(6 + 3) =$

56. $2 + 4 - 2 + 5 =$

57. $9(10 + 5) =$

58. $6 \times 2 + 9 =$

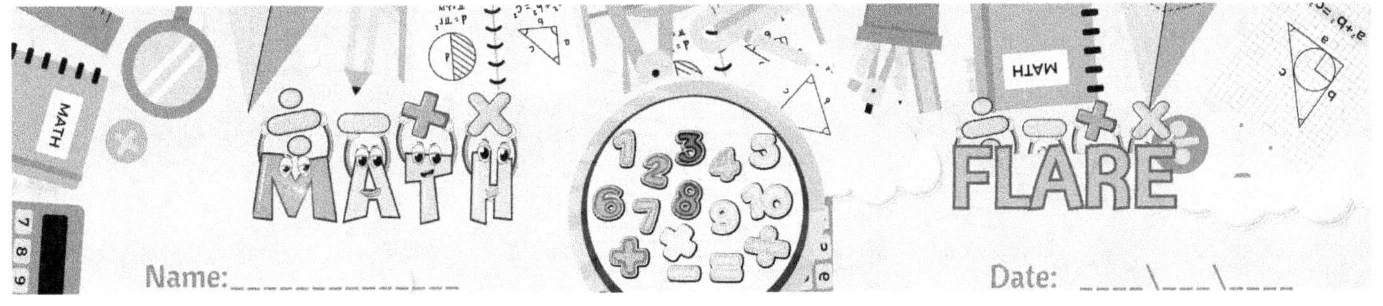

59. $1 + 9 + 10 =$

60. $(3^2) \times (8^2) + 1 =$

61. $4(7 + 3) =$

62. $(2 + 7)^2 =$

63. $(8 + 1) \times (8 + 6) =$

64. $6 \times (3 + 5) =$

65. $3 \times 7 \times 9 =$

66. $7 \times 8 + 1 =$

67. $(4 \times 2) - (4 + 1) =$

68. $(8 + 2)^2 =$

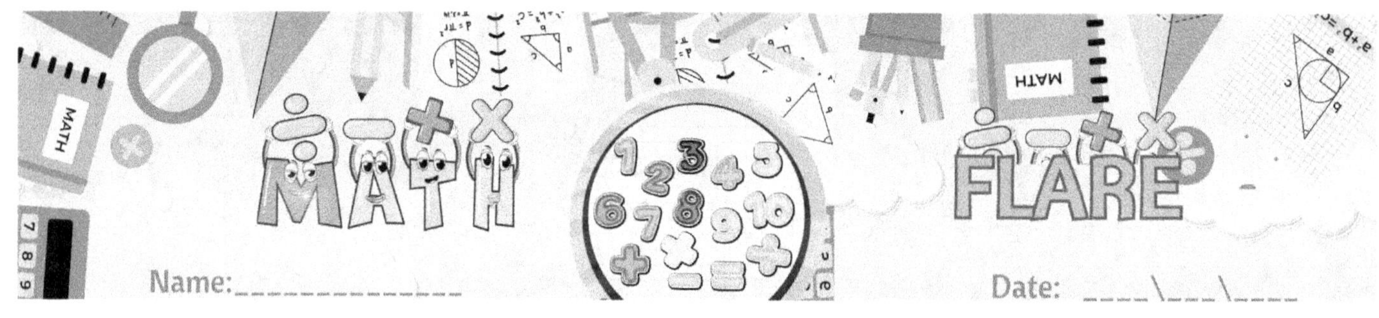

69. $9 \times 3 =$

70. $(9 + 2) \div 5 =$

71. $(4 \times 3) - (7 + 1) =$

72. $(6 + 7)^2 + (9 + 2)^2 =$

73. $(4 \times 6) - (4 + 3) =$

74. $4 + 9 + 3 =$

75. $(8 + 10)(4 + 5) =$

76. $1 \times 5 =$

77. $2 + 10 + 10 =$

78. $(7 + 7)^2 + (3 + 10)^2 =$

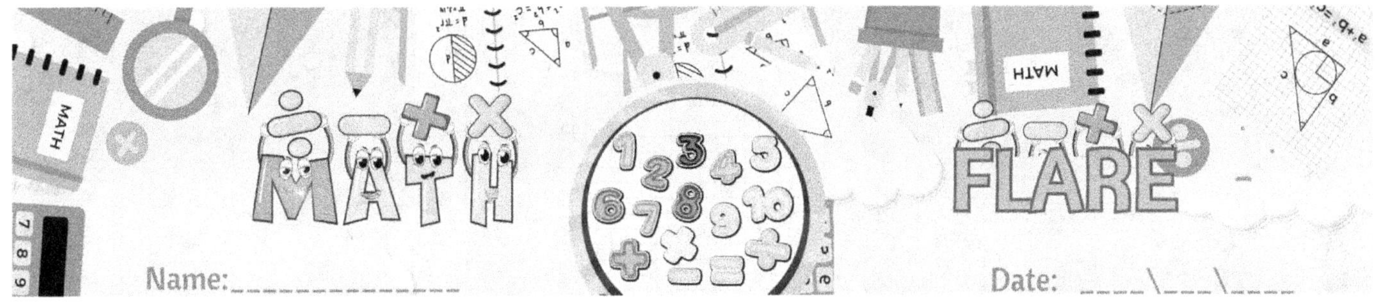

79. $(1 \times 3) - (5 + 9) =$

80. $9 + 4 + 2 + 3 =$

81. $(6 \times 5) - (7 + 10) =$

82. $10 + 5 + 5 + 5 =$

83. $(10 + 9)^2 + (1 + 3)^2 =$

84. $5 + 4 + 10 =$

85. $(9 + 4)(2 + 10) =$

86. $3 + 3 + 7 =$

87. $4 \times (9 + 5) =$

88. $10 + 1 + 1 =$

89. $(2 \times 6) - (5 + 10) =$

90. $7 + 1 + 3 =$

91. $(5 + 8)^2 =$

92. $6 \times 1 \times 1 =$

93. $7 + 6^2 + 1 + 9^2 =$

94. $(7^2) \times (1^2) + 6 =$

95. $8 \times 4 =$

96. $(6 + 5) \div 8 =$

97. $5 \times 10 + 10 =$

98. $(9 \times 2) - (8 + 5) =$

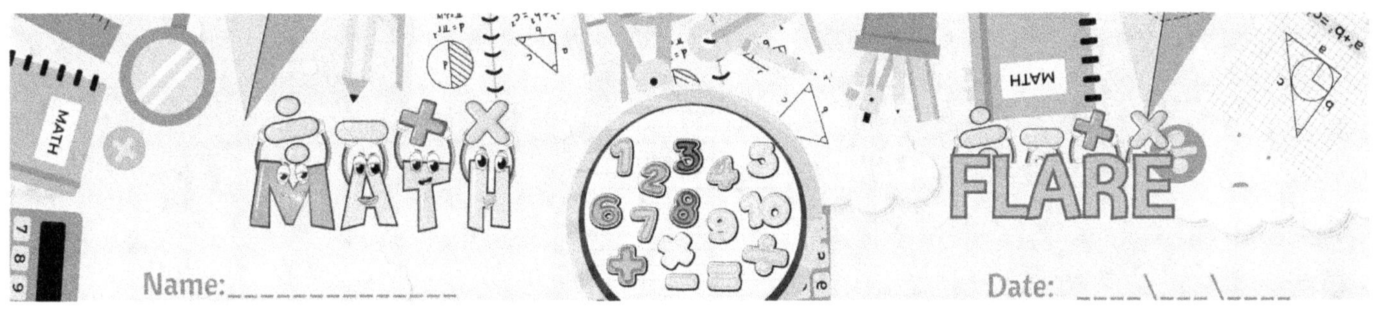

Combining and Distributing Terms

1. -6m + 6m

2. 2n + n

3. 3a - 1 + 3a

4. -3m - 4 - 5m

5. 1 - 4a + 4a

6. 1 + 4x + 3x

7. -2x - 3x

8. 3x - 2 + 8x - 5

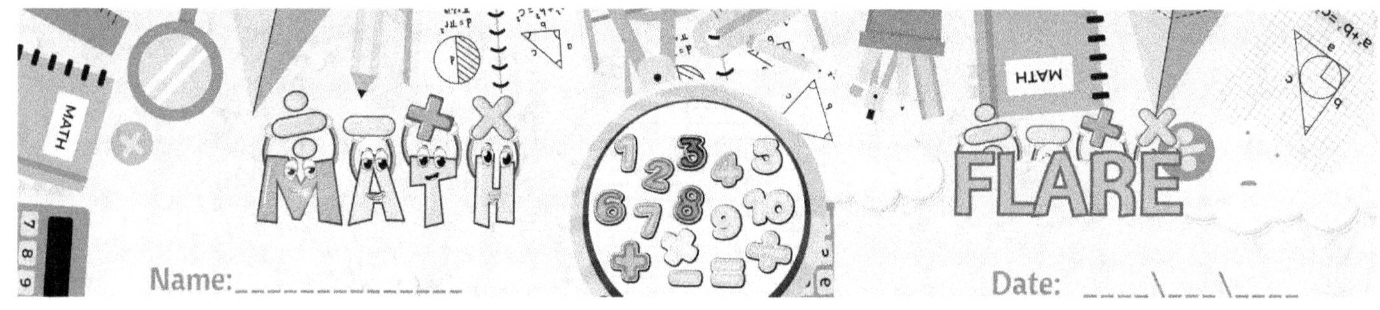

9. 1 + 6n + 2n

10. 4a + 6 + 3 + 5a

11. n - 5 + 4

12. 3 - 4x - 2x - 2

13. 7a + 5a

14. 1 + 8n + 8 + 7n

15. x - 3x

16. 5b - 6b

17. n + 5 + 6n

18. 2 + 5v + 7v - 3

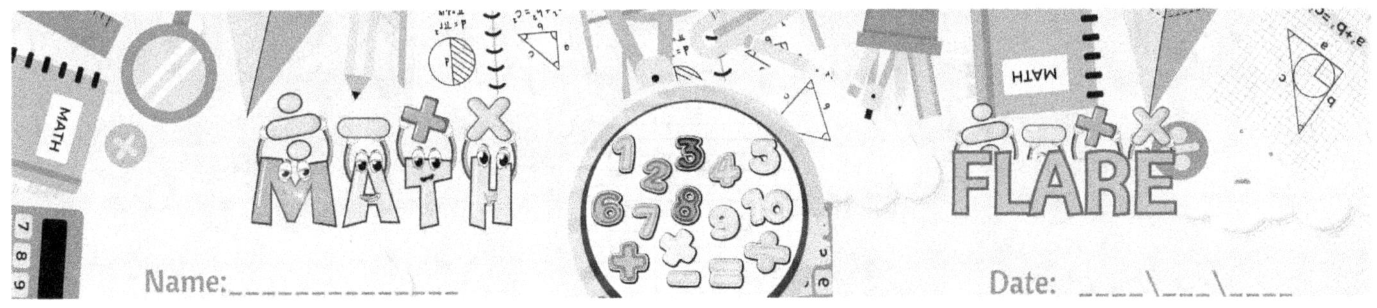

19. 1 - 4n + 3n

20. 8 + 4n - 8

21. -3r + r

22. 6r + r

23. 2a - 3a

24. -8 + 8r + 1 - 2r

25. -6n + 7n

26. 6 + 6 p + 2 p

27. -2x - 6 - x

28. n - 7 + 2 + n

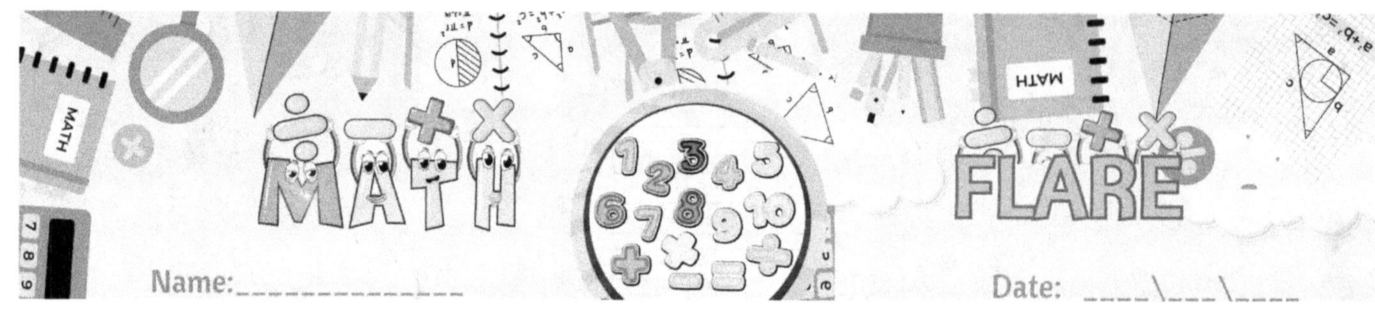

29. -7n - 3n

30. 3x - 5 - 7x

31. 2 + 8x - 2x

32. 6 p - 2 p

33. 1 - r + 7 + 4r

34. m - 3 + m - 5

35. p - 4 p

36. m + 8 + 7m + 8

37. 4k + 8k

38. -4v - 8v

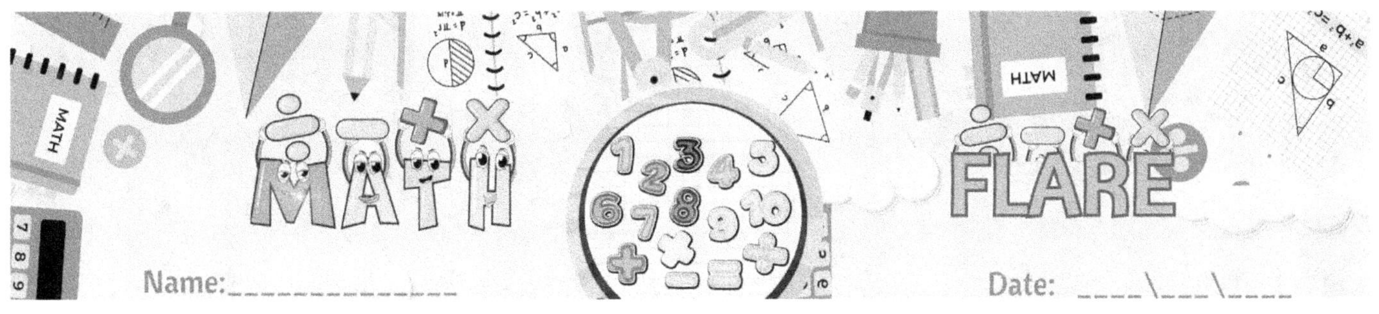

39. -7a - 5a

40. 4 - 3m + 2m

41. -6(p + 5)

42. -2(p + 7)

43. -(8x + 7)

44. (x - 6) × -1

45. -6(6x - 6)

46. (7n - 5) × -1

47. -3(-4x - 7)

48. (1 + 6n) × -7

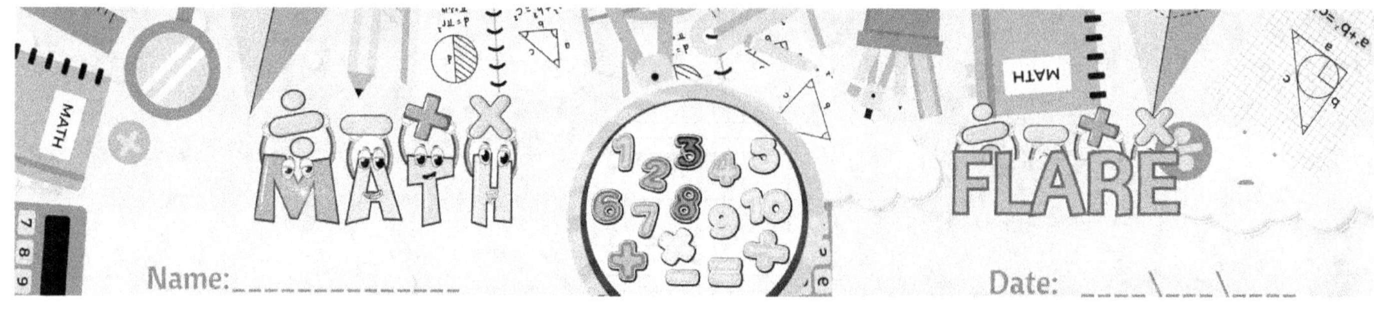

49. -4(5 - 7n)

54. (p - 2) × -6

50. -(4r + 1)

55. -4(5x + 7)

51. -8(1 - 8n)

56. (-8 - 8a) × -2

52. (-7 - 3 p) × -1

57. -4(5n + 6)

53. (a - 4) × -1

58. (5 - 5x) × -7

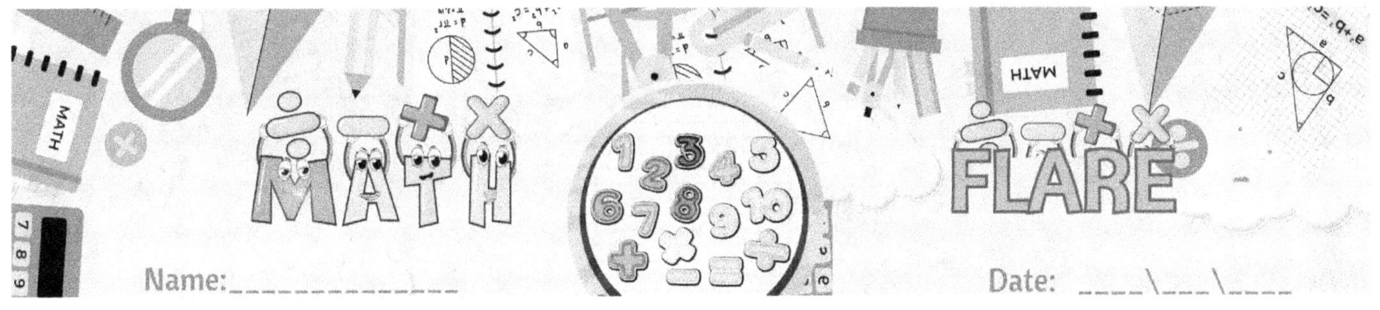

59. $-2(p + 4)$

64. $-7 - 6(2x + 6)$

60. $-8(6b - 6)$

65. $-(2x + 1) + 2x$

61. $-4 - 3(7 + 6a)$

66. $-7(5b + 3) - 3b$

62. $(2 - 5b) \times -5 - 2$

67. $-4(8 - 8a) + 3$

63. $-4 + (-3k + 8) \times -3$

68. $-3 - 6(-6v - 8)$

69. -3 - 8(-7x - 4)

70. (1 - 7 p) × -3 - 3 p

71. -8 + (8n + 7) × -3

72. -6(1 - 8x) - 2x

73. 3 - 5(3a - 4)

74. 6b - 7(4b - 5)

75. -6x - 5(x + 4)

76. 7x - 3(8 + 7x)

77. -(6r + 1) - 3r

78. -(k - 6) - 2

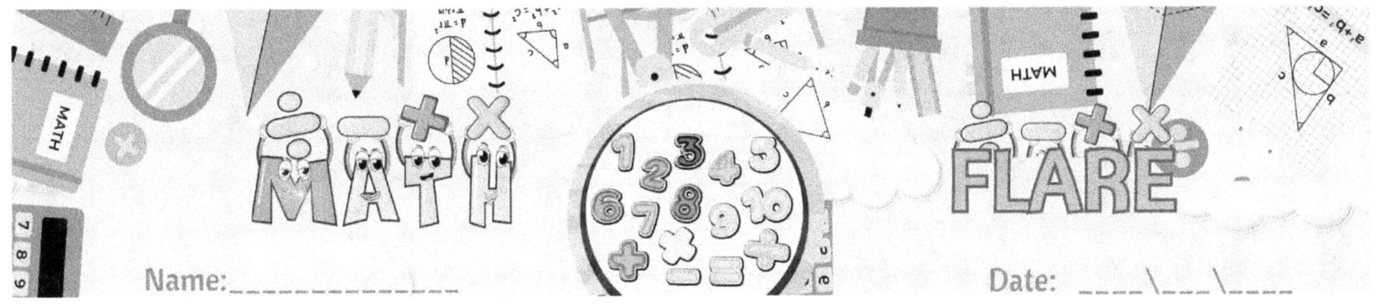

79. -3 + (3 - x) × -3

84. -2(1 - 7n) - 7(3n - 3)

80. -(-2 p - 5) - 3 p

85. -6(-5 - 4b) - 8(-b - 7)

81. -7(8x + 7) - 3(2 - 7x)

86. -7(3 - 7r) + (1 + 3r) × -2

82. (-7 - 8a) × -4 + (8a - 7) × -3

87. (p + 3) × -4 - 6(p - 5)

83. -6(1 - n) - 7(7n - 3)

88. -6(m + 1) - 7(m - 4)

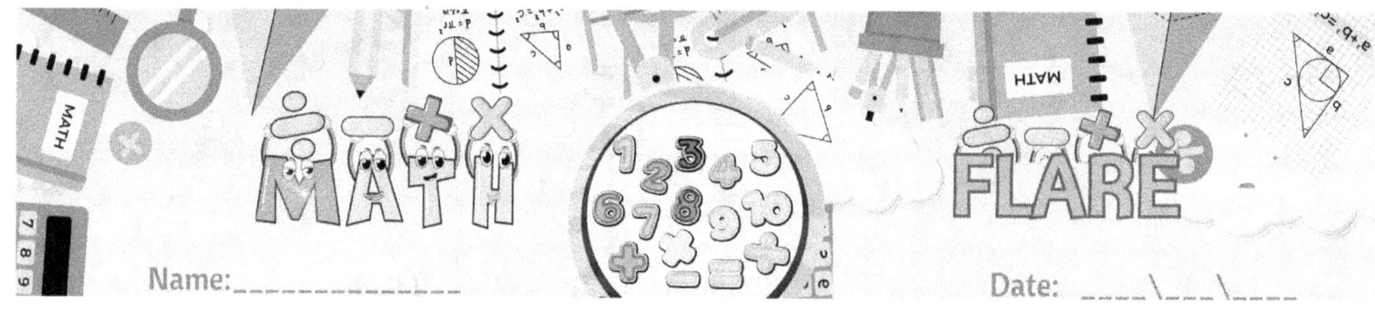

89. $-6(-n - 8) - 7(7n - 1)$

94. $-3(1 + 7r) - 4(1 - 4r)$

90. $(5 - 4x) \times -5 - 2(x + 2)$

95. $-6(b + 1) - (3 + 3b)$

91. $(a + 4) \times -2 + (a + 7) \times -7$

96. $(1 + 6m) \times -5 - 3(3m + 2)$

92. $-2(-5p + 1) - 7(2 + p)$

97. $(1 + 4p) \times -4 - 7(4p + 7)$

93. $-2(x - 7) - 5(-6 + 6x)$

98. $(b - 4) \times -6 + (1 + 5b) \times -8$

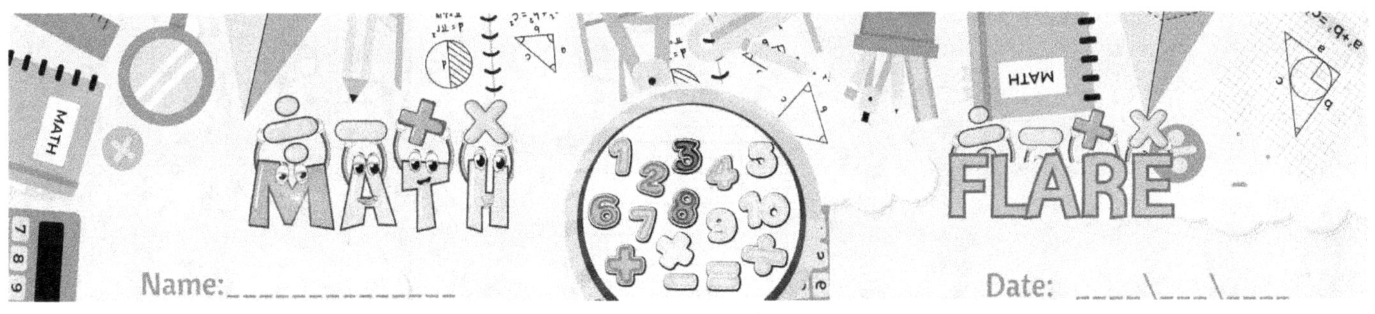

Solving One-Step Equations

Solve for the variable.

1. $\dfrac{b}{2} = 5$

2. $-1 + a = 6$

3. $54 = 6s$

4. $\dfrac{s}{3} = 2$

5. $1 = \dfrac{s}{1}$

6. $-4s = -8$

7. $b + 4 = 10$

8. $-5 = -7 + z$

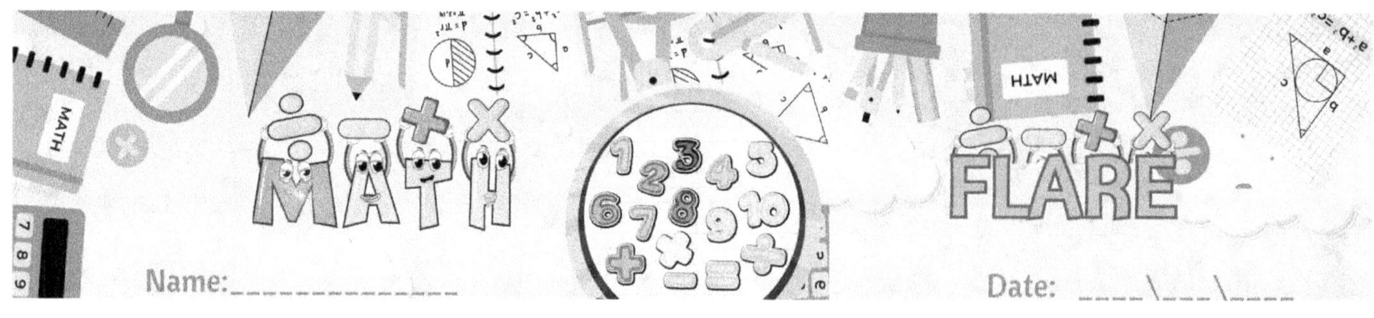

9. $13 = k + 5$

10. $-9a = -81$

11. $-10m = -100$

12. $-3 = -4 + s$

13. $5 = a - 1$

14. $-2 + a = 4$

15. $-30 = -5k$

16. $3 = x - 2$

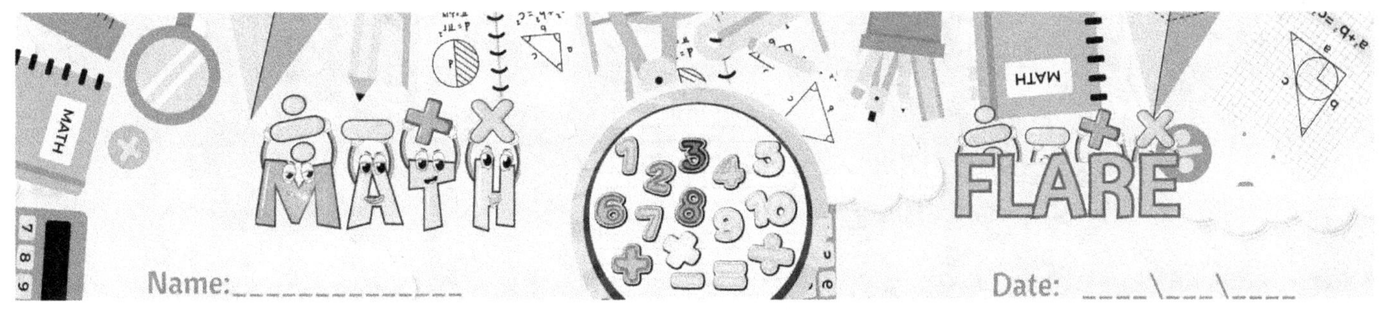

17. $-10 + y = -7$

18. $1 = b - 8$

19. $-8 + s = 1$

20. $2 = m - 7$

21. $14 = b + 8$

22. $2 = \dfrac{s}{4}$

23. $10 = \dfrac{b}{1}$

24. $16 = 2b$

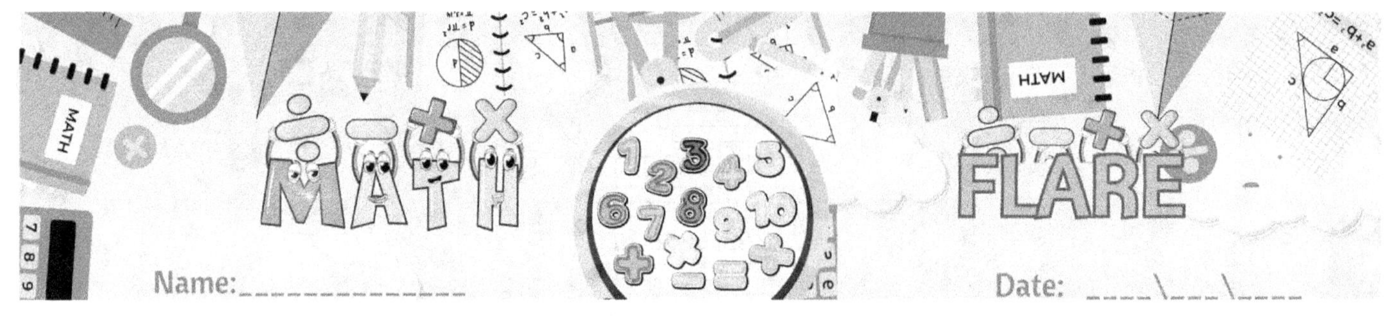

Name:________________   Date: _______________

25. $4 = \dfrac{x}{1}$

26. $-6 = -z$

27. $7 = a + 1$

28. $x - 6 = -5$

29. $\dfrac{m}{1} = 8$

30. $2 = \dfrac{a}{5}$

31. $\dfrac{y}{1} = 6$

32. $-50 = -10a$

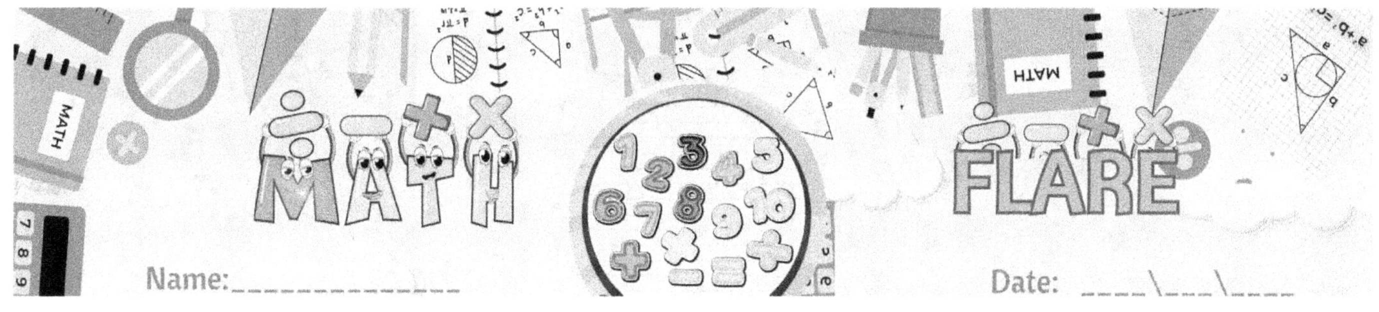

33. $60 = 10a$

34. $m + 3 = 6$

35. $k - 7 = -5$

36. $\dfrac{m}{6} = 1$

37. $5k = 25$

38. $-24 = -4z$

39. $1 = \dfrac{m}{4}$

40. $\dfrac{s}{9} = 1$

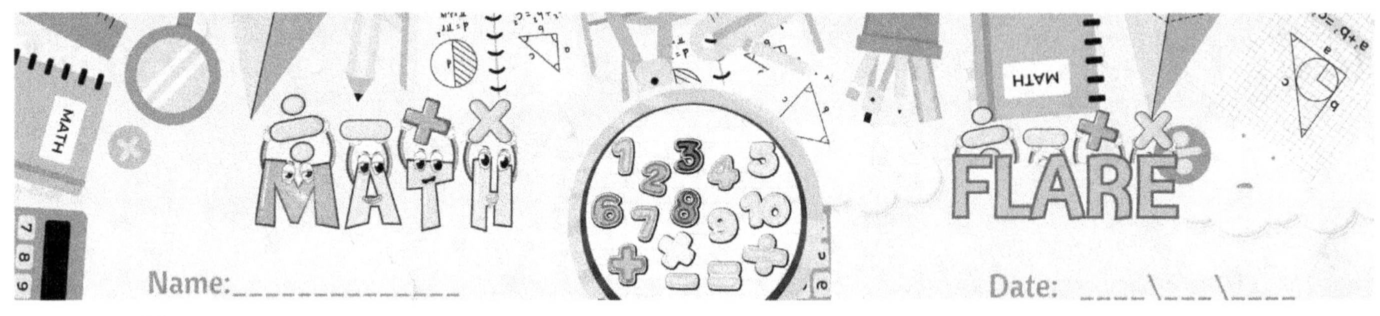

41. $\dfrac{x}{3} = 3$

42. $13 = x + 6$

43. $3 = \dfrac{y}{2}$

44. $9z = 72$

45. $2 = m - 2$

46. $\dfrac{b}{2} = 2$

47. $-2 = a - 4$

48. $z + 7 = 14$

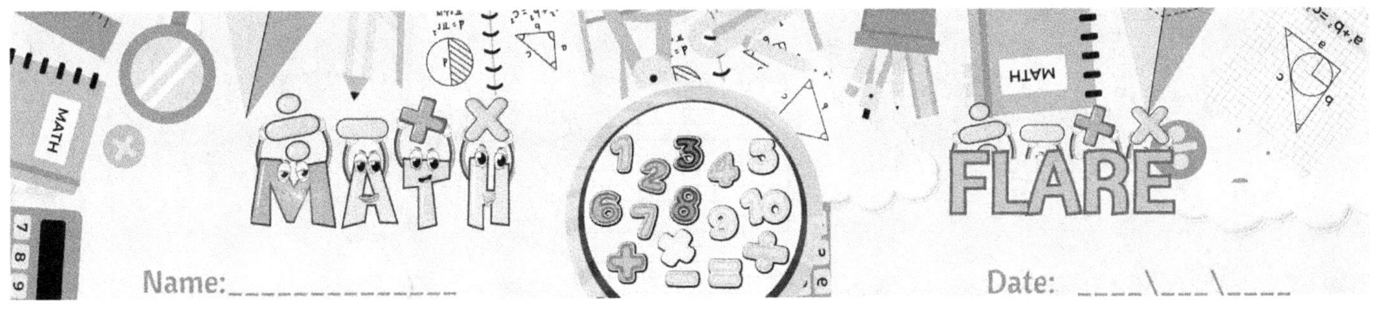

49. $13 = x + 9$

50. $-8 + y = 0$

51. $m + 2 = 12$

52. $-2 + s = 2$

53. $-3 = b - 7$

54. $12 = 6x$

55. $5 = x - 2$

56. $9 = y + 1$

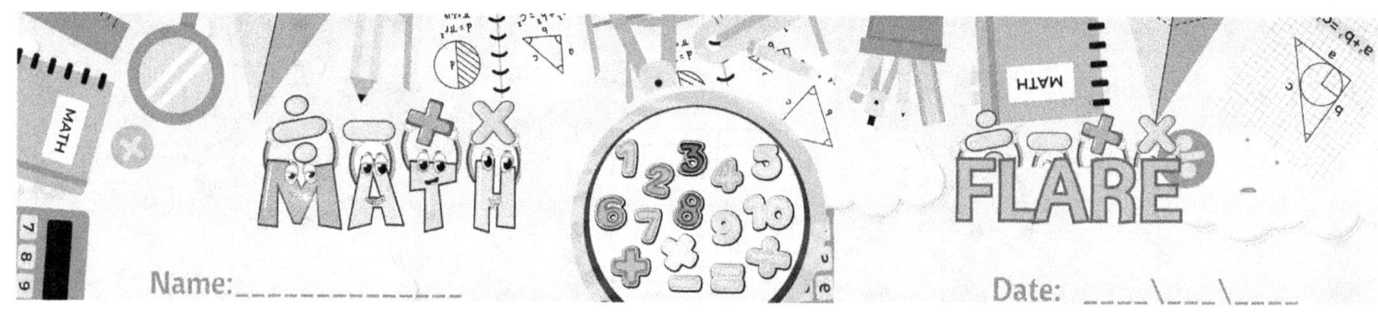

Solving Two-Step Equations

Solve for the variable.

1. $9.8 = \dfrac{x}{-4} + 10$

2. $(-3 + a) - 1 = 5$

3. $(2 + z)8 = 64$

4. $20 = \dfrac{10 + a}{1}$

5. $5 = \dfrac{6 + a}{3}$

6. $-8(2 + z) = -48$

7. $36 = 9(1 + a)$

8. $-5(6 + s) = -80$

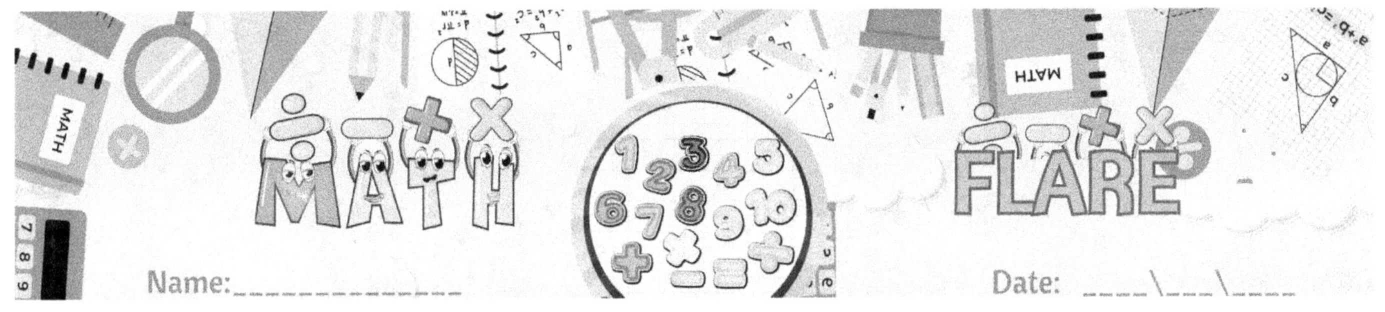

9. $\dfrac{y}{3} - 1 = 1$

10. $\dfrac{m}{4} - 4 = -3$

11. $1\dfrac{s}{5} = 2$

12. $4 = 9 - \dfrac{k}{2}$

13. $-2m - 3 = -11$

14. $-3 = 3(5 - x)$

15. $35 = 5(1 + m)$

16. $54 = 9\dfrac{m}{1}$

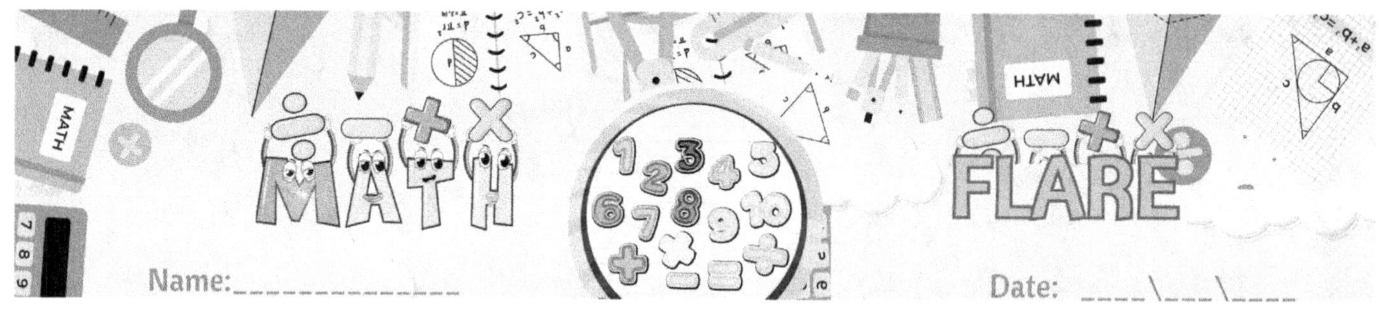

17. $9 - \dfrac{x}{1} = 5$

18. $(1 - a) - 10 = -14$

19. $70 = 10(9 - s)$

20. $\dfrac{k}{-1} + 6 = 0$

21. $-6 = \dfrac{b}{1} - 10$

22. $11 = \dfrac{a}{2} + 9$

23. $\dfrac{a}{2} - 10 = -8$

24. $-8 \dfrac{k}{-9} = 8$

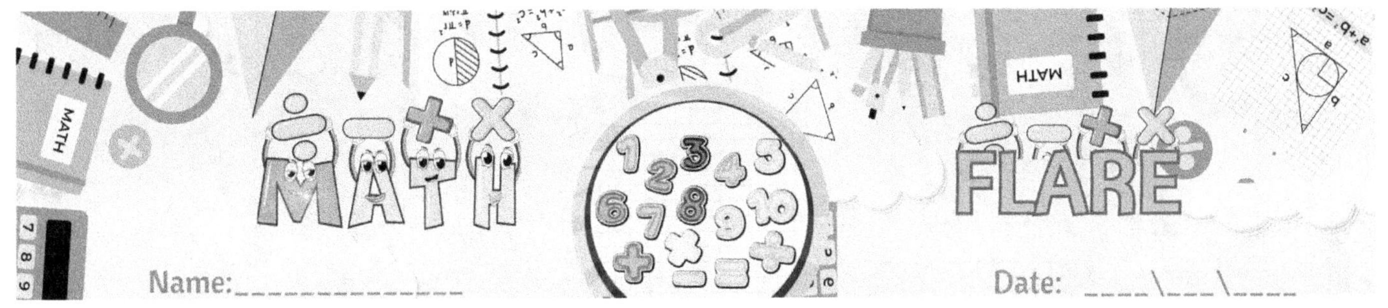

25. $\dfrac{6+z}{2} = 7$

26. $27 = 9k + 9$

27. $\dfrac{-4+b}{1} = 5$

28. $7(-10 + b) = -7$

29. $\dfrac{b}{1} + 1 = 2$

30. $-35 = -10s - 5$

31. $\dfrac{6+s}{2} = 6$

32. $6\dfrac{-b}{10} = -6$

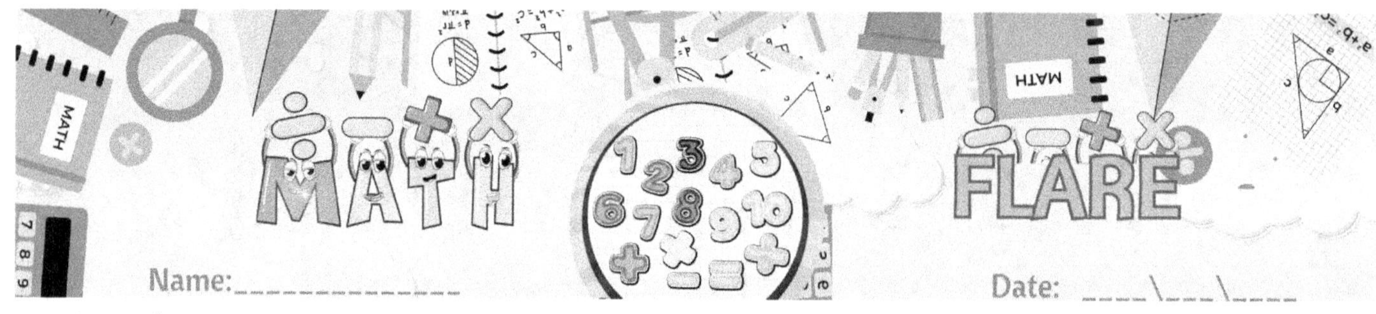

33. $\dfrac{k}{10} - 4 = -3$

34. $36 = 7s + 1$

35. $8\dfrac{x}{6} = 8$

36. $-2y - 4 = -18$

37. $\dfrac{a}{2} - 8 = -6$

38. $9y - 1 = 26$

39. $12 = \dfrac{4 + k}{1}$

40. $-1(5 + x) = -7$

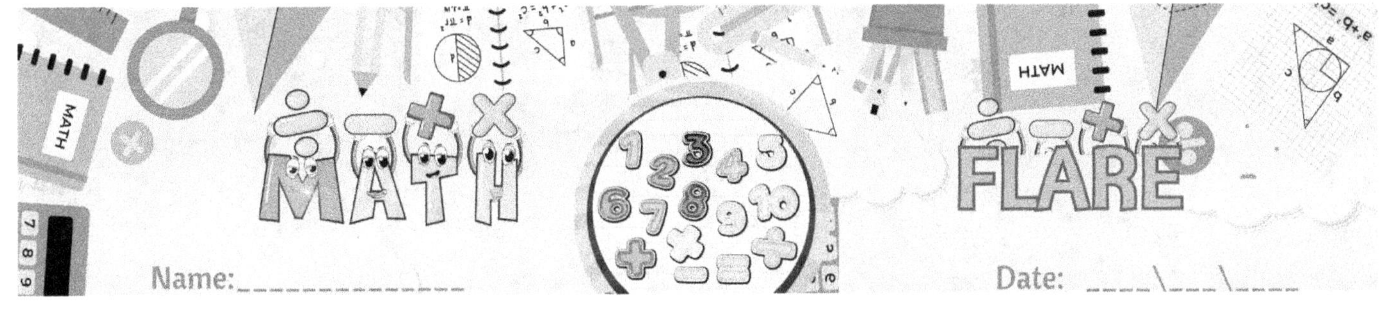

41. $4 = -1\dfrac{-x}{1}$

42. $6\dfrac{z}{6} = 6$

43. $\dfrac{10+s}{1} = 18$

44. $12 = k + 9$

45. $-9 = 9\dfrac{-k}{8}$

46. $9(3 + a) = 90$

47. $\dfrac{a}{4} - 1 = 0$

48. $-48 = 8(2 - y)$

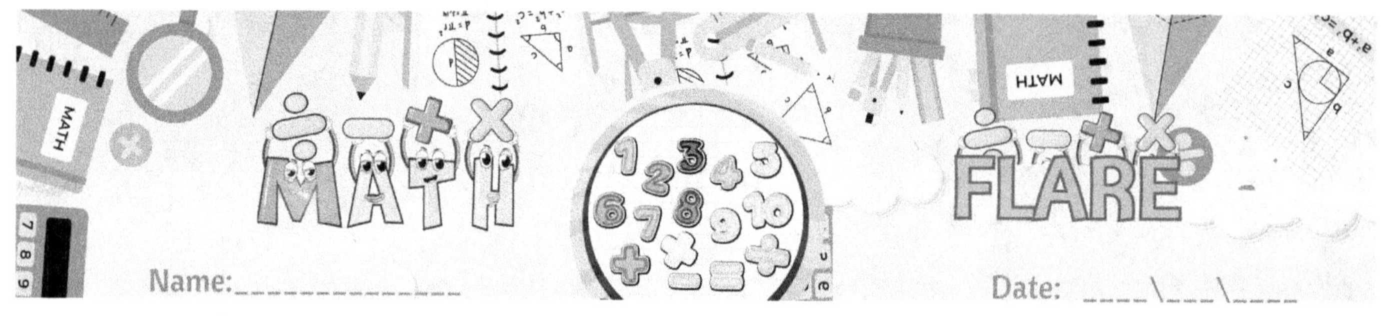

49. $6 = \dfrac{4+m}{2}$

50. $140 = 10(7+s)$

51. $31 = 4m+3$

52. $-7 = (-3+m)-5$

53. $\dfrac{s}{1}+4 = 5$

54. $3(-10+y) = -12$

55. $8(2+b) = 48$

56. $-54 = 6\dfrac{-a}{1}$

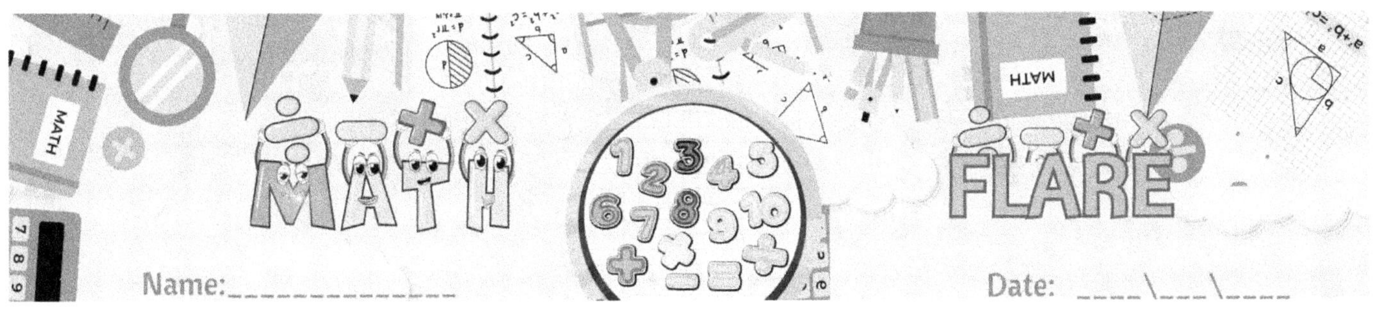

Solving Multi-Step Equations

Solve for the variable.

1. $-6 = -4b + 9 - b$

2. $12 = k + 8 + 3k$

3. $30 = -m + 9 + 8m$

4. $-2s + 8 + 10 = 12$

5. $-24 = -3 - 5y + 4$

6. $m + 9 + 4m = 29$

7. $4x - x = 15$

8. $5 + k + 9k = 65$

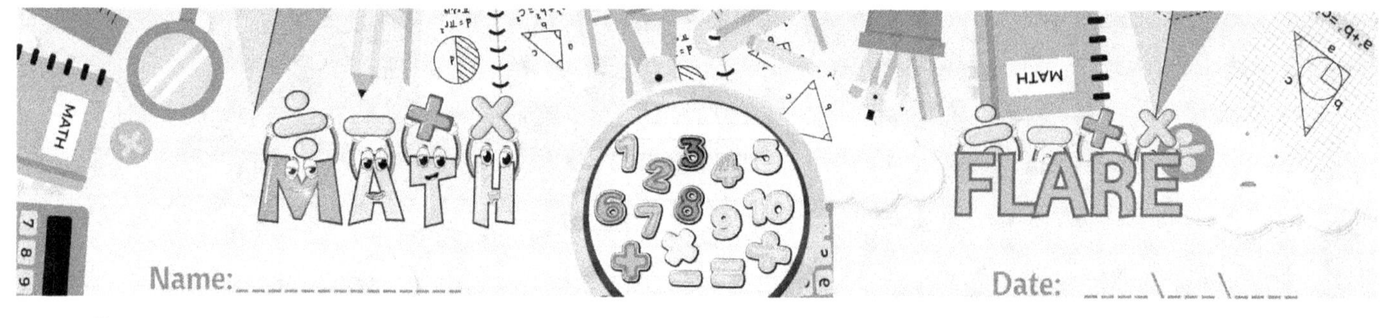

9. $-3 = 4b - 5b$

10. $20 = -3y + 5y$

11. $10 - 8z - 6 = -68$

12. $-111 = -10y - 6 - 5$

13. $k + 5 + 8k = 23$

14. $-7x - x = -32$

15. $b + 7 - 2b = 3$

16. $-8s - 5 - s = -77$

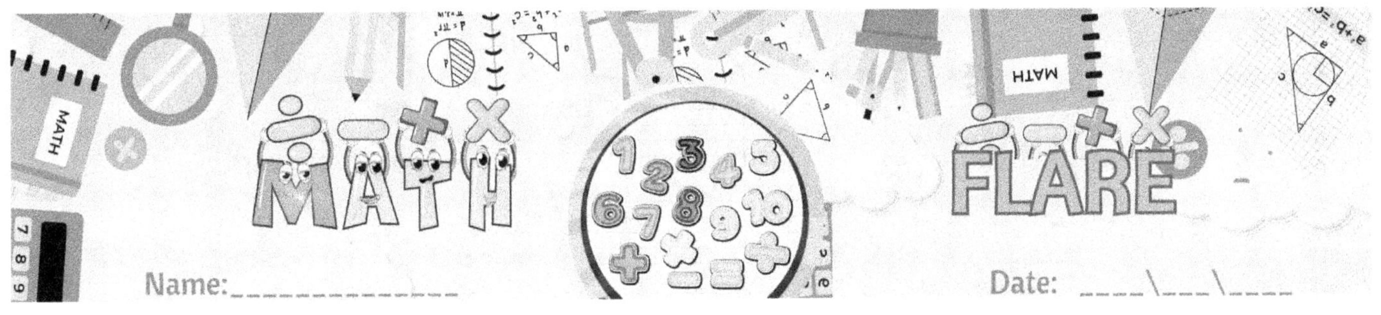

17. $-32 = -1 - 3z - 4$

18. $4b - 8 + 3 = 31$

19. $10 = 3z - 10 + z$

20. $-8 + 7z - 8 = 40$

21. $-4s - s = -5$

22. $-8a + 6 + 8 = -26$

23. $10b - 9 + 6 = 77$

24. $-8z + 3 - 2 = -15$

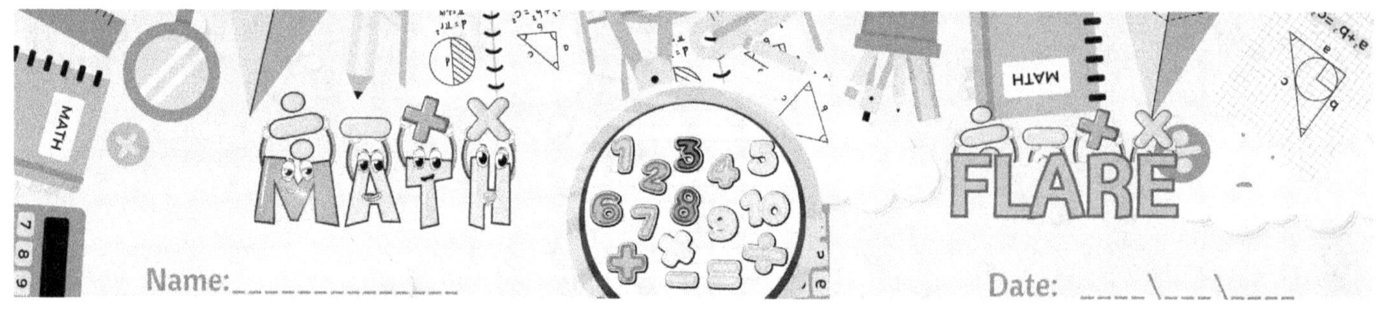

25. $b - 5 - 7b = -23$

26. $-8 + 10z - 1 = 21$

27. $5 + 6k + 2k = 61$

28. $-8 = -8 - 3x + 3$

29. $6 = 7a - 10 + a$

30. $k - 10 + 7k = 46$

31. $-1 + z + 9 = 11$

32. $-4 = -3b + 2b$

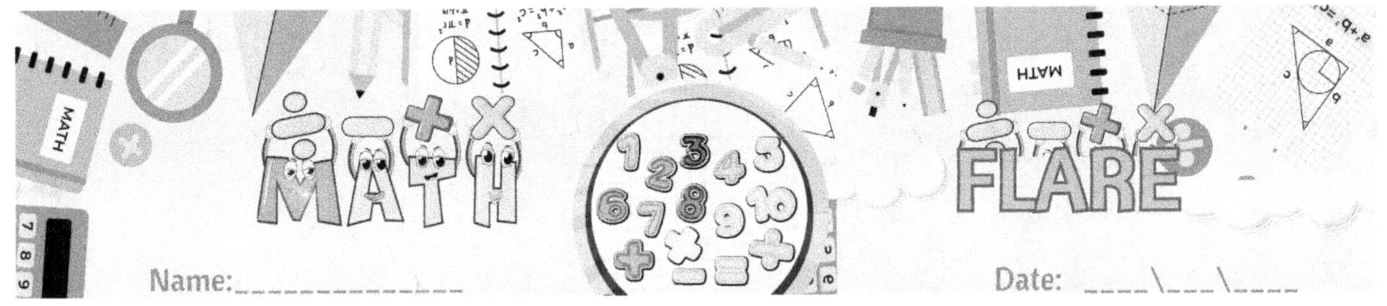

33. $-47 = -5k + 1 - k$

34. $7 + 10k + 3k = 20$

35. $21 = 5b + 9 + b$

36. $9 + m + 3m = 29$

37. $-y + 6 + 2y = 12$

38. $-51 = 3 - b - 5b$

39. $9b + 2 + b = 52$

40. $5 - 9m - 4 = -44$

41. $6 + 2s + 5s = 41$

42. $-61 = -9b + 9 - b$

43. $-9a - 8 - a = -108$

44. $78 = 6 + 6b + 3b$

45. $-9z + z = -64$

46. $6m - m = 15$

47. $22 = 1 + 2x + x$

48. $5k + 10k = 150$

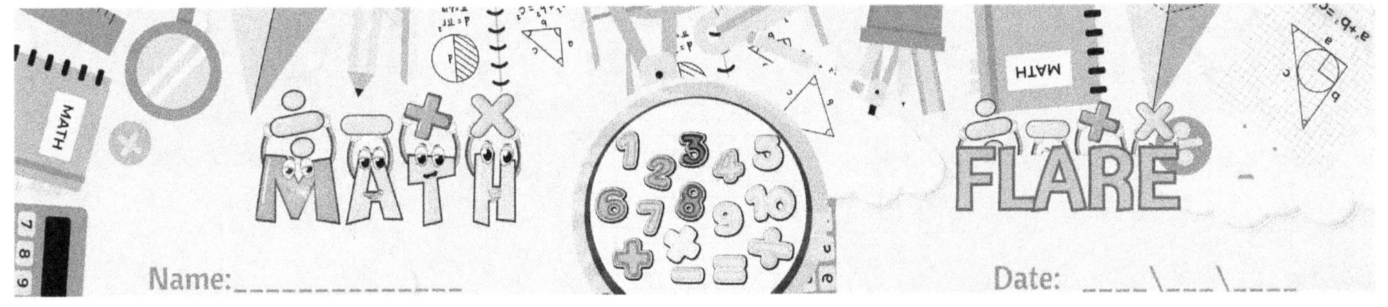

49. $-a + 5a = 32$

50. $a + 3 + 4a = 38$

51. $-18 = -3z - 7 - 5$

52. $-1 - b + 10 = 2$

53. $19 = 3z - 5 + z$

54. $-63 = -7 - s - 6s$

55. $-8z - 3 - z = -12$

56. $-9 = -s + 7 - s$

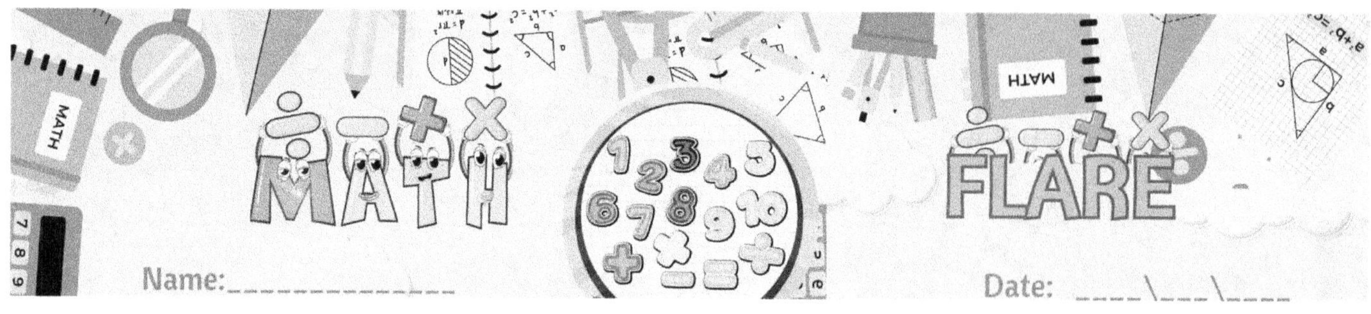

Equations: (One Side)

Solve the equations for the variable.

1. $-3 \times m = -15$

2. $k - 1 = 11$

3. $k - -5 = 7$

4. $16y + -1 = 95$

5. $16 + y = 22$

6. $k \times -4 = 24$

7. $18 + m = 34$

8. $13m + -1 = 259$

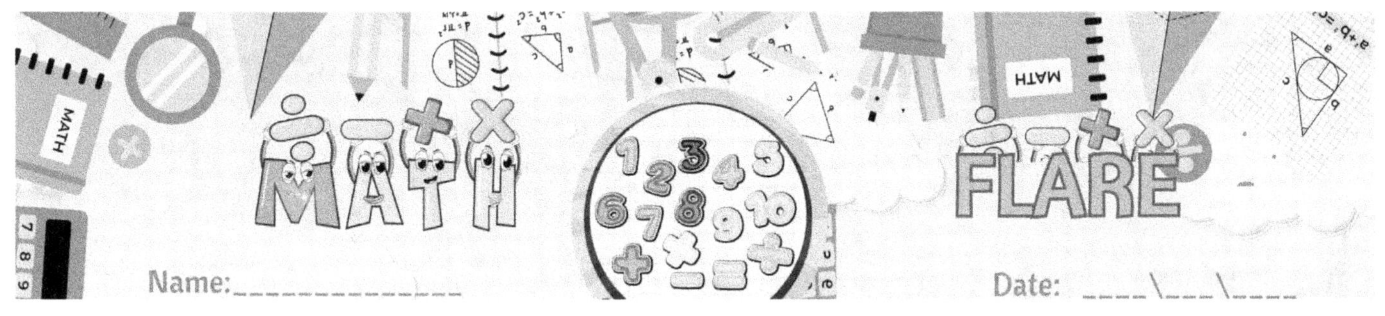

9. $2m - 16 = 12$

10. $11 \times k = 11$

11. $6y + 16 = 16$

12. $0 + 9y = 117$

13. $z \div 13 = 13$

14. $10 + -7y = 45$

15. $14 + k = 20$

16. $6x + 1 = 61$

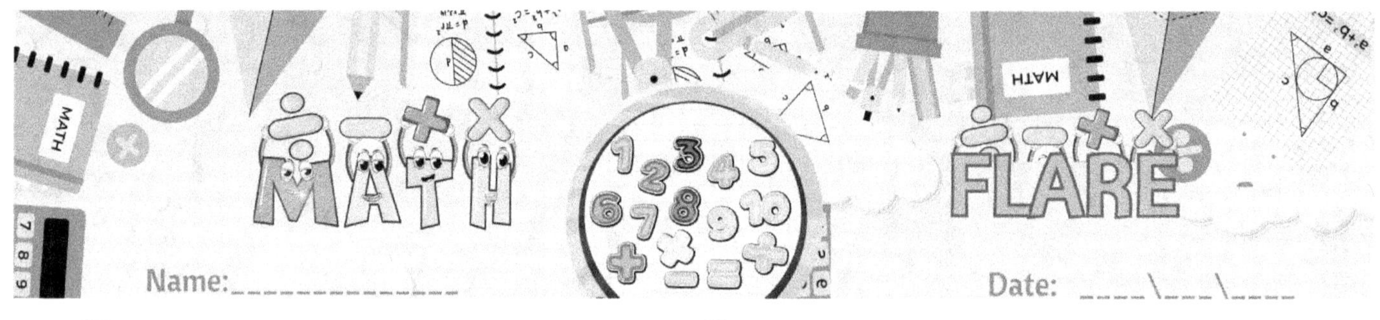

17. $3 \times z = -27$

18. $-6 + 1y = -5$

19. $9 - k = 18$

20. $-7m + 18 = 53$

21. $11x + 10 = -12$

22. $0 + x = -6$

23. $-120 \div m = 15$

24. $49 \div z = -7$

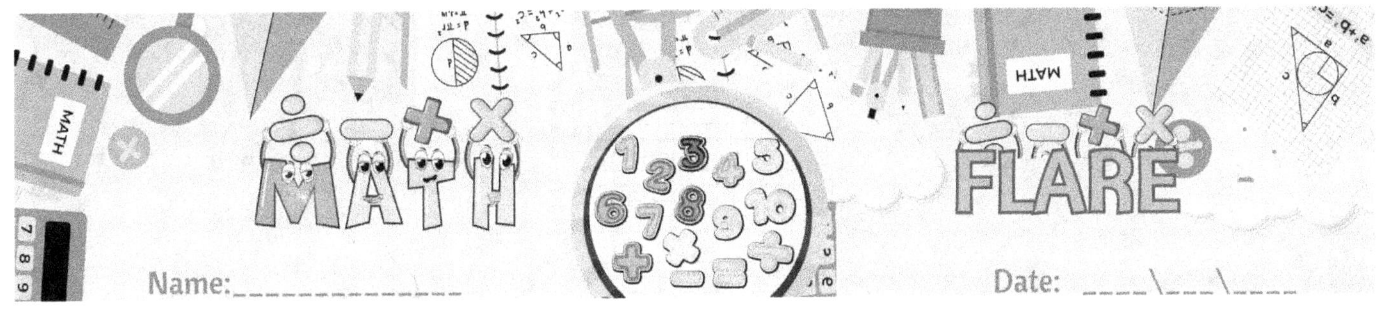

25. $z \times 1 = 8$

26. $10 \times z = -30$

27. $13 - 0y = 13$

28. $323 \div m = 17$

29. $360 \div x = 18$

30. $11 - k = 14$

31. $-7m - -7 = 0$

32. $15 + -9k = -30$

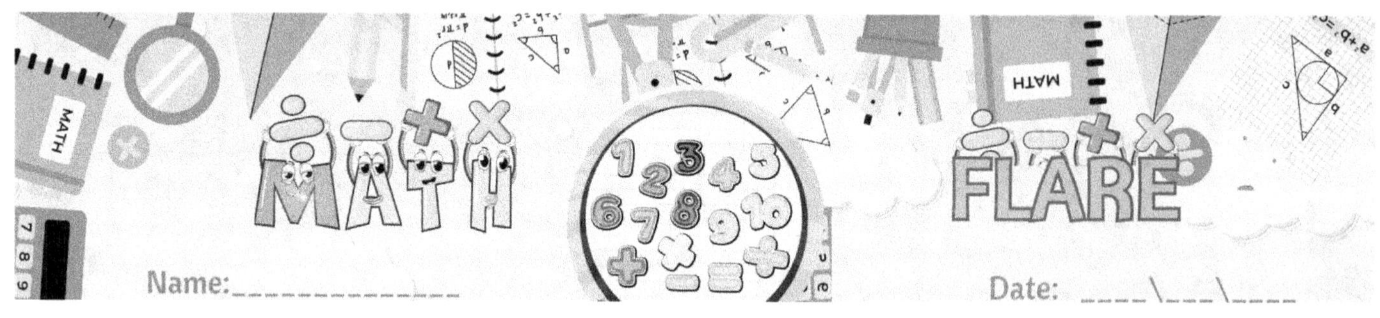

33. $-9 + z = -6$

34. $x \times 4 = 52$

35. $z \times 15 = 285$

36. $x \times 15 = -150$

37. $k - 7 = 13$

38. $m + -3 = -6$

39. $4 + x = -6$

40. $y \div -5 = 18$

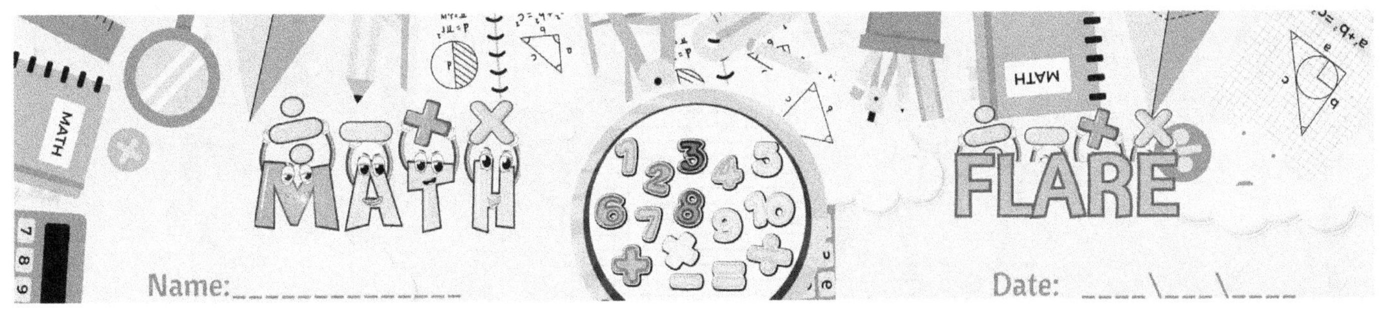

41. $z \div 16 = -3$

42. $z \times 14 = -70$

43. $z + 20 = 23$

44. $17y - 15 = 172$

45. $-8 + m = -11$

46. $16x - -7 = 295$

47. $17m - 13 = 4$

48. $k \times 6 = 72$

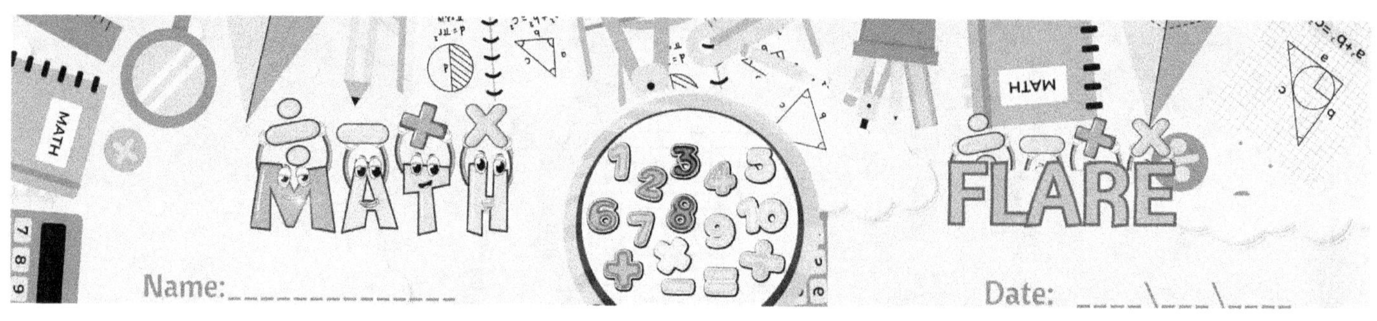

49. $m - -9 = 2$

50. $15 + -9y = -120$

51. $z \times -4 = 16$

52. $-4 - -1k = 14$

53. $34 - -4k = 6$

54. $k - -7 = 26$

55. $k - 1 = 0$

56. $9y - -1 = 10$

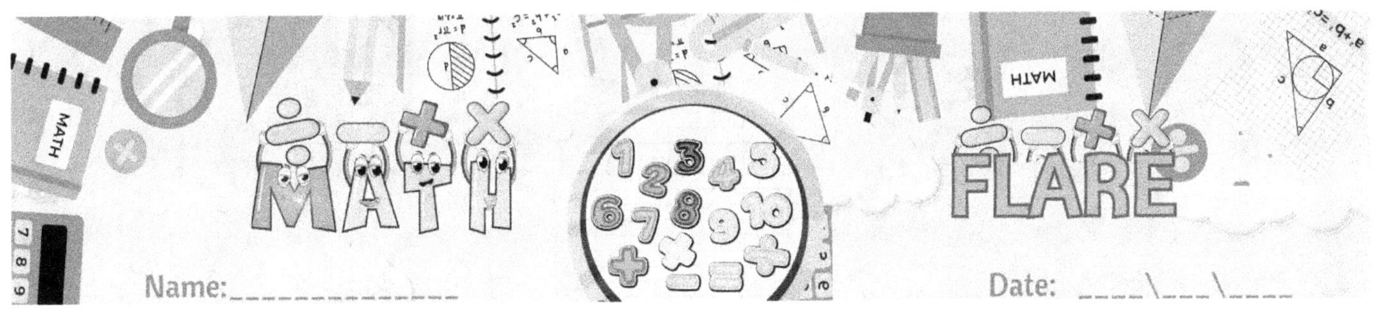

Equations (Two Sides)
Solve for the variable.

1. $-21 - -2s = -6 + -1s$

2. $5a + -5 = -7 + 7a$

3. $-1 + 1b = -15 - -8b$

4. $2s + 2 = 8 - s$

5. $9 + -7z + 1 = -27 + z + 5$

6. $-98 - 4k = 9k + 6$

7. $-10s + 8 = -46 - s$

8. $6 + 8s = 24 - -6s$

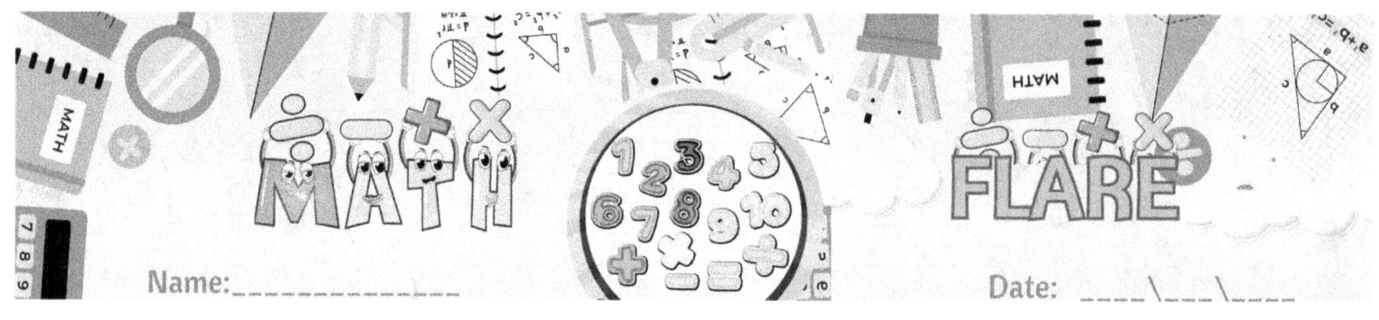

9. $-4 + 2z = 2 + z$

10. $55 + k = -10k$

11. $3k = 12 - k$

12. $-38 - -8y = 6 + -3y$

13. $4k = 25 - k$

14. $-57 - -2a = 9a + 6$

15. $-8 + 8m = 46 - m$

16. $3a = -4 + a$

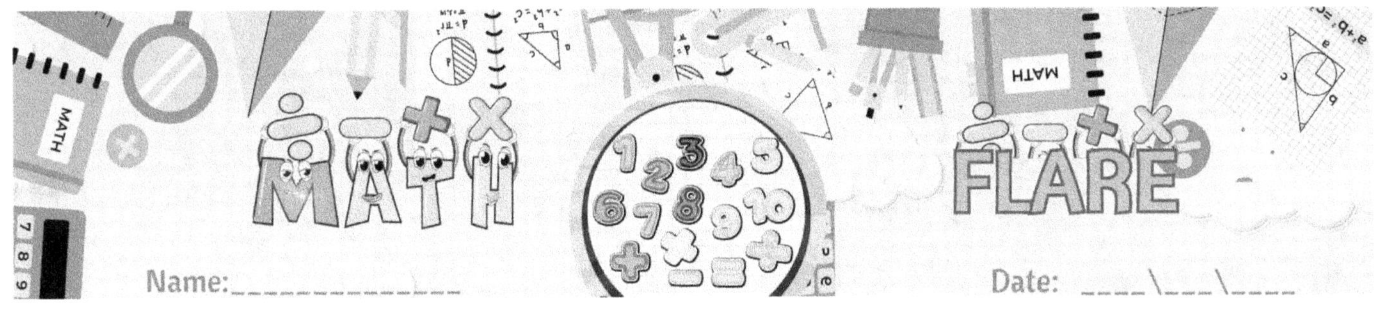

17. $-9x + 24 = 1x + -6$

18. $9 - z = 2z$

19. $-2m = -7 - m$

20. $-10 + -5m + 5 = 35 + m + 14$

21. $-69 - 2b = 10b + -9$

22. $7z + 5 = 29 + z$

23. $65 + s + -4 = -7 + 9s + 4$

24. $1 + 5z + 4 = -31 + z + 8$

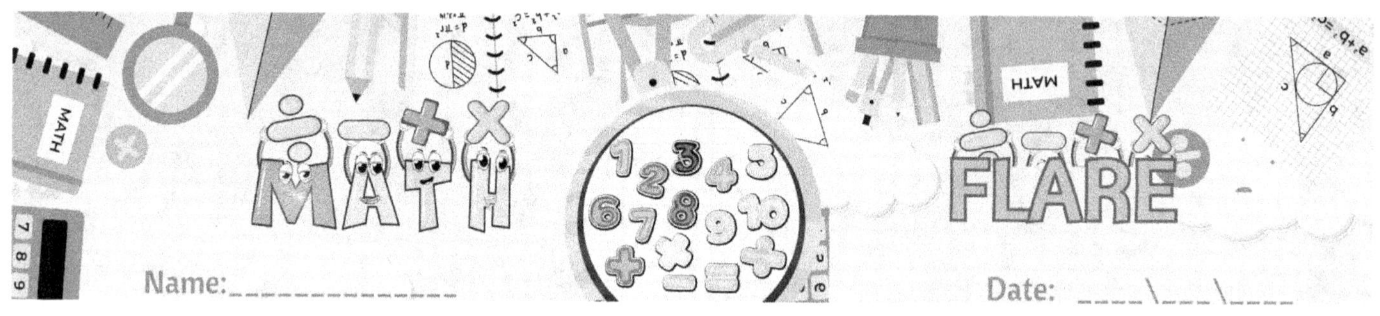

25. $-4 + 10s = 32 - 8s$

26. $5y = 6 - y$

27. $17 - k = 7 + -6k + -10$

28. $80 + s = -7s$

29. $-9 + -3m + 3 = -18 - m + -2$

30. $-3m = 2 - m$

31. $-3 + b = 2b$

32. $-3 + -4b + -7 = -27 - b + 2$

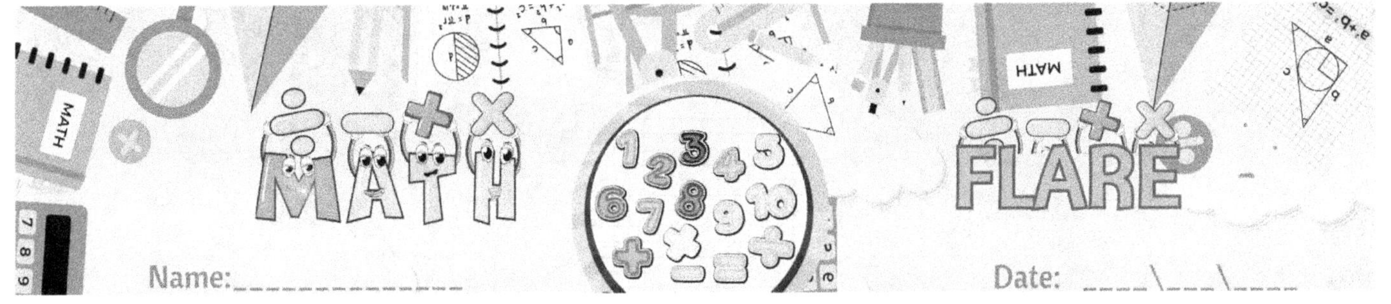

33. $-2 + 1m = 25 + -8m$

34. $32 - -9s = 8 + -3s$

35. $-3 - y = -3 + -2y + -4$

36. $-1 + -8b + -8 = -64 + b + -8$

37. $158 - 9y = 10y + 6$

38. $7 + k = 2k$

39. $-5b + -5 = 51 - -9b$

40. $-8 + a + 4 = 10 + 2a + -5$

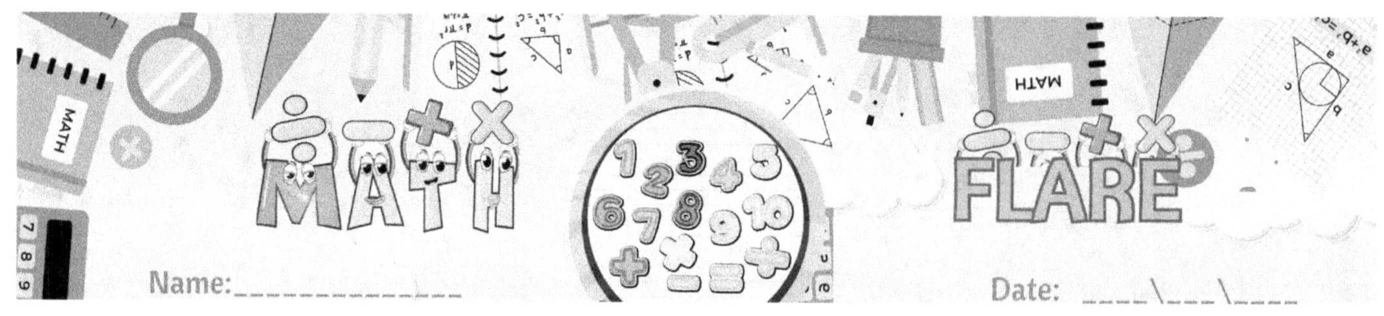

41. $-2 + -2s + -1 = 21 + s$

42. $-6z + 4 = 43 - -7z$

43. $67 + z + -9 = 1 + 6z + 7$

44. $2 + b + 8 = 9 + 3b + -1$

45. $-7b + 4 = 52 - b$

46. $55 + z + 15 = -9 + -8z + 7$

47. $2k = 3 - k$

48. $-7 + -2y + 5 = -29 + y$

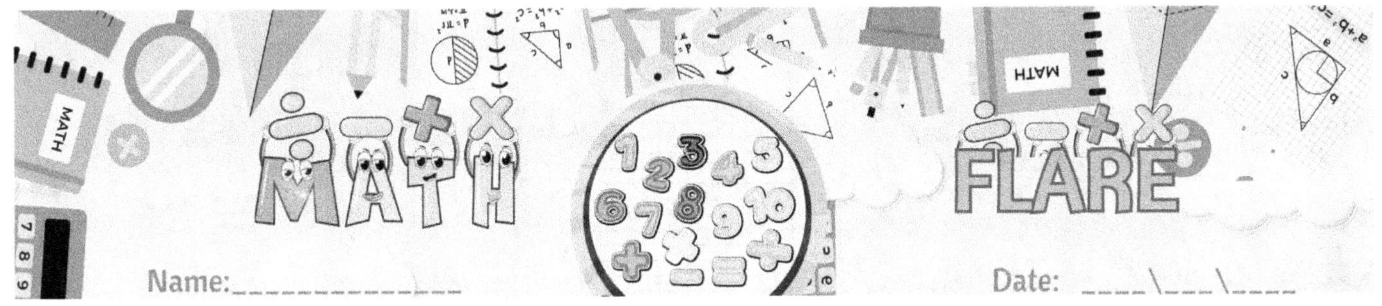

49. $-27 - y = 4 + 5y + -7$

50. $-30 - y = 9y$

51. $31 + 2x = 10x + 7$

52. $5 + 9b = 13 + b$

53. $3 + -2x + 5 = 23 + x + 15$

54. $16 + z = 4 + -5z$

55. $46 - y = 8y + 1$

56. $-1 + 10s = -4s + -113$

Simplify Expressions

1. $-5y + 10y + 16 - 14y$

2. $15y + y$

3. $5y - 2 - 9y + 17$

4. $-x + 12x$

5. $9k - 9k + 16 + 11$

6. $18 + 16m - 16m$

7. $7 - 10m + 4 - 11m + 8 - 12m$

8. $7 - 16k + 5 - 7k + 19 - 9k$

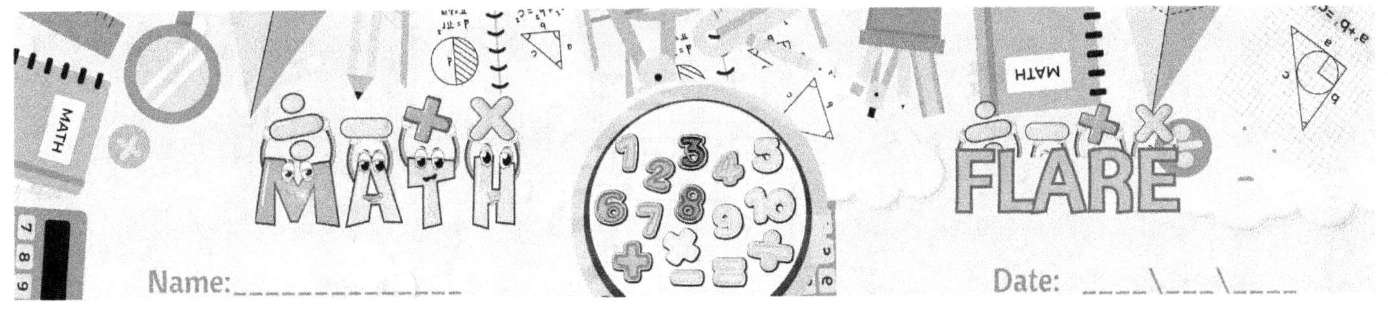

9. $15k - 5k + 4k - 6 + 12$

10. $-15 + 11y - 19y - 17 + 5y$

11. $k + 13 - 2k + 4 + 9k + 3$

12. $15y + 5y$

13. $-15 + 6k - 20k - 11 + 2k$

14. $-2y + 4 + 5y + 11 + 12y - 14$

15. $4z - z$

16. $15k + 1 - k - 17 + 16k - 2$

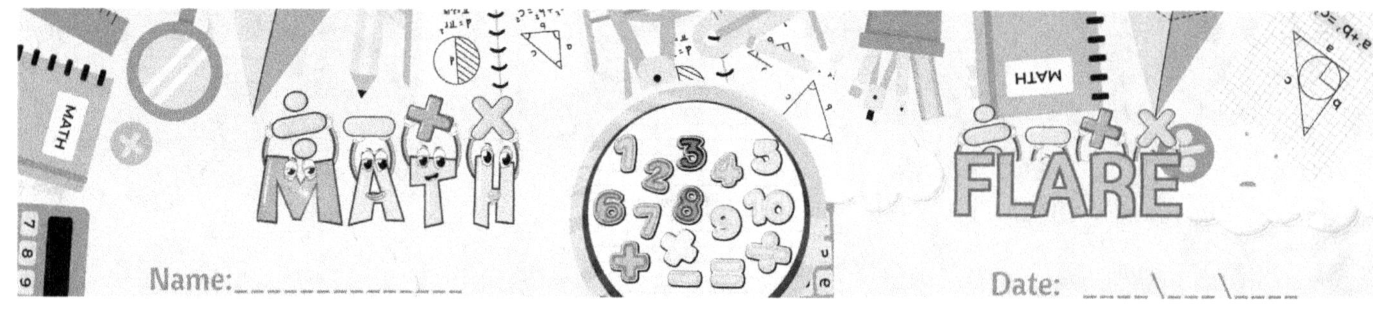

17. $-7z - 7 - 6z$

18. $14z - 9z$

19. $-y - 5y$

20. $5m + 11 - 19 - 20m + 9m$

21. $-7m + 14m + 10 - 7m$

22. $-15z - 15 + 9 - 13z$

23. $-10 + 17y - 20y - 2 + 14y$

24. $13y - 13y + 19y - 9 + 13$

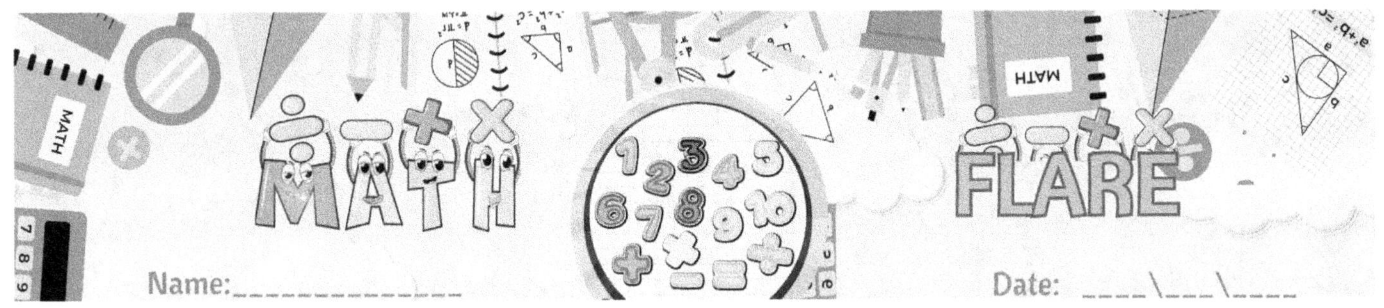

25. $6x + 8 - 20x + 9 + x + 6$

26. $-12x - 5 + 6x$

27. $-z - 4z$

28. $-x - 8x$

29. $8m + m$

30. $y - 15y$

31. $-12y + 14 + 4y + 17 + 20y - 17$

32. $-4k - 8 + 1 - 6k$

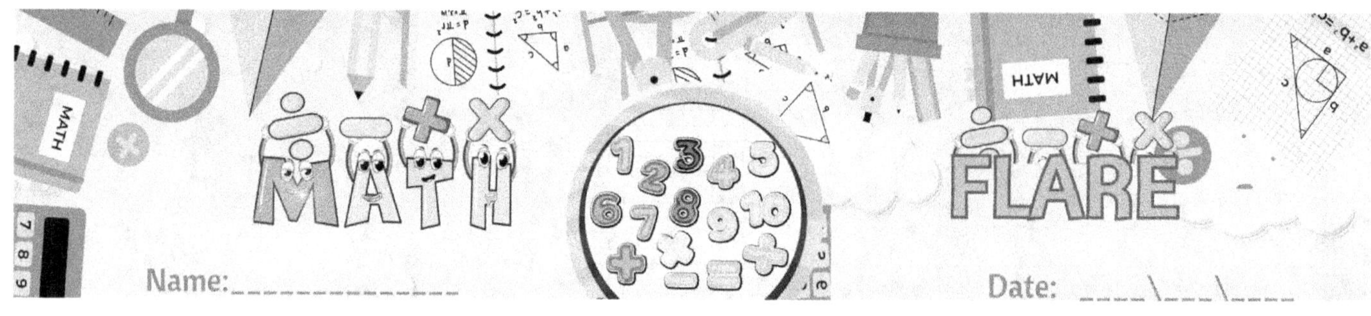

33. $-2z + 14 + 16z$

34. $-5y - 8 - 7 - 12y$

35. $-9 + 17z - 5z - 11 + 4z$

36. $-17k + 7 + 6k + 1 + 6k - 4$

37. $18 + 15k - 5 + 11k$

38. $20m + m$

39. $-18z + 5 - 3z$

40. $20k - 7 - 10k + 5$

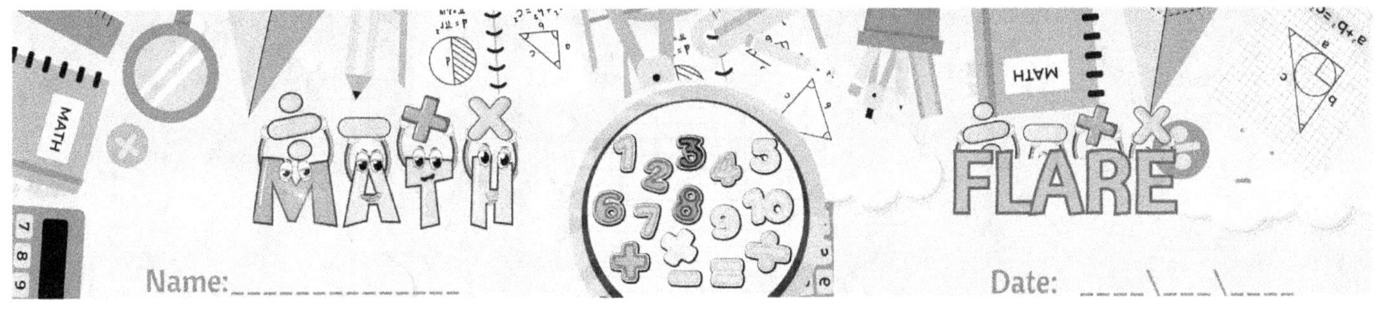

41. $3k - 2k + 1 + 4$

42. $-4k + 5k$

43. $m + 7m$

44. $17y - 3 - 5y + 2$

45. $20 + 20z - 3z$

46. $-20y + y + 11 - 8y$

47. $15m - 14m + 13 + 6$

48. $6y + 18 - 8y - 17 + 5y - 20$

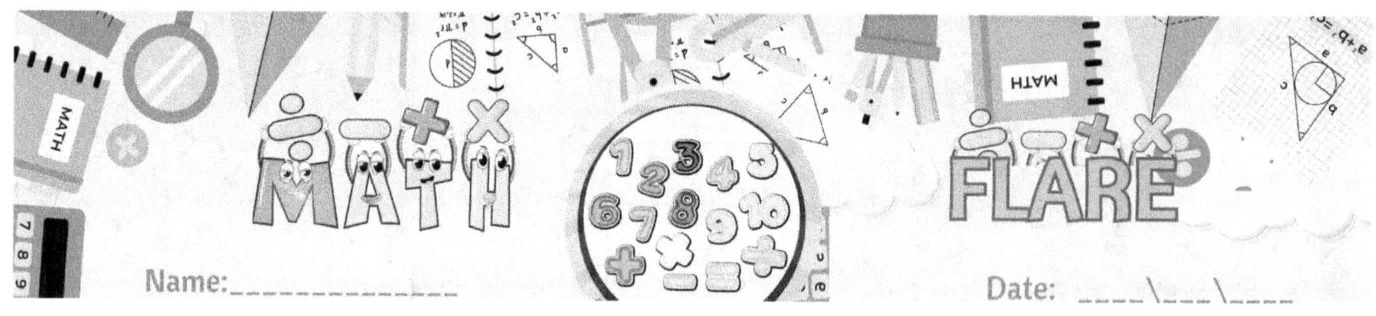

49. $20 + 6k - 15 + 14k$

50. $-8 - 7m + 4m - 12 + 16m$

51. $12x + x$

52. $3 + 20z - 4 + 10z$

53. $2 + 3k - 14 + 6k$

54. $-10 + 10 - 10y + 14y - 20 + 19y$

55. $14z - z$

56. $20 - 3(-z + 18)$

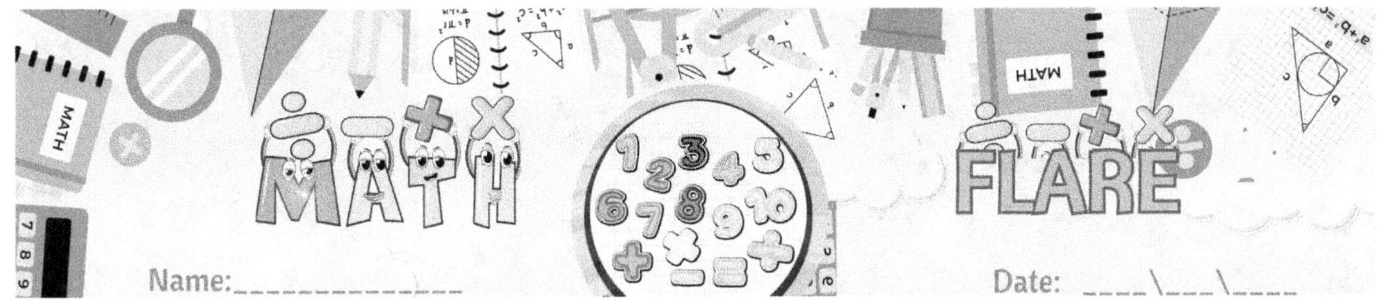

57. $8 + 6z - 15 + 6z$

58. $5z + 19 + 2z + 10 + 4z + 7$

59. $-20z - 18 + 15z$

60. $3x + 7x$

61. $-m + 5m$

62. $5y + 14 + 6y + 5 + 19y + 10$

63. $12y - 3 + 6y - 10 + 16y + 5$

64. $-6 + 8m - 10m - 2 + 11m$

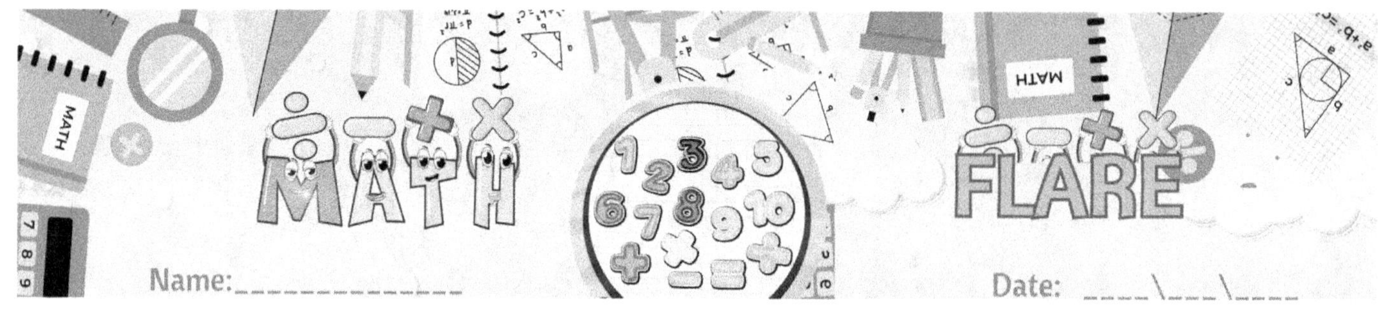

65. $9z - 16 + 8z - 20 + 6z + 17$

66. $k + 18 + 19k$

67. $15y - 7 + 4y - 2 + 7y + 2$

68. $m + 5m$

69. $-10z + 10z$

70. $-z + 11 - 18z$

71. $14 + 10k - 15 + 18k$

72. $-19y + 17 - 5y$

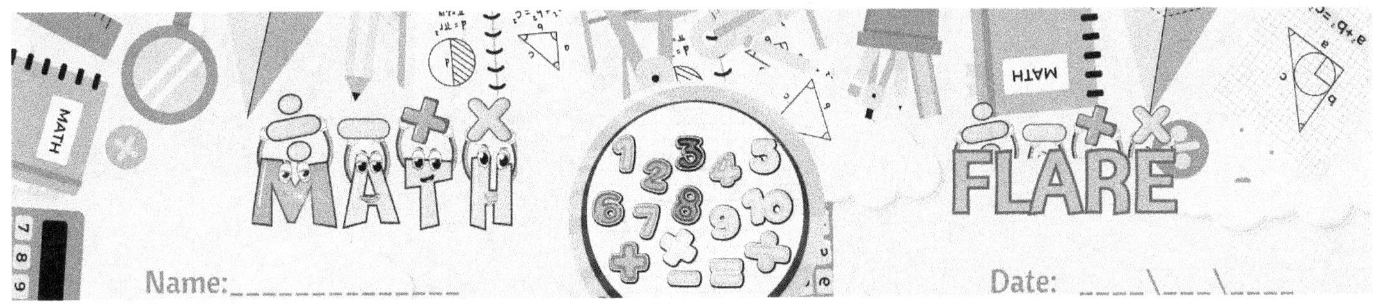

73. $-14 + 7 - 6z + 3z - 18 + 14z$

74. $-2 + 8x - 3x - 13 + 3x$

75. $-20m - 10m$

76. $-10k - 1 + 18k$

77. $11x - 7 - 9x + 9$

78. $3z + 4z$

79. $4 + 18z + 8 + 7z$

80. $17y + 16 + 15y$

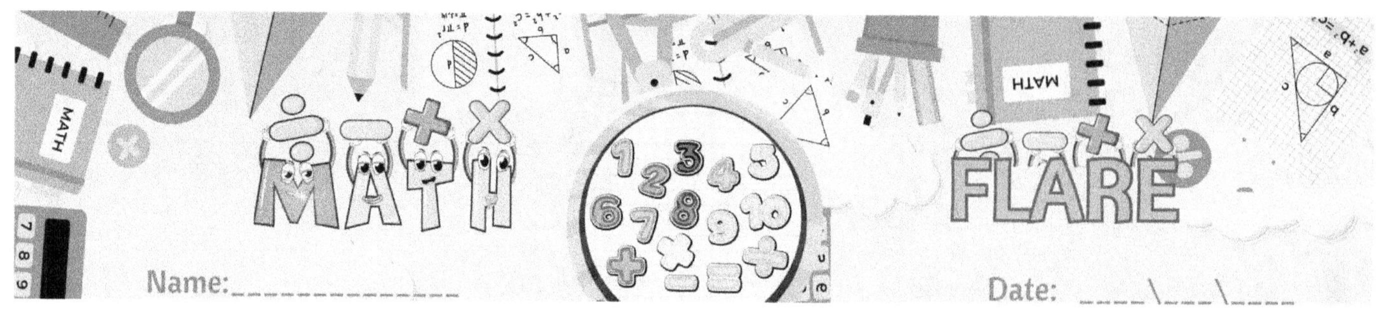

81. $2m + 12 + 17m + 8 + 13m + 8$

82. $-8m - 11 + 10m$

83. $8x - 8x + 2x - 19 + 19$

84. $15 + 19k + 18 + 11k$

85. $-20k + k$

86. $-11 + 19y + 18 - 16y$

87. $6z - 6z$

88. $12 + 15k + 16 + 9k$

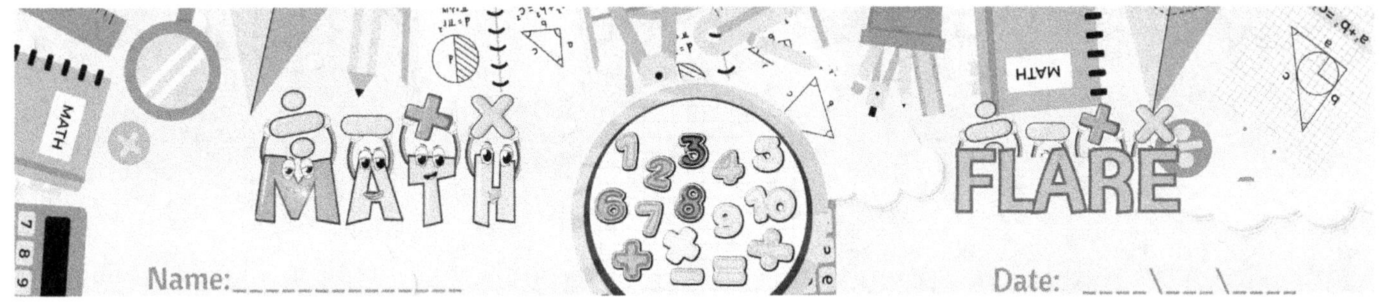

89. $-1 - 3z + 19 - z$

90. $-3 + 13k - 16k - 19 - 10k$

91. $-13 + 9k + 2 - 15k$

92. $-16 + 18m - 3m - 17 + 7m$

93. $10m - 10 - 13m + 20 - 5$

94. $-5x - x$

95. $-11z + 7 + 10z$

96. $m - 12m + 17m + 1 + 17$

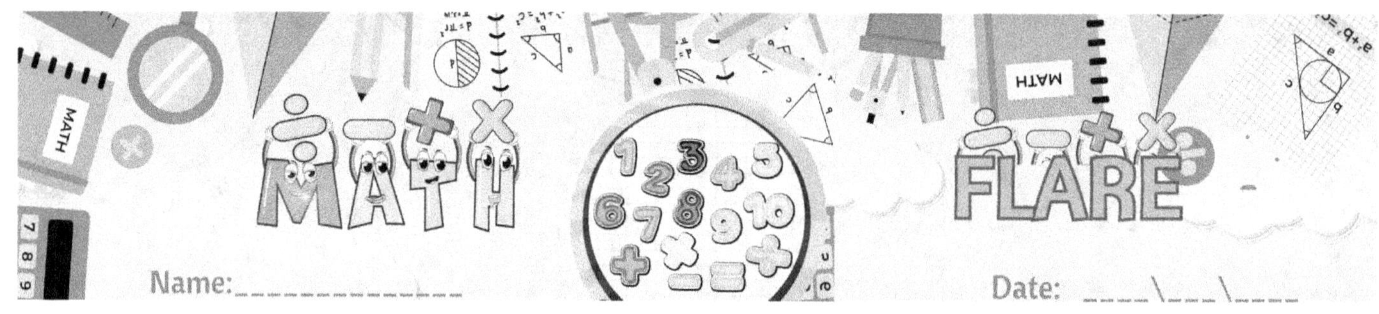

97. $-8m - 4 - 15m$

98. $20 + 2k - 8 + 18k$

99. $4 + 12z - 18z + 18 - 13z$

100. $-13z + z$

101. $14z + 9 - 9 - 4z + 8z$

102. $9 + 20z + 10 + 7z$

103. $19z - 11z + 18 + 16$

104. $m - 3m$

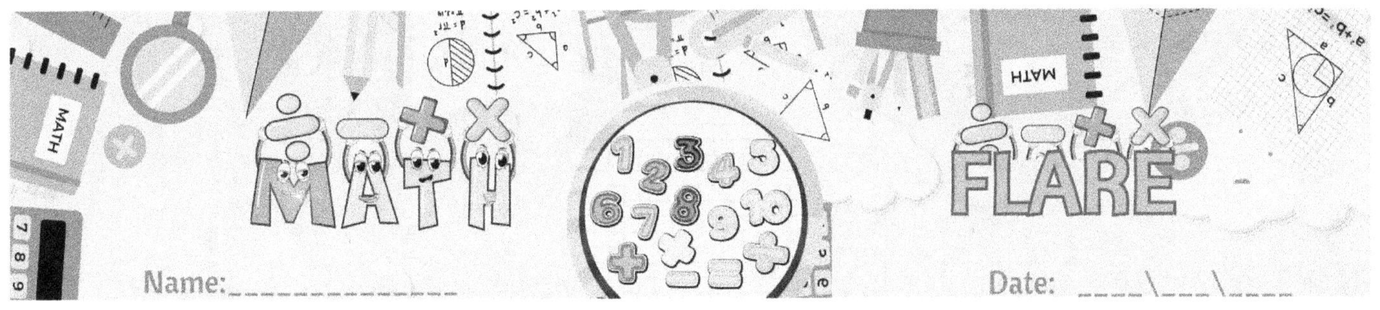

Simplifying Equations

Simplify the following equations when the value of $n = 2$

1. $3n - 9 + (-9)n =$

2. $n(-10 + n) =$

3. $8n - n =$

4. $4 + (-1)n =$

5. $-1n + 5n - 0 =$

6. $-8n + (-6) =$

7. $-2(-2 + n) =$

8. $8(10 + n) =$

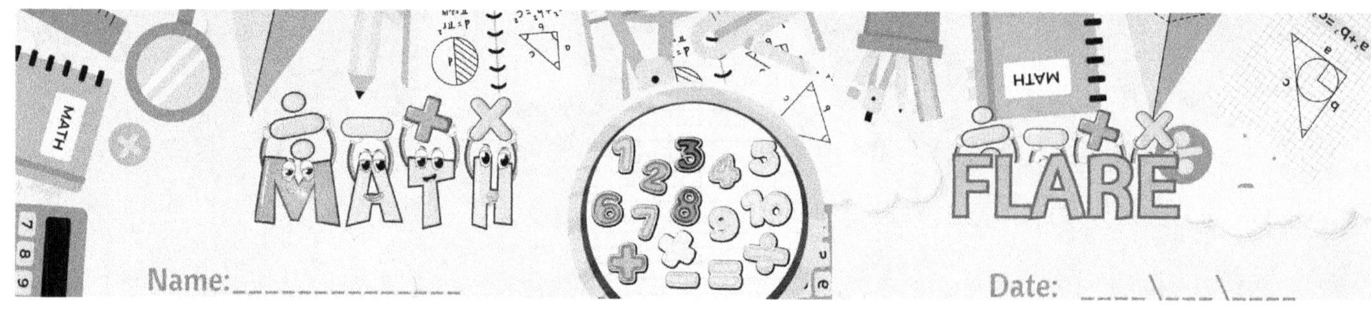

Simplifying Equations

Simplify the following equations when the value of $n = -10$

1. $2(0 + n) =$

2. $-8n + (-6) =$

3. $-3n + (-2)n + (-6)n =$

4. $8n + 7 - 3n =$

5. $4 - n =$

6. $n \div 4 =$

7. $9(-10 + n) =$

8. $4n + 0 =$

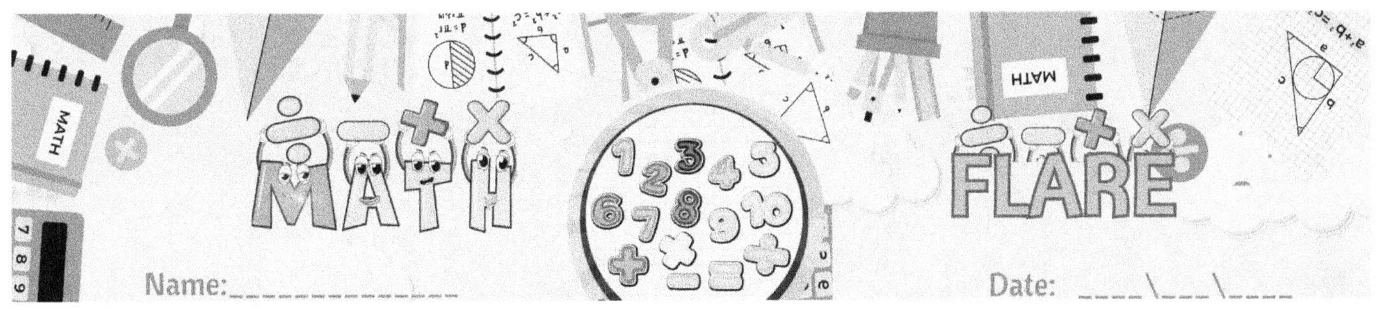

Simplifying Equations

Simplify the following equations when the value of n = -4

1. $n + 3n + (-1)n =$

2. $n(-2 + n) =$

3. $9n + n =$

4. $-4n - 4 + 2n =$

5. $n \div (-8) =$

6. $5^2 + n^2 =$

7. $0n + n =$

8. $5n + 7 - 5n =$

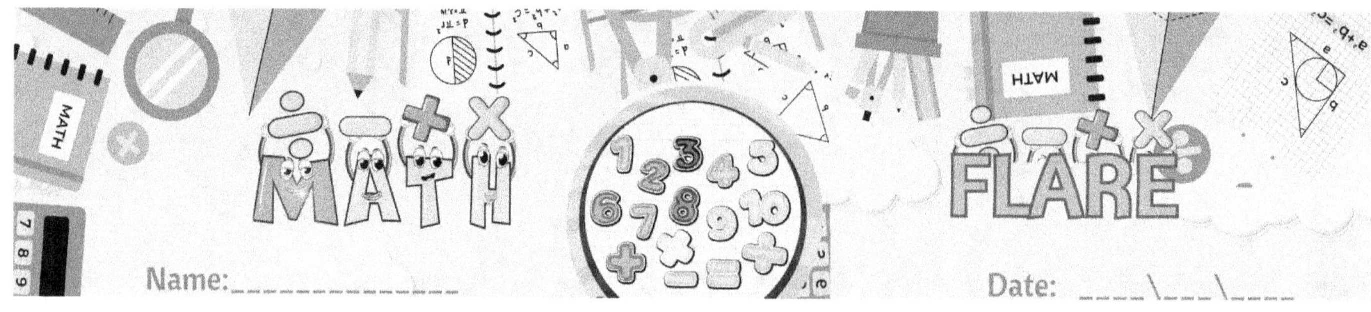

Simplifying Equations

Simplify the following equations when the value of $n = -8$

1. $8 - n =$

2. $-10^1 + n^3 =$

3. $1 + n =$

4. $-8 \div n =$

5. $n + (-10) + n =$

6. $n + (-10) =$

7. $9n + (-4) =$

8. $2(8 - n) =$

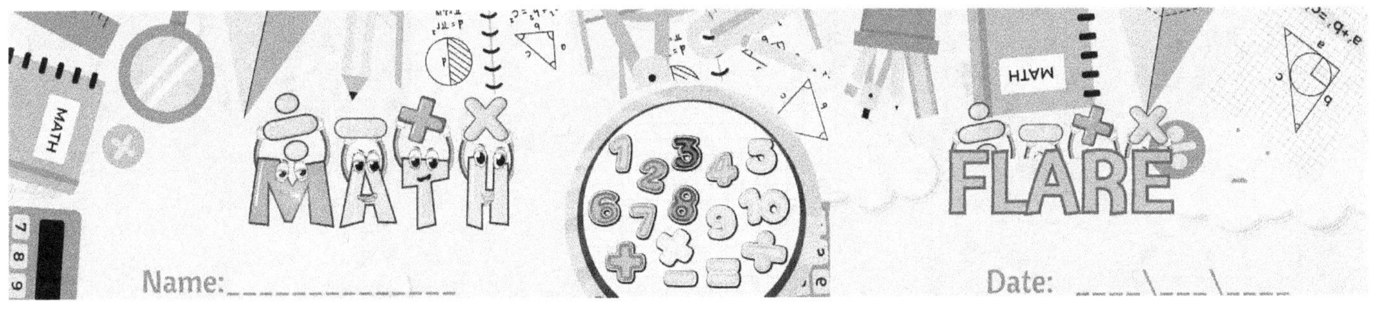

Simplifying Equations

Simplify the following equations when the value of n = 4

1. $-4n + (-6) =$

2. $5n^3 + 5n^2 =$

3. $-9n + (-8) =$

4. $n + 8 + 8n =$

5. $5(6n) =$

6. $0(2 - n) =$

7. $n \div (-6) =$

8. $0 - n =$

Simplifying Equations

Simplify the following equations when the value of n = -7

1. $-8n + 10n + 10n =$

2. $-3(9 - n) =$

3. $2n + (-9) =$

4. $-8 + (-10)n =$

5. $4n - 1 + 7n =$

6. $n + 4 =$

7. $-4 + n =$

8. $n(6 + n) =$

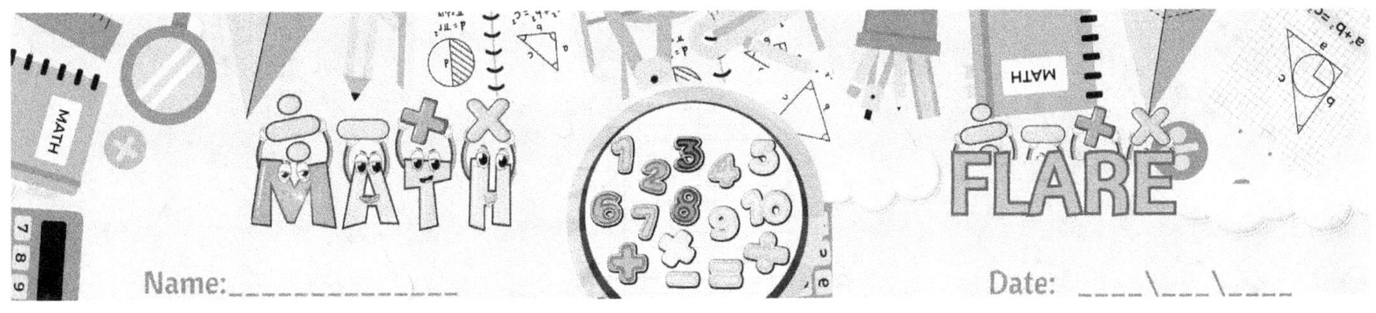

Simplifying Equations

Simplify the following equations when the value of n = -5

1. n – (-6) =

2. -8 ÷ n =

3. 0 + (-7n + (-3)) =

4. -9n + 4 =

5. -1n + 10 =

6. 3n + 6n – (-8) =

7. 5 + n =

8. 10(-5 + n) =

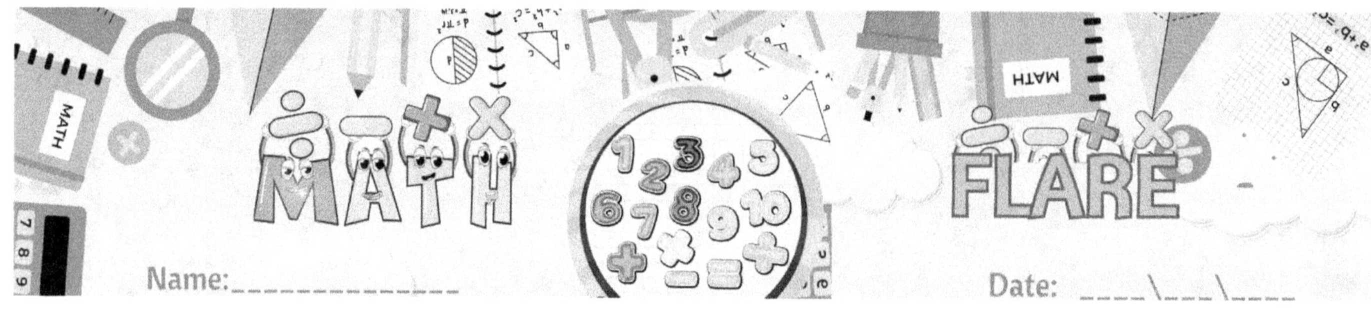

Simplifying Equations

Simplify the following equations when the value of $n = -8$

1. $n^1 + n - 4 =$

2. $-3^2 + n^1 =$

3. $10n + 3n - 4 =$

4. $-10 \div n + 3 =$

5. $-3n - (-8) + 4n =$

6. $0 + (n + 10) =$

7. $3(2n) =$

8. $n - 8 =$

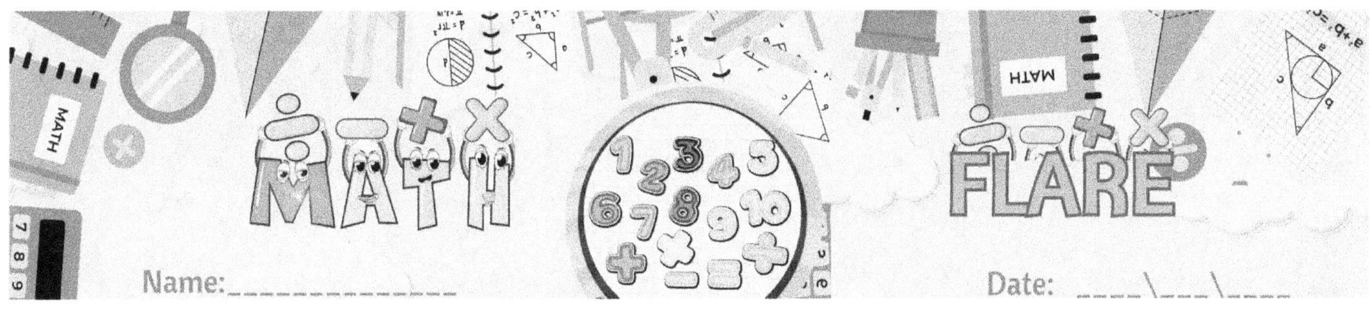

Simplifying Equations

Simplify the following equations when the value of $n = -2$

1. $7n + 1 =$

2. $-2^3 + n^2 =$

3. $10 + (3n + (-3)) =$

4. $n + (-9) =$

5. $9 \div n + (-10) =$

6. $4 + 5n =$

7. $5^1 + n^2 =$

8. $6 \div n + (-5) =$

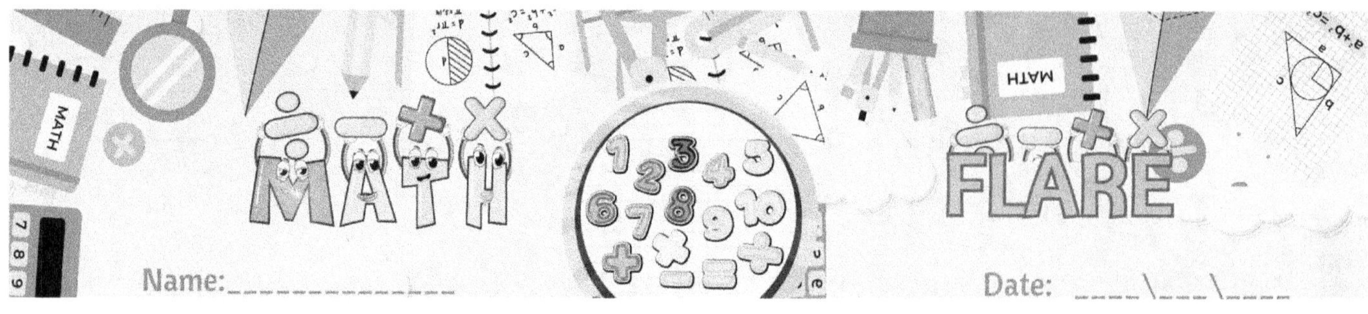

Simplifying Equations

Simplify the following equations when the value of $n = 5$

1. $-4n + 5n + (-5)n =$

2. $-6 - n =$

3. $-2n^2 + 2n^2 =$

4. $-6n - (-1) + 4n =$

5. $-9(-6 + n) =$

6. $8n^2 + (-1)n^1 =$

7. $-5n + (-2) =$

8. $n^2 + n - 0 =$

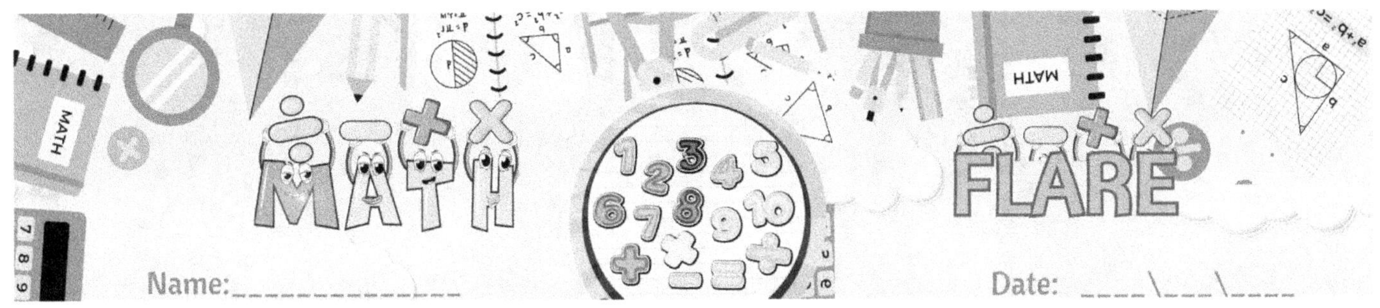

Verbal Algebra Expressions

1. Two times the sum of a number and six times the number is 70. Find the number.

2. A number diminished by 5 is 3. Find the number.

3. Four times a number increased by 6 is 18. Find the number.

4. Five times a number equals 2 less than seven times the number. What is the number?

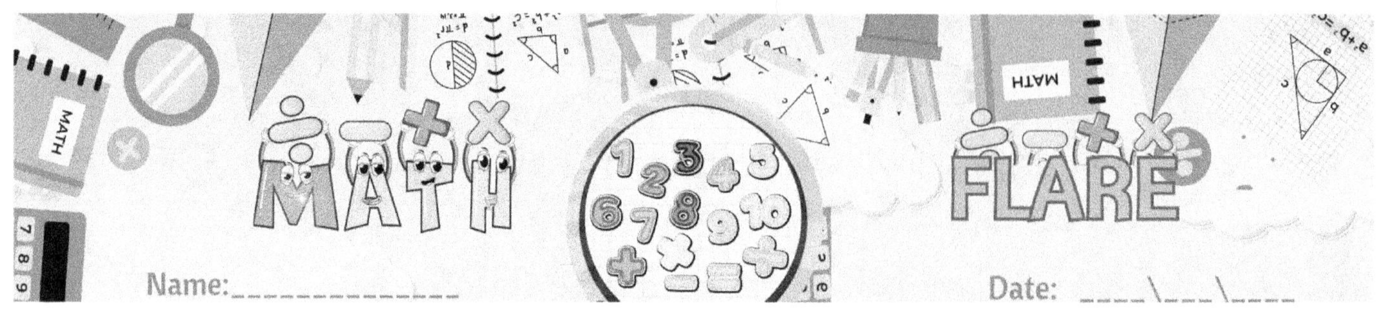

Name:_________________   Date: _______________

5. The difference of two numbers is 62. The larger number is 8 more than ten times the smaller number. What are the numbers?

6. The sum of four consecutive numbers is 10. What are the numbers?

7. Three times a number is 6. What is the number?

8. Eight is equal to the quotient of a number and 4. Find the number.

9. The sum of two numbers is 8. The larger number is three times the smaller number. What are the numbers?

10. The sum of two consecutive even numbers is 14. What are the numbers?

11. One less than a number is 2. Find the number.

12. The sum of two numbers is 12. The difference of the same two numbers is six. Find the numbers.

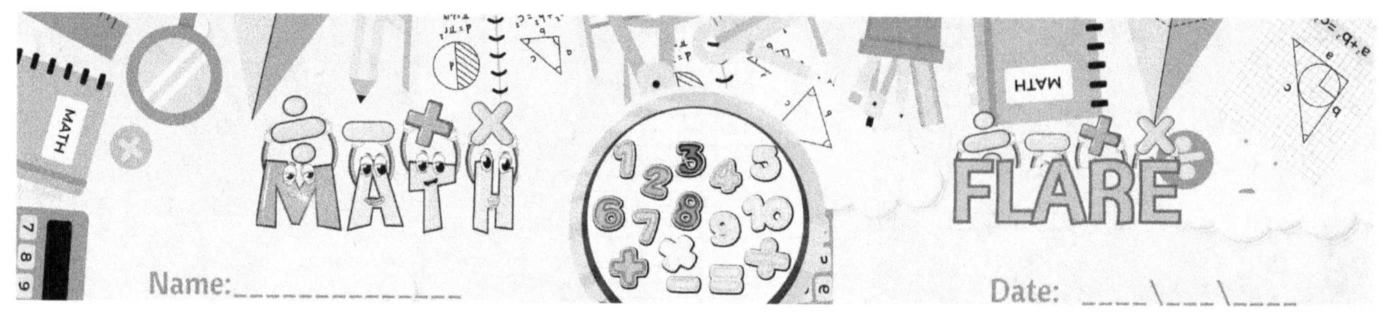

13. The sum of three numbers is 52. The largest number is seven times the smallest, and the smallest is seven less than the middle number. Find the numbers.

14. Six more than a number is 10. What is the number?

15. The greater of two numbers is 7 less than three times the smaller number. Their sum is 29. Find the numbers.

16. The sum of a number and four is 11. Find the number.

17. One less than eight times a number is 63. Find the number.

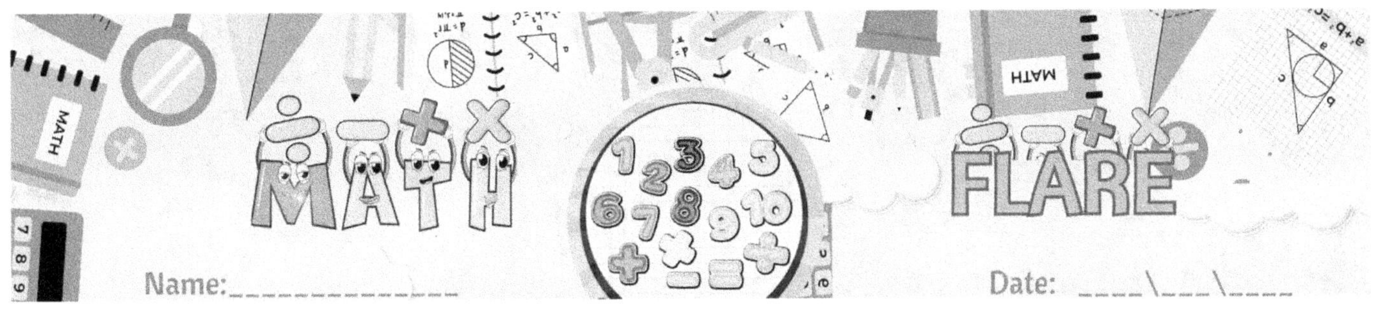

18.   Two more than a number is 11. What is the number?

19.   The sum of the largest and nine times the smallest of three consecutive numbers is equal to 22. Find the numbers.

20.   The sum of the first and third of three consecutive numbers is 18. Find the numbers.

21.   A number increased by two is 11. Find the number.

22.   Four times the sum of a number and six times the number is 56. Find the number.

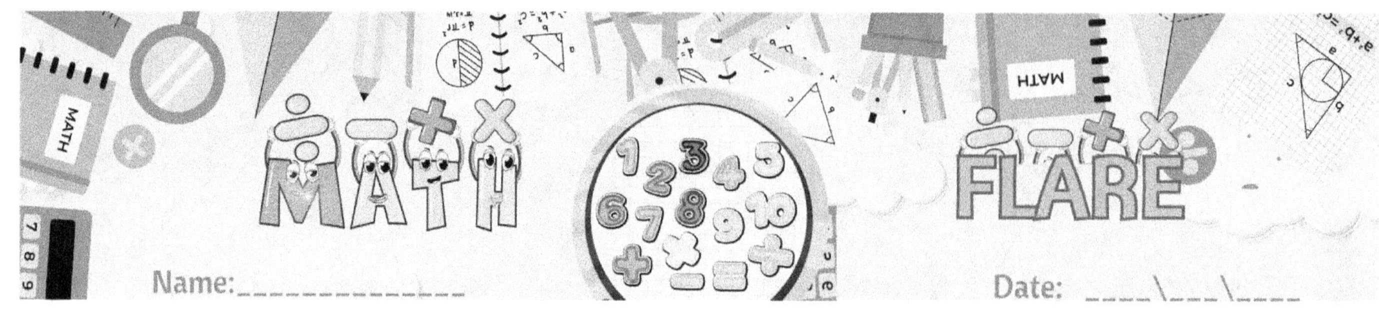

23.   The product of six and a number is 18. What is the number?

24.   The product of six and a number is 24. What is the number?

25.   The sum of a number and six is 12. Find the number.

26.   The quotient of a number and three is 5. Find the number.

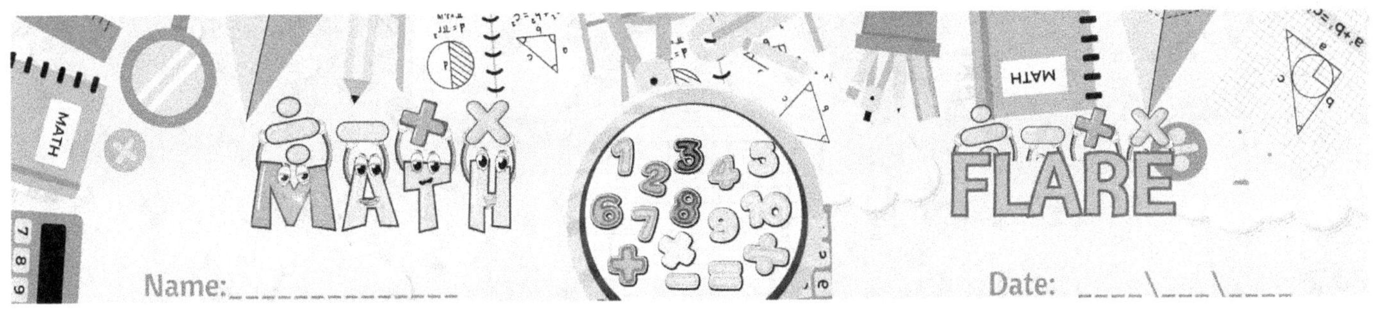

27. One number is two more than another number. The sum of the larger number and twice the smaller number is 17. Find the numbers?

28. When a number is divided by eight, the result is 3. What is the number?

29. Four times the sum of a number and three times the number is 144. Find the number.

30. Seven less than a number is 4. Find the number.

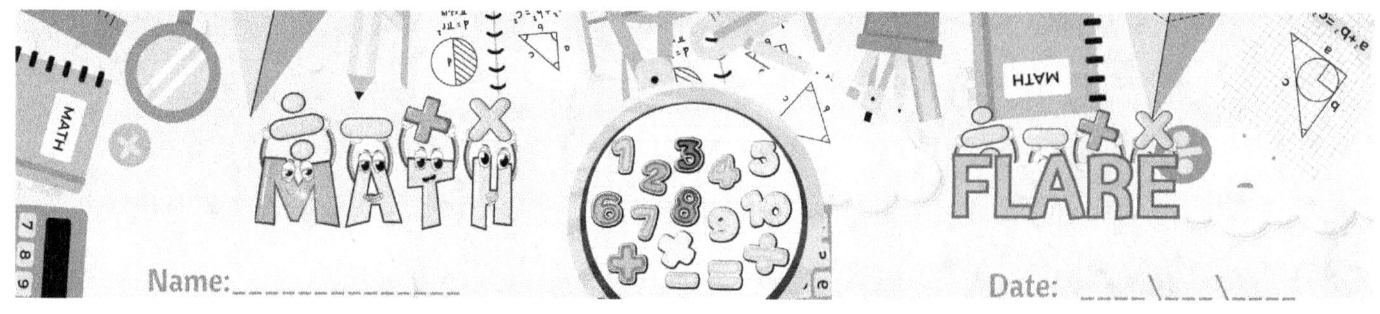

31. One less than seven times a number is 69. Find the number.

32. 40 is equal to the product of eight and some number. Find the number.

33. Four times the difference of 7 minus a number is 20. What is the number?

34. One number is 7 more than another number. The sum of twice the larger number and nine times the smaller is 36. What are the numbers?

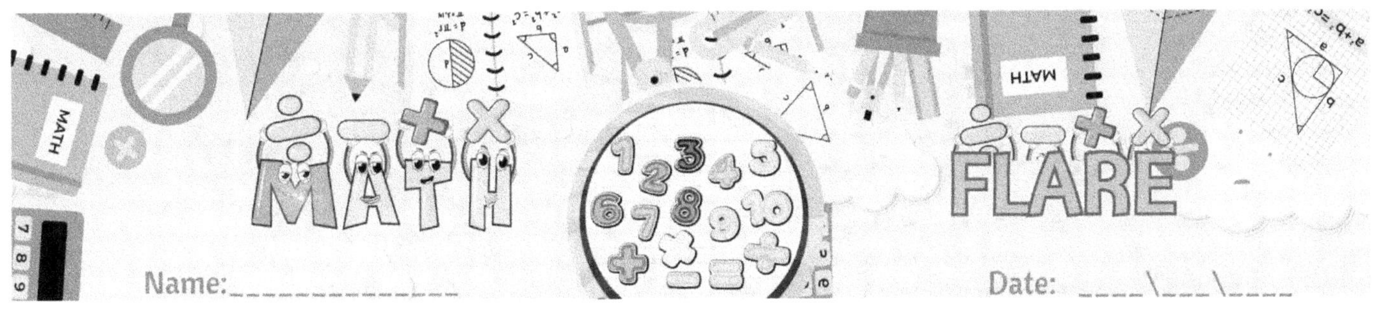

35. The product of three and some number is equal to the sum of that number and 18. What is the number?

36. The sum of the largest and three times the smallest of three consecutive numbers is equal to 34. Find the numbers.

37. The difference of two numbers is 12. The larger number is 3 more than four times the smaller number. What are the numbers?

38. The product of two numbers is 12. One number is four less than the other. What are the numbers?

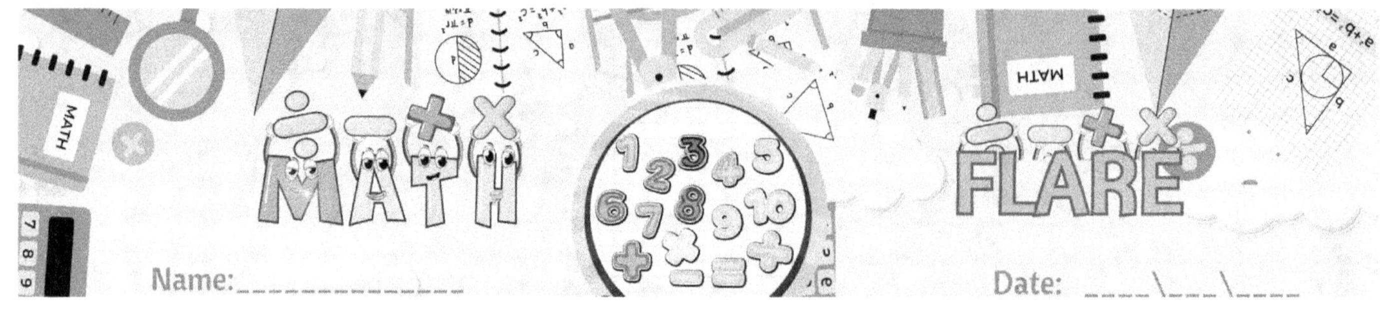

39.   The sum of a number and three is 6. Find the number.

40.   The difference of a number and seven is equal to 4. What is the number?

41.   The sum of two numbers is 4. One number is two less than the other. Find the numbers.

42.   Find two consecutive even integers such that three times the smaller decreased by the larger is 10.

43.   Twice a number is 6. What is the number?

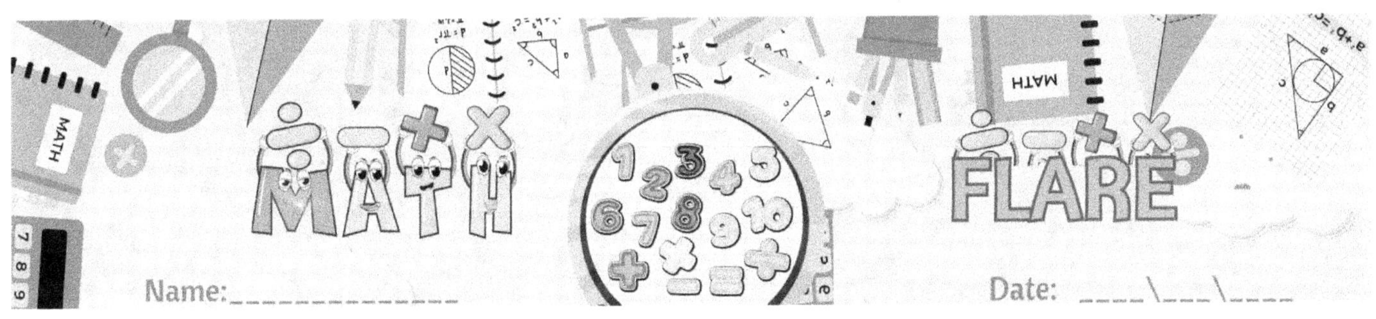

44.   Five more than twice a number is equal to the number increased by 7. What is the number?

45.   A number increased by one is 6. Find the number.

46.   One less than five times a number is 24. Find the number.

47.   Three times a number increased by 2 is 14. Find the number.

48.   Two more than twice a number is equal to the number increased by 5. What is the number?

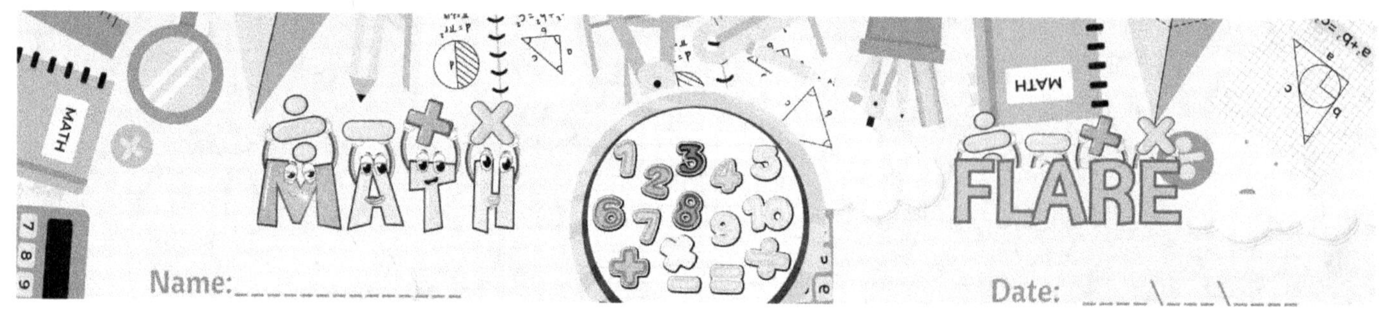

49.   Two times a number equals 18 less than five times the number. What is the number?

50.   The sum of two numbers is 27. The difference of the same two numbers is nine. Find the numbers.

51.   The product of four and a number is 32. What is the number?

52.   One less than five times a number is 54. Find the number.

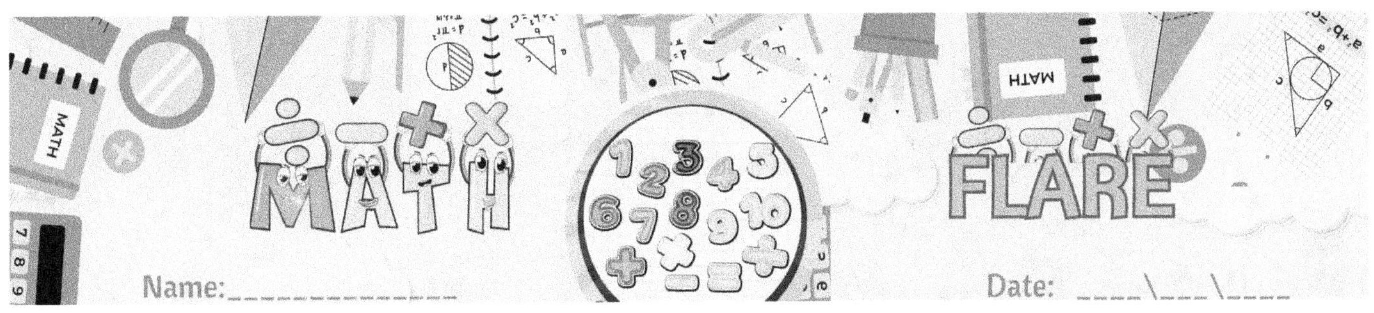

53. more than the second of three consecutive even integers is the same as the difference between the third and three times the first. Find the numbers.

54. Six more than a number is 7. What is the number?

55. The sum of two numbers is 11. The difference of the same two numbers is seven. Find the numbers.

56. Find two consecutive odd integers such that four times the larger decreased by the smaller is 17.

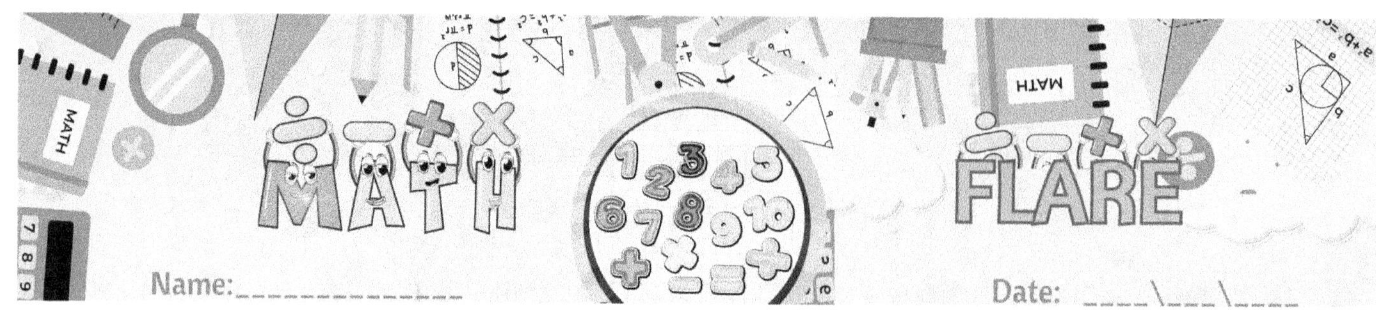

57. One number is five times another. Their sum is 24. Find the numbers.

58. Three times a number equals 24 less than six times the number. What is the number?

59. The sum of four consecutive numbers is 26. What are the numbers?

60. The product of two numbers is 5. One number is four less than the other. What are the numbers?

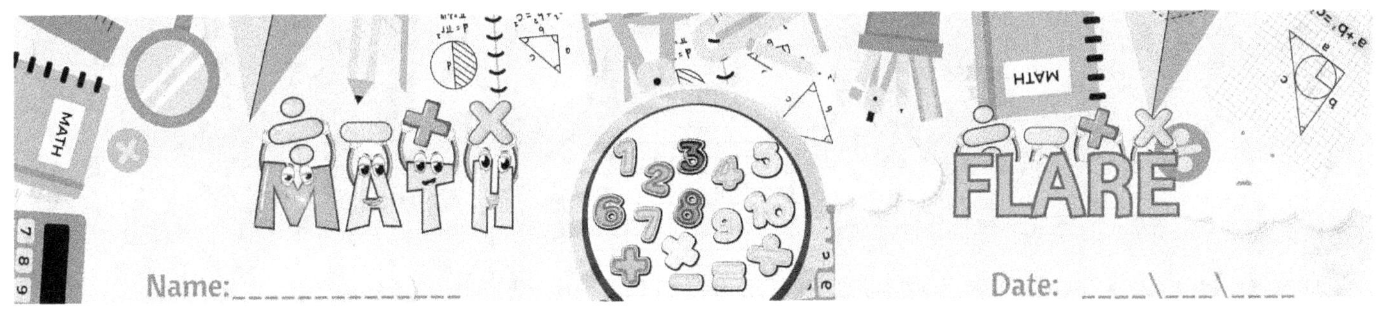

Solving Inequalities

1. $-2 - x < 0$

2. $15\,b < 18$

3. $k + 8 \geq -3$

4. $\dfrac{z}{1} \geq 5$

5. $15\,z \leq 9$

6. $-9 - m \leq -4$

7. $-2 + s < -7$

8. $\dfrac{s}{3} < -5$

9. $s + 7 > -7$

10. $\dfrac{x}{4} \geq -9$

11. $b - {-4} \geq 7$

12. $-8\,x < -16$

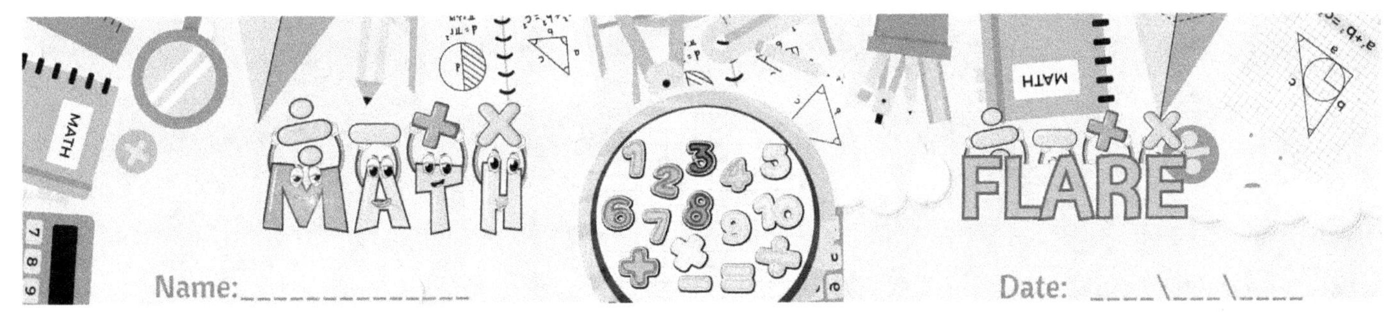

13.
$$-12\,y \ge 8$$

14.
$$\frac{b}{-8} < -7$$

15.
$$y - -8 \ge 1$$

16.
$$8 + x > 5$$

17.
$$-12\,s \ge 4$$

18.
$$2 + y \le 2$$

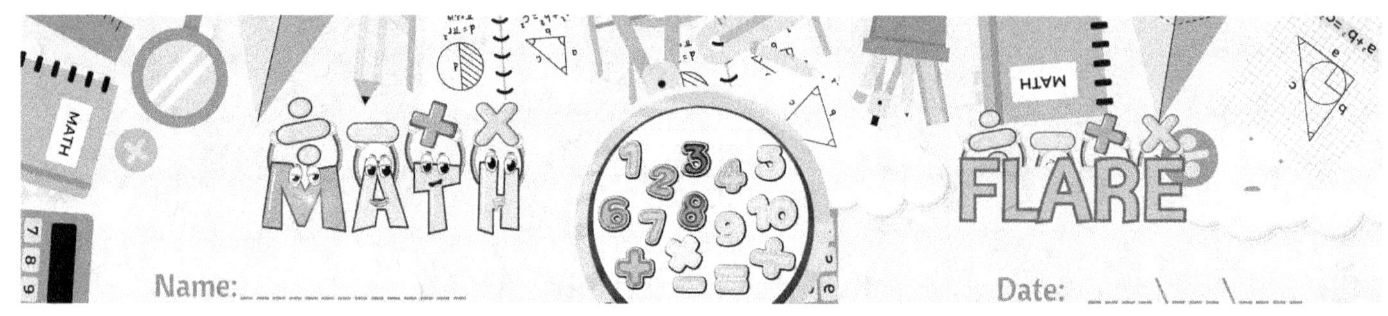

19.
$$\frac{b}{-9} > -4$$

20.
$$7 - s \geq 8$$

21.
$$x - 1 \geq 3$$

22.
$$-12\,x \leq 8$$

23.
$$-10 + a < -1$$

24.
$$\frac{m}{-8} < -2$$

MathFlare - Algebra 1 7th to 10th Grade

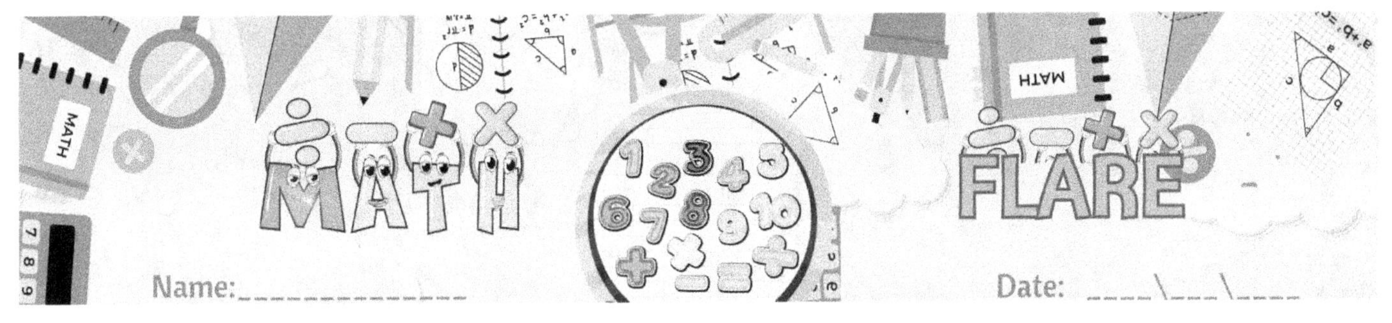

25. $-5 - s \le -3$

26. $-24\,y > -8$

27. $-5 + k \le 9$

28. $\dfrac{k}{2} \le 5$

29. $k + -6 < 4$

30. $\dfrac{y}{2} \ge -2$

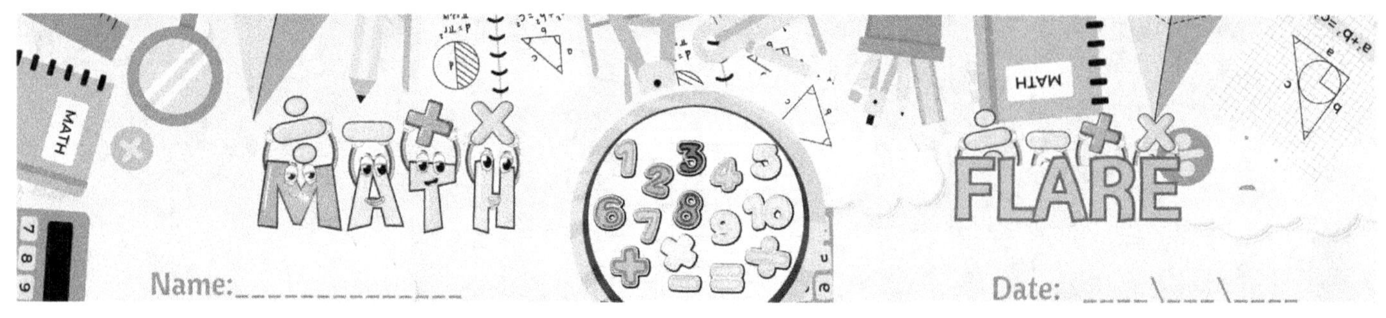

31.

$$y - 7 \leq 9$$

32.

$$10\,b \leq 12$$

33.

$$-3\,a \geq -6$$

34.

$$\frac{m}{6} \leq -3$$

35.

$$6 - a < 9$$

36.

$$5 + m > 6$$

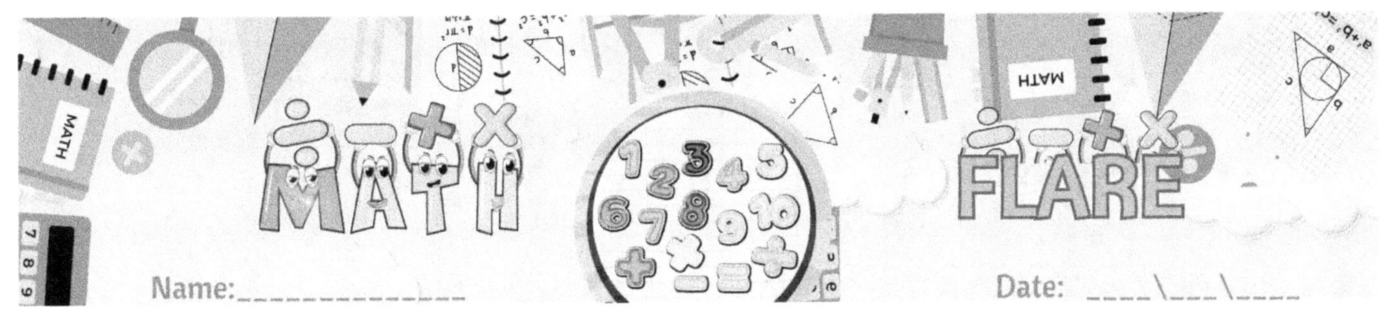

37. $z + -5 \leq 7$

38. $9b \leq 6$

39. $\dfrac{b}{3} \geq -3$

40. $k - -2 < 8$

41. $\dfrac{x}{-8} \leq -4$

42. $-9b \geq 18$

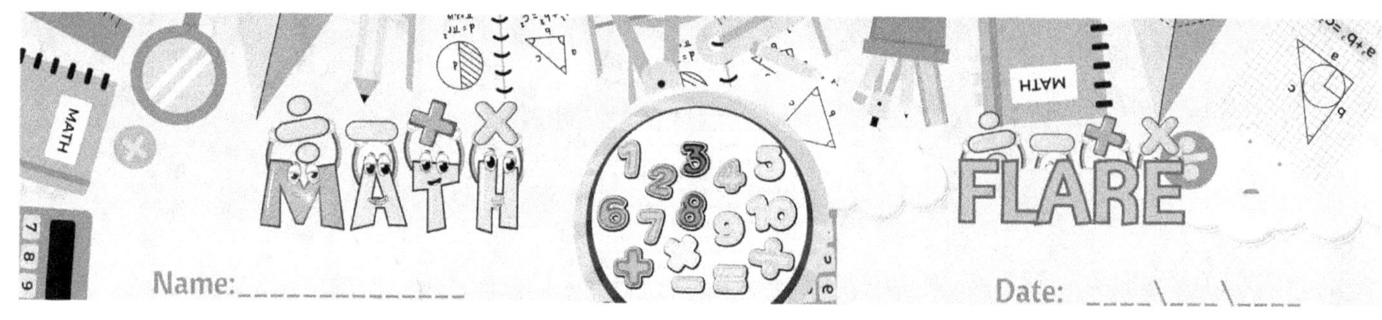

43.
$$1 + y \leq 4$$

44.
$$x - -8 \leq -7$$

45.
$$a + -9 \geq 9$$

46.
$$\frac{k}{6} \leq 8$$

47.
$$-1 - z > 3$$

48.
$$1\,m \geq 4$$

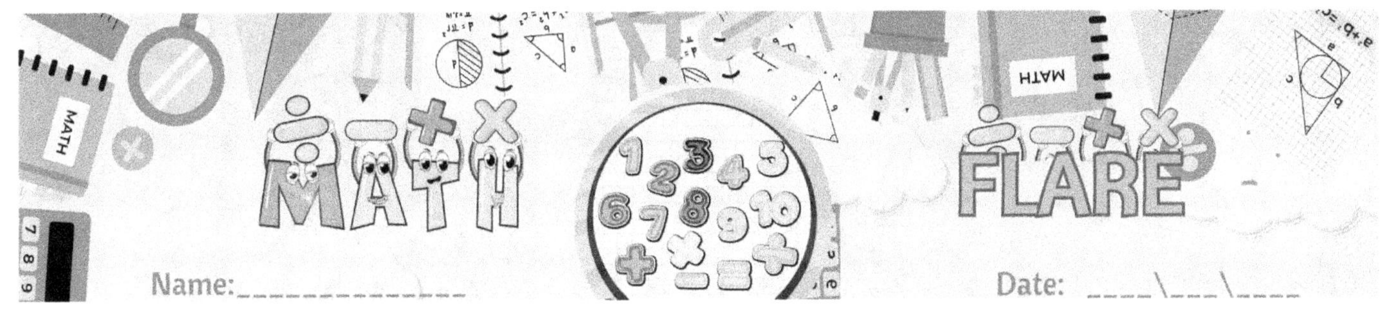

49.

$$-1\,s \le -5$$

50.

$$2 - k \ge 5$$

51.

$$\frac{y}{4} \ge -4$$

52.

$$-1 + y \le -8$$

53.

$$-6\,z \ge -4$$

54.

$$\frac{a}{5} < 5$$

55.
$$x + -2 > 8$$

56.
$$z - -2 > 1$$

57.
$$-2 + a > 4$$

58.
$$3\,y \geq -9$$

59.
$$k - -8 > -3$$

60.
$$\frac{a}{-6} \leq -2$$

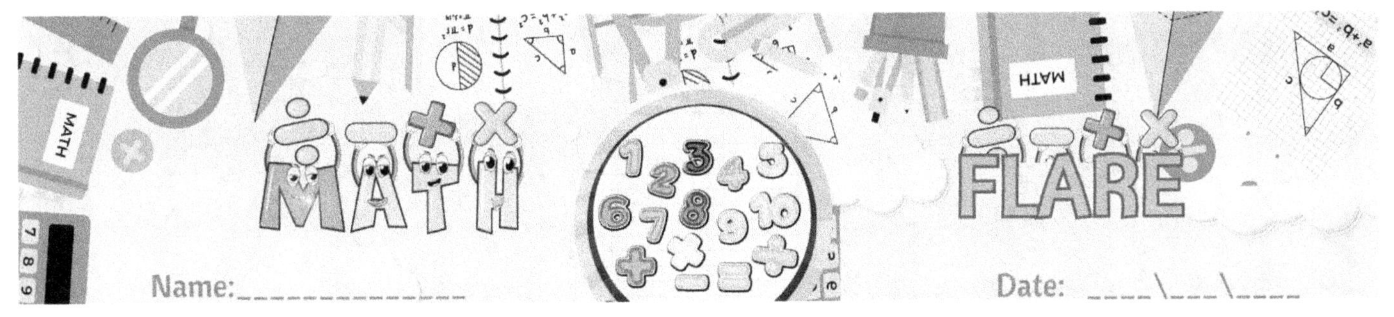

61. $-2 + b < 2$

62. $7 - b < 9$

63. $\dfrac{b}{8} \geq -2$

64. $-3y \leq -4$

65. $2z > -4$

66. $\dfrac{z}{7} > 2$

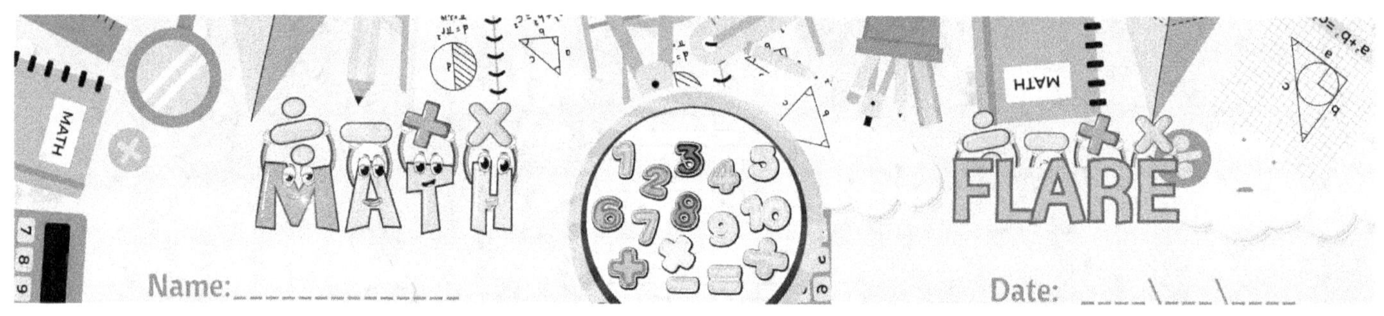

67. $1 + x > 1$

68. $m - 8 \leq 9$

69. $-9 + a < -6$

70. $2m > -6$

71. $\dfrac{x}{-1} > -8$

72. $k - {-5} > 6$

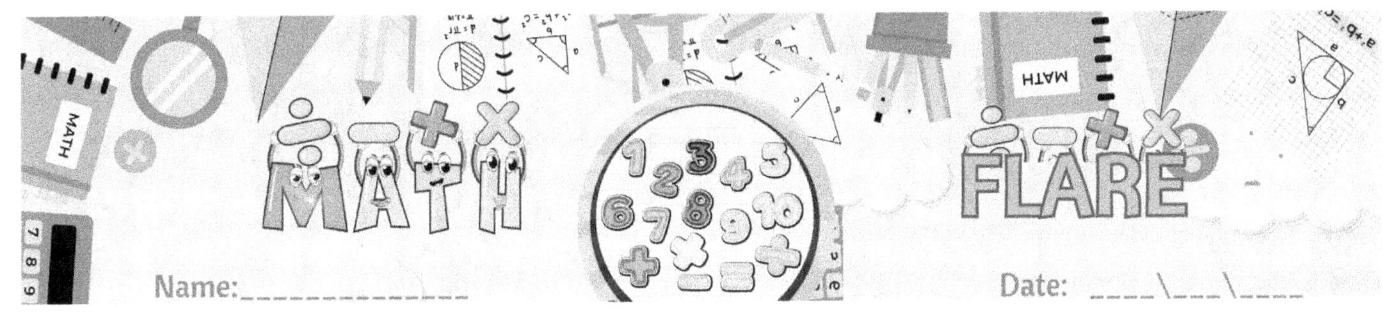

73. $x + 4 > 9$

74. $\dfrac{z}{-8} > -5$

75. $3 - y \geq 9$

76. $9\,s < 6$

77. $z + 6 > -7$

78. $\dfrac{m}{-6} \leq -5$

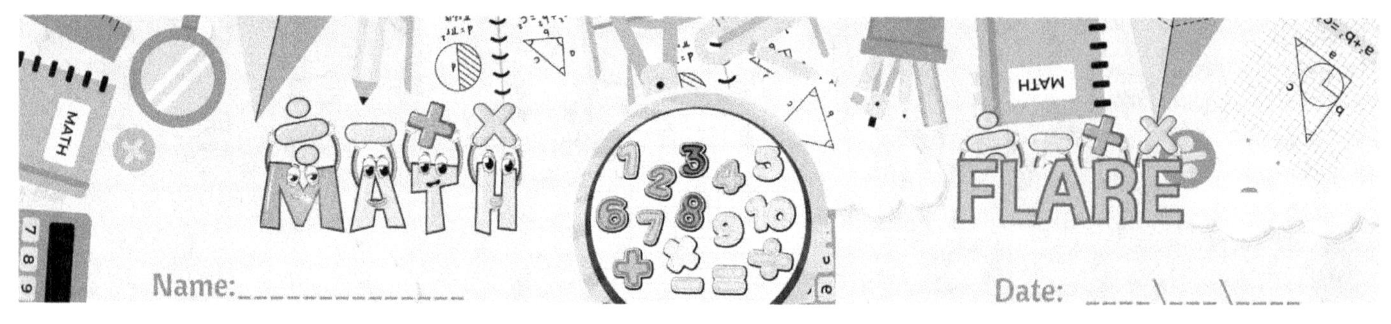

79.

$$21\,k \geq -6$$

80.

$$-1 - b < 4$$

81.

$$y + 5 \leq -4$$

82.

$$1\,y \geq -3$$

83.

$$\frac{y}{2} < 1$$

84.

$$a - 1 > 3$$

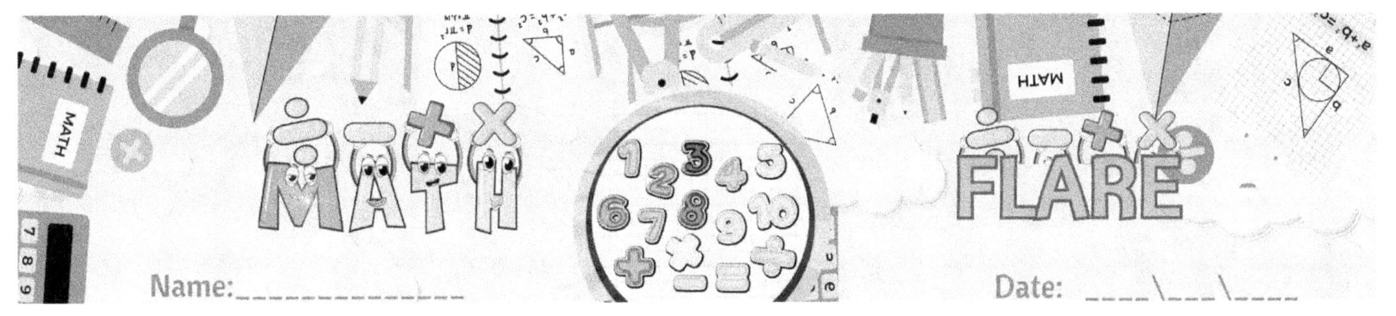

85.

$$-5 + z > -2$$

86.

$$4 - a \geq 5$$

87.

$$\frac{k}{-8} \leq -3$$

88.

$$2z > 6$$

89.

$$-4x \leq 6$$

90.

$$\frac{b}{5} \geq -7$$

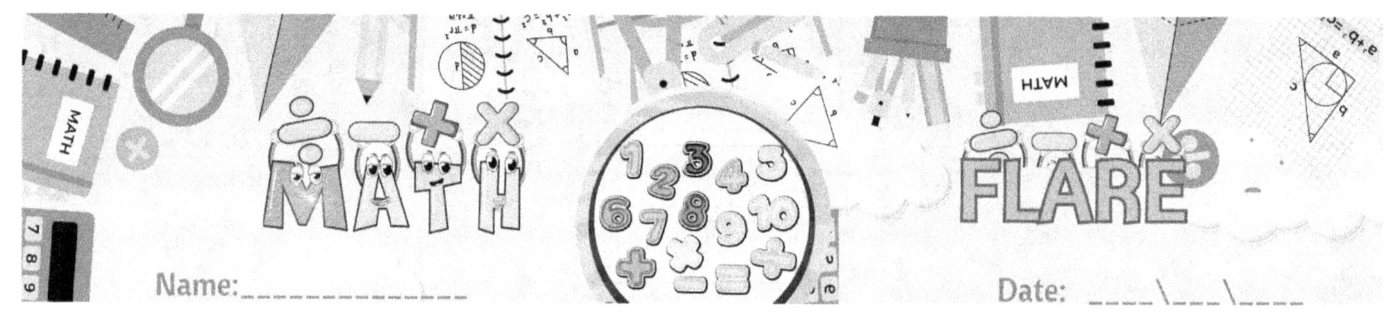

91.

$$k - 1 \leq 9$$

92.

$$a + 3 \geq 6$$

93.

$$-4\,y \geq 4$$

94.

$$\frac{a}{1} \leq -2$$

95.

$$3 - a \geq 5$$

96.

$$s + {-5} \leq 2$$

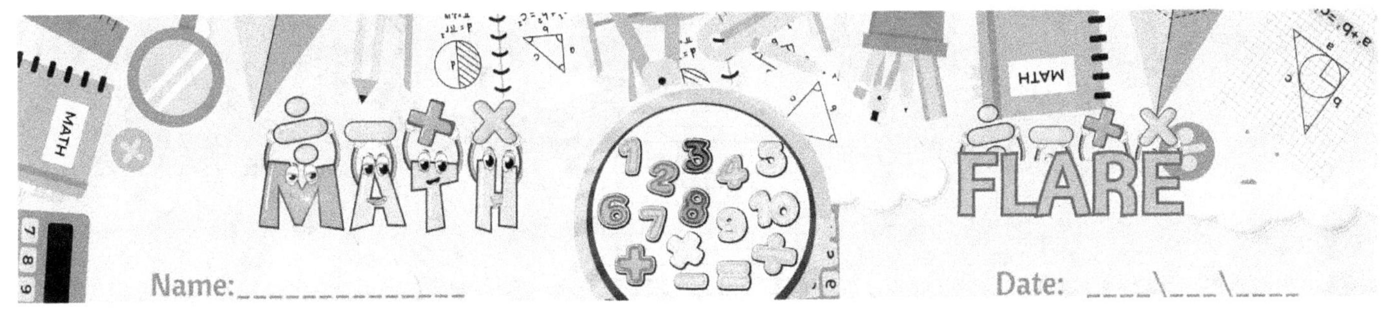

97. $2 + z \geq -7$

98. $z - 5 < 7$

99. $\dfrac{y}{-3} > -3$

100. $12\,a < 15$

101. $\dfrac{x}{8} \leq -2$

102. $1 - m < 4$

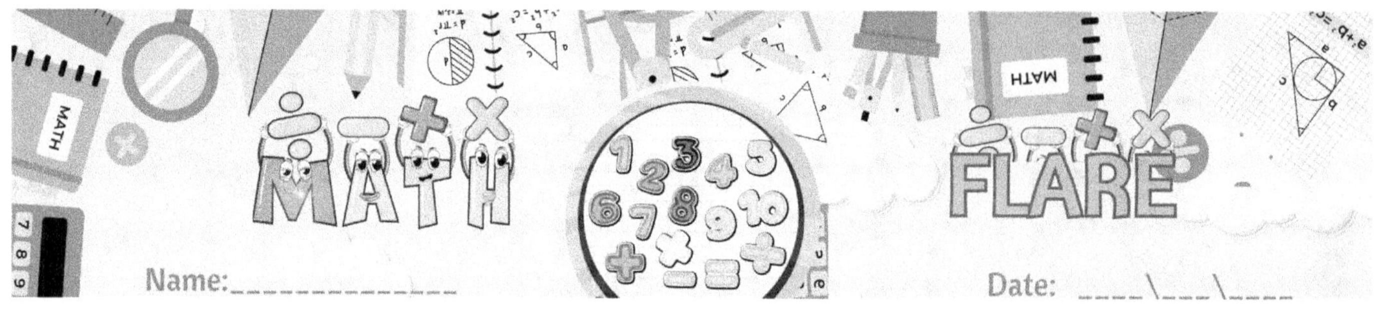

Standard Linear Equations

1. -6x + -7 = -55

2. -1x + -6 = -16

3. 9x + 4 = -23

4. -10x + 1 = 51

5. 10x + 5 = -65

6. -2x + 5 = -13

7. 2x + 5 = -7

8. 8x + 5 = -43

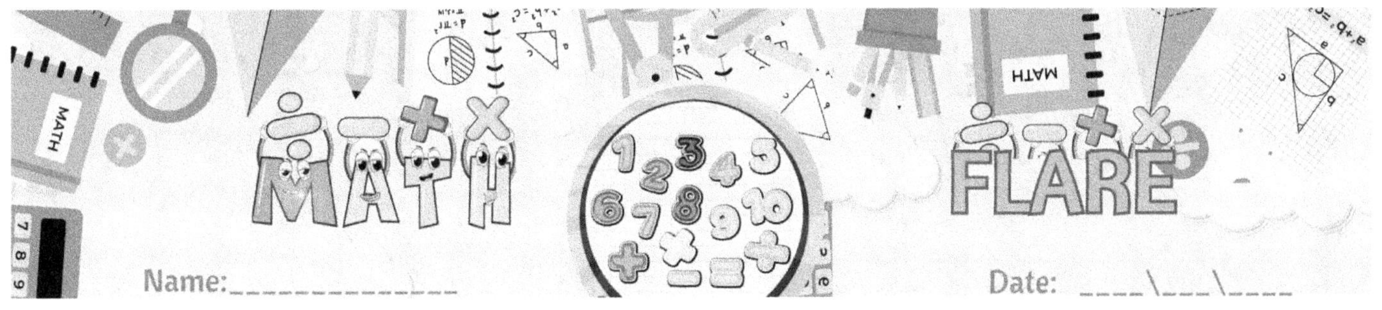

9. 3x + 0 = -27

14. 3x + 10 = -14

10. -6x + 3 = -21

15. -7x + 4 = -3

11. 5x + -4 = 41

16. 5x + -6 = 9

12. -2x + -7 = -19

17. -1x + 10 = 5

13. -3x + 7 = 22

18. 8x + -7 = -71

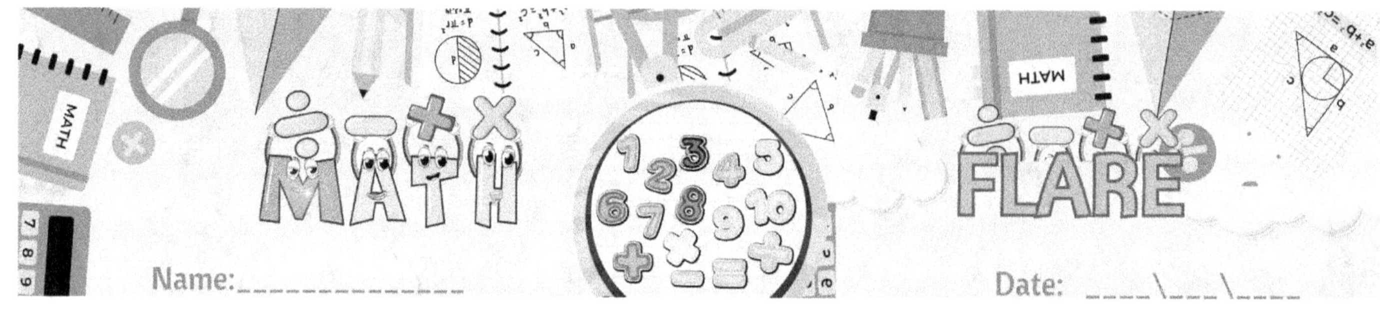

19. $3x + -10 = -37$

20. $-2x + -4 = -20$

21. $6x + -6 = 42$

22. $10x + -8 = 12$

23. $-10x + 3 = 63$

24. $-9x + -4 = 59$

25. $-8x + -10 = -2$

26. $10x + -6 = -6$

27. $8x + 5 = 61$

28. $-1x + 1 = 4$

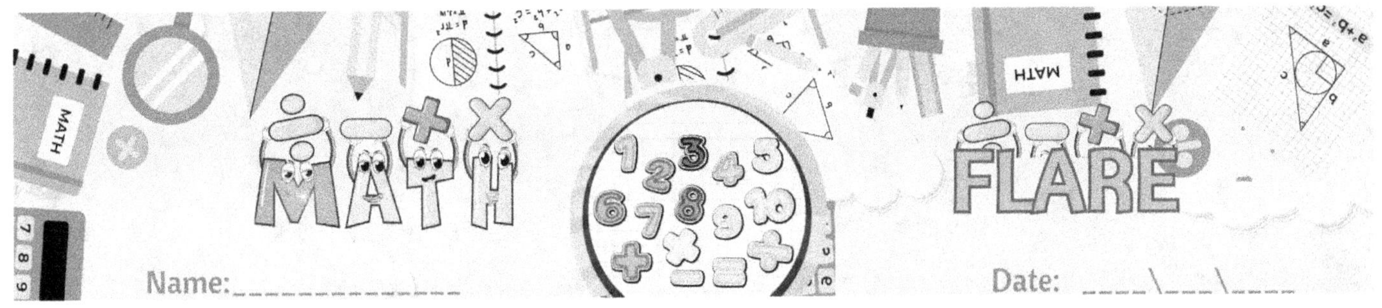

29. $6x + 9 = -9$

30. $-4x + -5 = -29$

31. $-7x + -5 = 65$

32. $3x + -2 = 7$

33. $7x + -3 = 46$

34. $10x + -1 = 39$

35. $3x + 4 = 25$

36. $-3x + 2 = 29$

37. $-3x + 4 = -23$

38. $-5x + 2 = -38$

39. $10x + 8 = 18$

40. $3x + -9 = -30$

41. $2x + 5 = -13$

42. $-3x + 5 = 14$

43. $6x + 3 = -33$

44. $-7x + 2 = -68$

45. $2x + 3 = -15$

46. $-7x + 5 = 47$

47. $1x + -3 = -12$

48. $6x + 7 = 61$

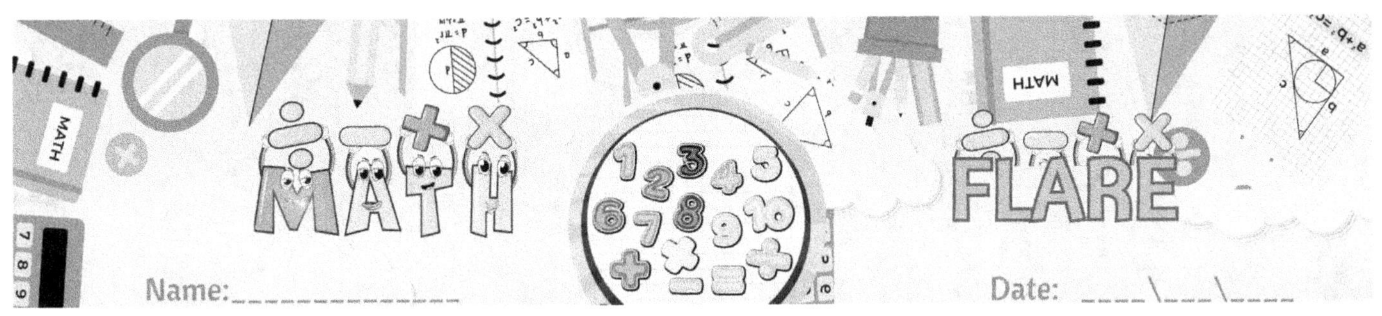

Find Slope from Two Points

1. (-3, -4) and (4, -11)

2. (8, 9) and (0, -7)

3. (0, -9) and (5, 1)

4. (1, -6) and (-6, -6)

5. (-2, 4) and (8, -6)

6. (-2, 3) and (8, 13)

7. (-9, -92) and (-1, -12)

8. (-2, 12) and (-7, 37)

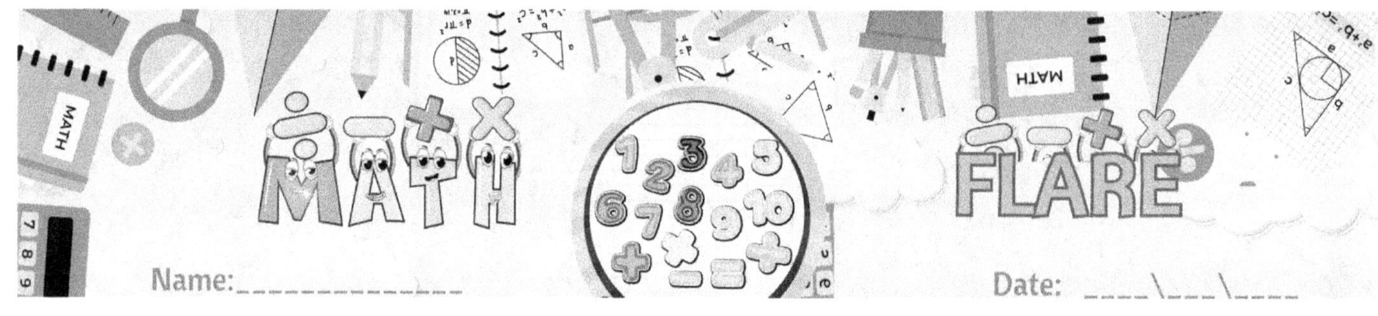

9. (-5, -32) and (-7, -44)

10. (-7, -45) and (1, 11)

11. (-4, 32) and (2, -10)

12. (-7, 39) and (6, -52)

13. (8, 12) and (3, 2)

14. (-7, -9) and (-8, -9)

15. (-8, 62) and (2, -18)

16. (7, -31) and (9, -39)

17. (-4, 1) and (-1, 4)

18. (-3, 11) and (-9, 47)

19. (-6, 36) and (-10, 64)

20. (0, 10) and (10, 60)

21. (-7, 63) and (-1, 3)

22. (2, 9) and (-7, -36)

23. (5, -1) and (2, -4)

24. (7, 23) and (2, 13)

25. (-3, 17) and (-8, 32)

26. (-1, 1) and (-2, 9)

27. (2, -3) and (-2, 5)

28. (-3, 17) and (2, 2)

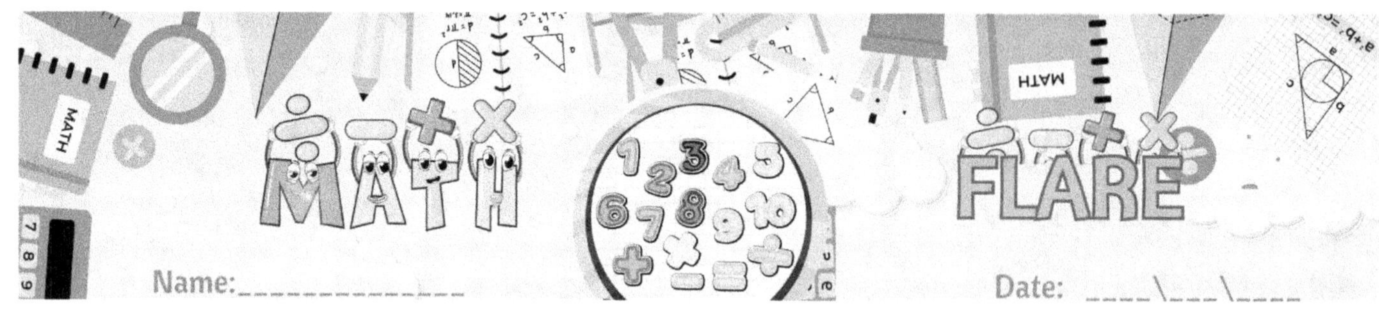

29. (-4, -10) and (1, 0)

30. (8, -63) and (-6, 63)

31. (1, 10) and (6, 45)

32. (-9, 8) and (2, -14)

33. (-7, -1) and (7, -1)

34. (-9, -28) and (-2, -14)

35. (5, -6) and (10, -11)

36. (2, -4) and (6, -4)

37. (8, -46) and (-9, 39)

38. (-9, 58) and (-1, 10)

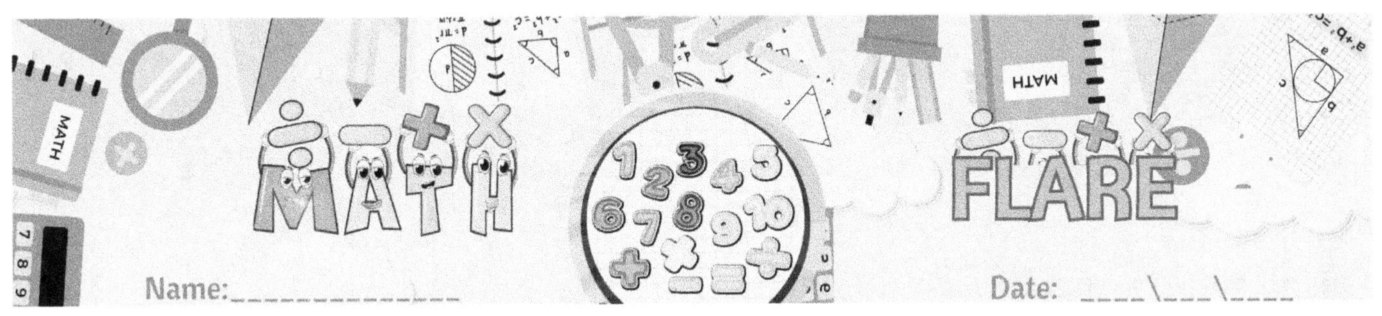

39. (-8, 43) and (-8, 43)

40. (1, 14) and (5, 30)

41. (0, -3) and (-7, -59)

42. (3, -21) and (8, -61)

43. (-3, -24) and (-4, -34)

44. (10, -54) and (-7, 31)

45. (9, -4) and (3, 2)

46. (5, -9) and (0, 6)

47. (10, 70) and (-4, -28)

48. (4, -28) and (4, -28)

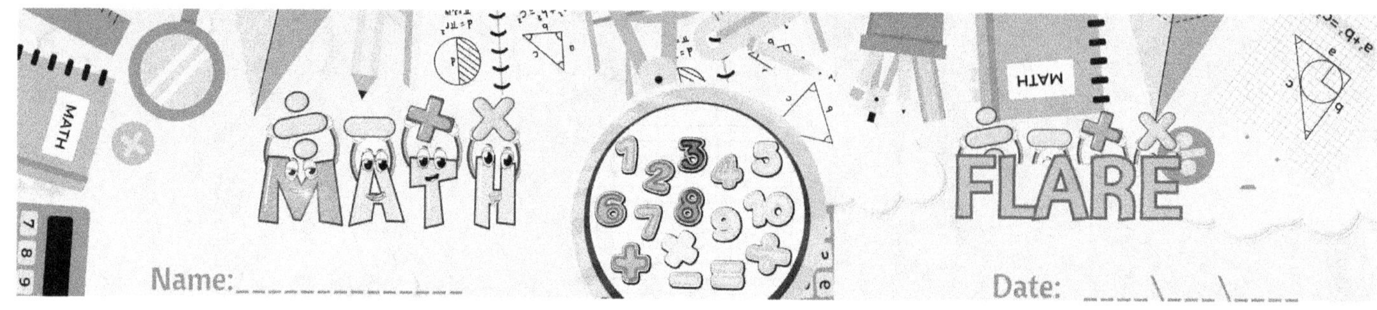

Plotting Lines
Plot and draw the lines.

1.

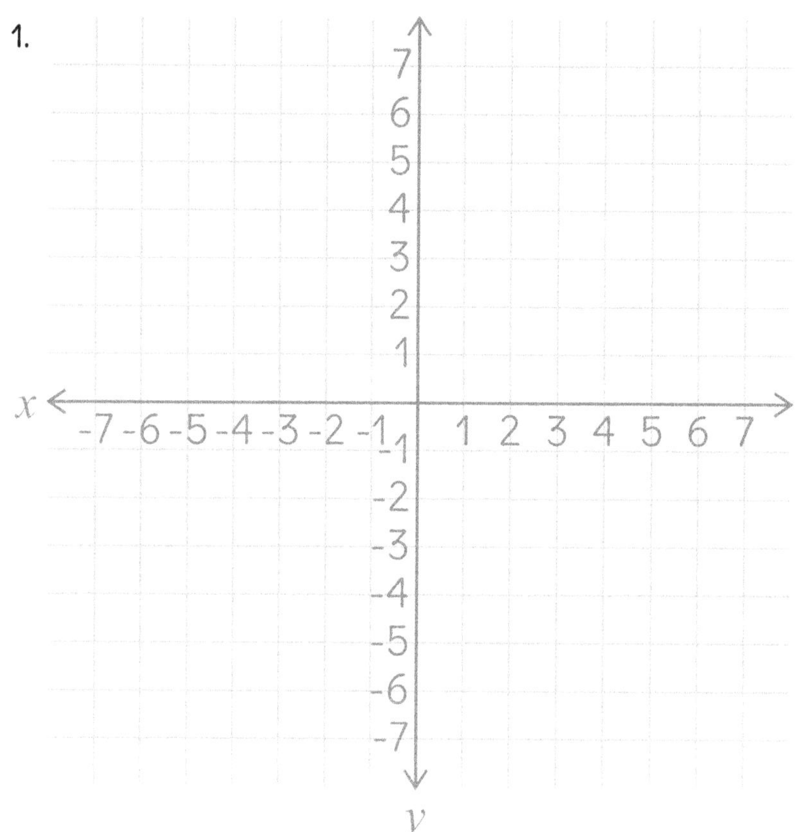

A = (-1, -4)   B = (0, -6)

C = (-2, -2)   D = (-6, 6)

E = (-4, 2)   F = (-3, 0)

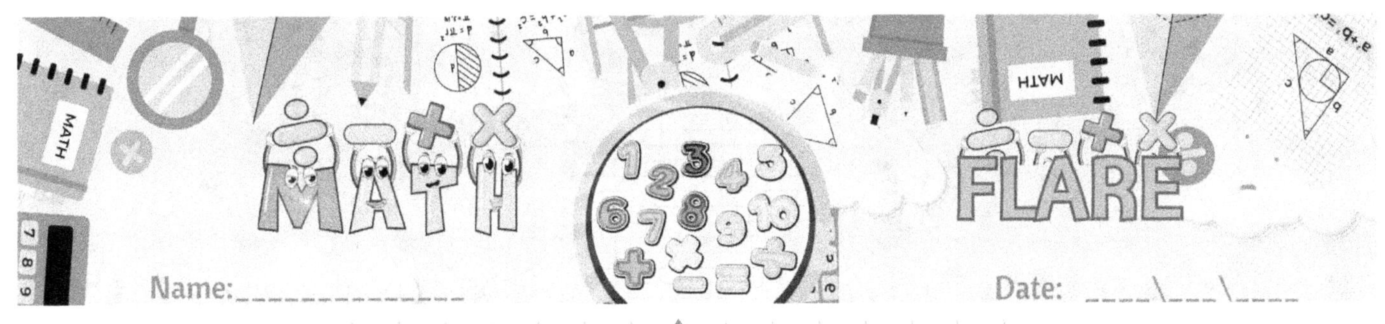

2.

A = (2, 2)   B = (0, 1)

C = (-4, -1)   D = (6, 4)

E = (-2, 0)   F = (4, 3)

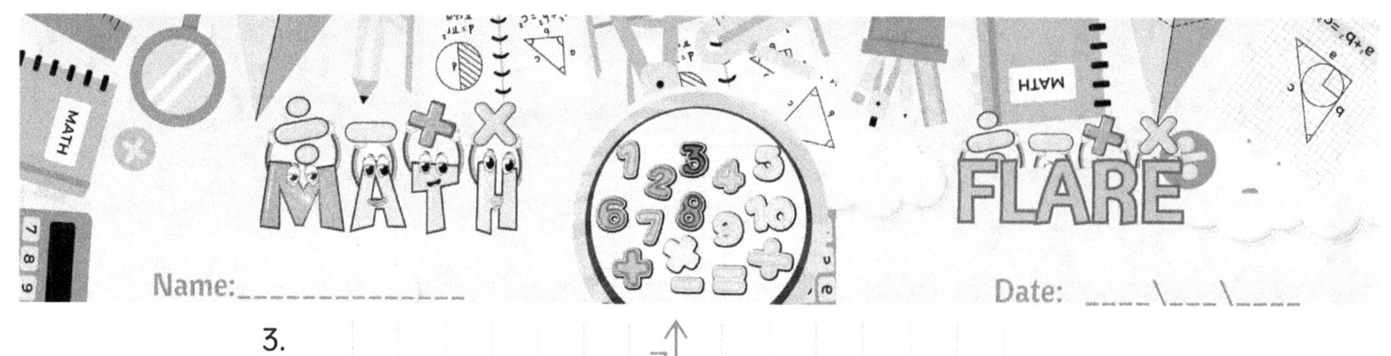

3.

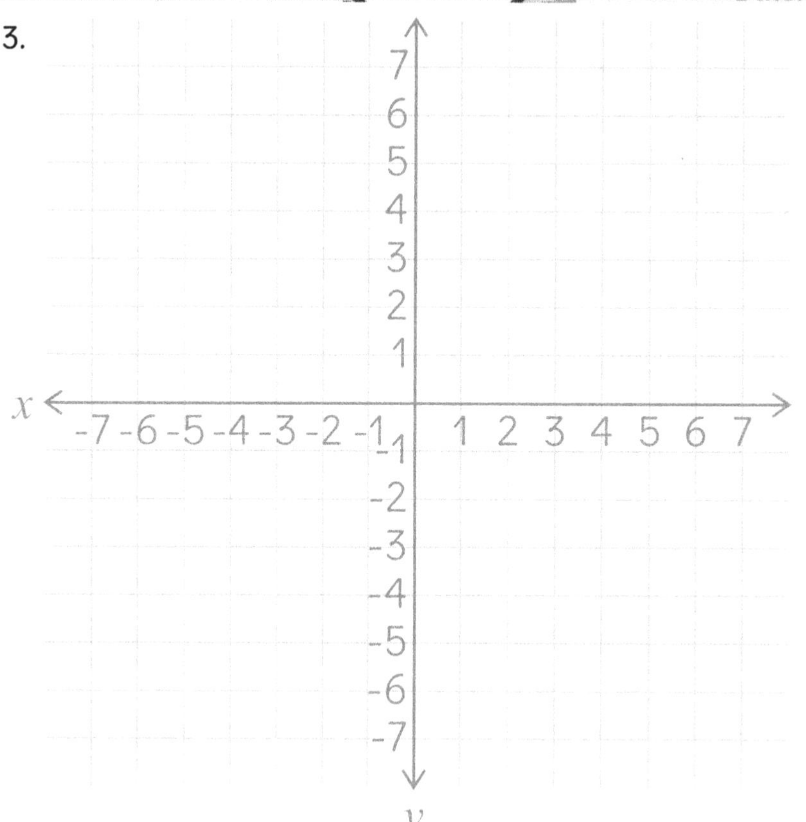

A = (-4, -3)   B = (0, 5)

C = (-6, -7)   D = (-3, -1)

E = (-2, 1)   F = (-5, -5)

Name:_________________   Date: _______________

4.

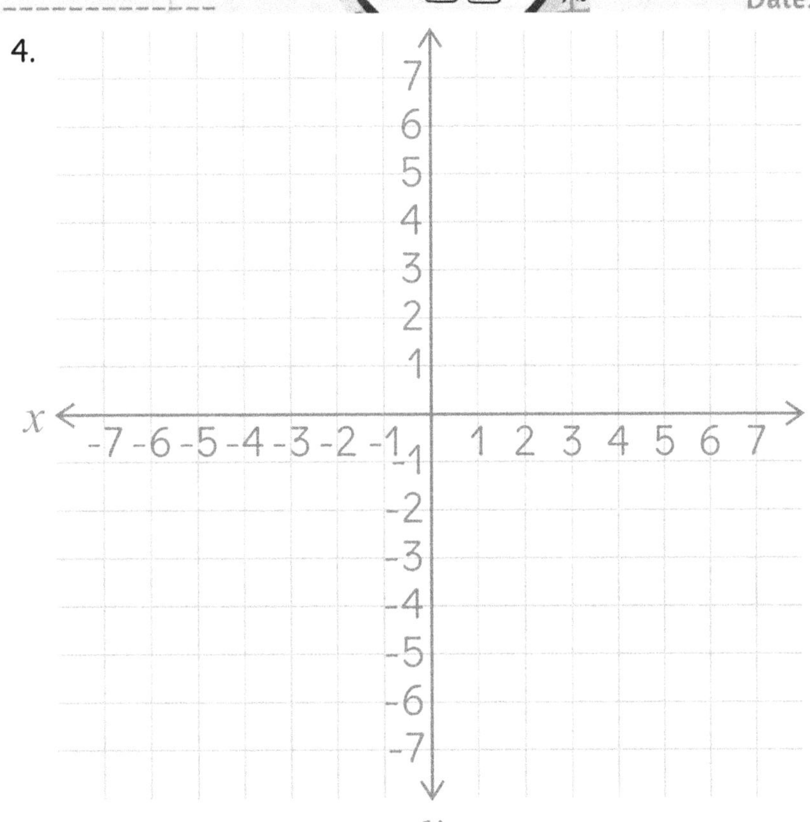

A = (-5, 6)   B = (-1, -2)

C = (-4, 4)   D = (-3, 2)

E = (1, -6)   F = (0, -4)

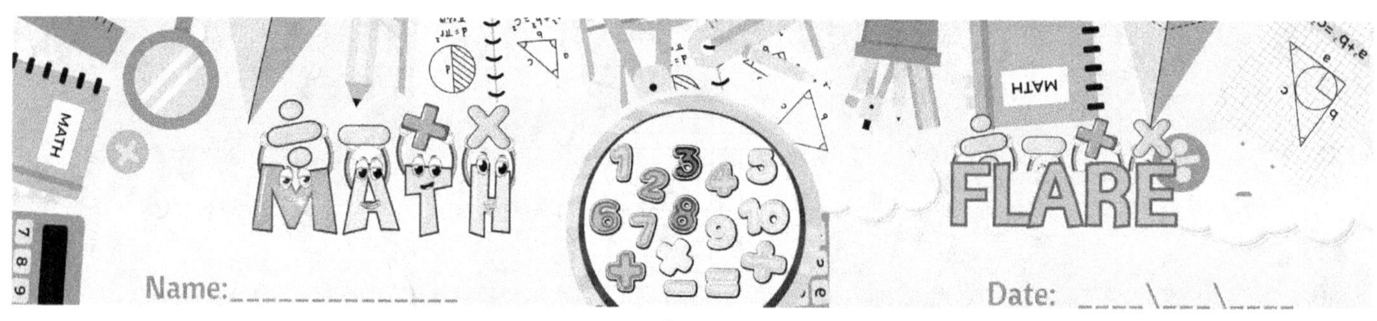

5.

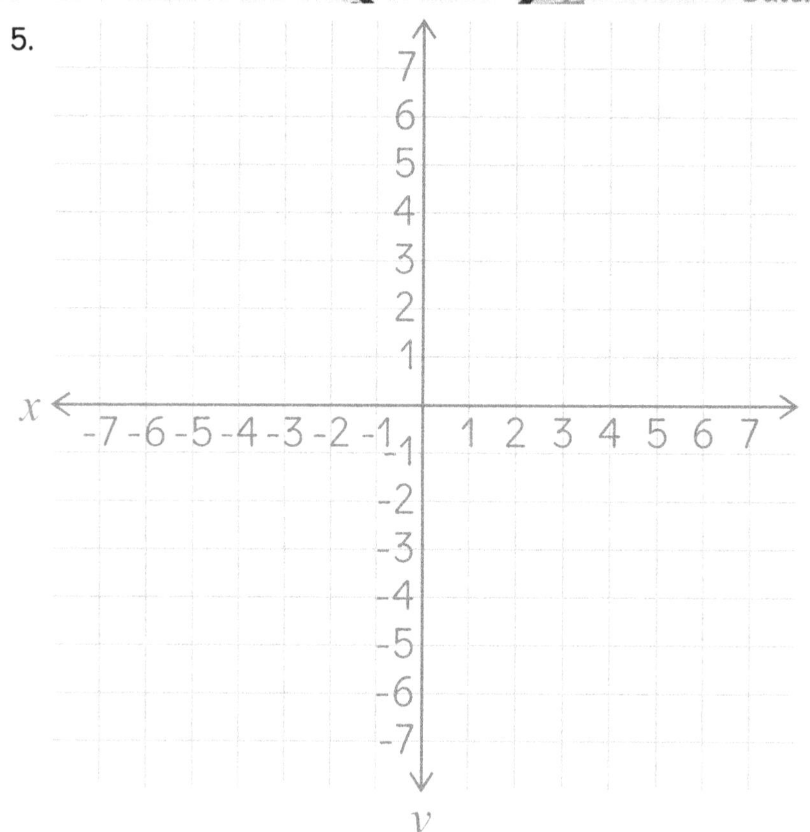

A = (-1, 2)   B = (1, 6)

C = (-2, 0)   D = (-5, -6)

E = (-4, -4)   F = (-3, -2)

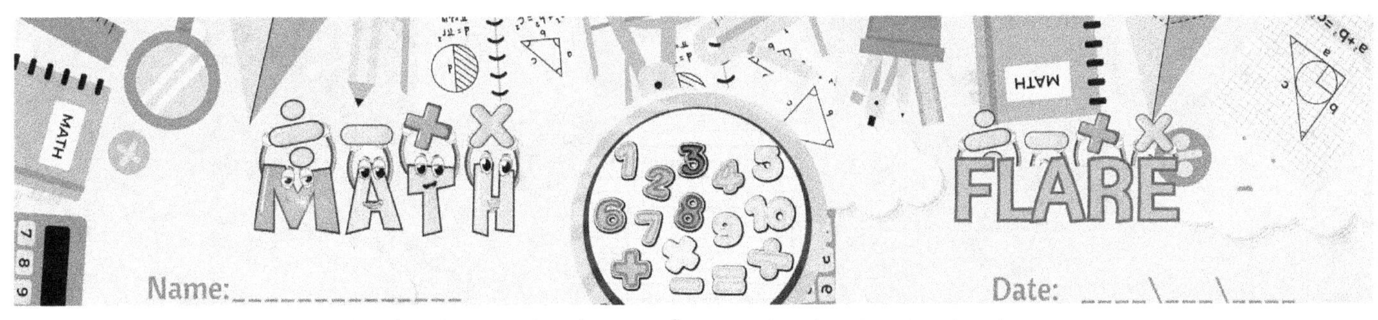

6.

A = (-6, -7)   B = (0, -4)

C = (-4, -6)   D = (2, -3)

E = (-2, -5)   F = (6, -1)

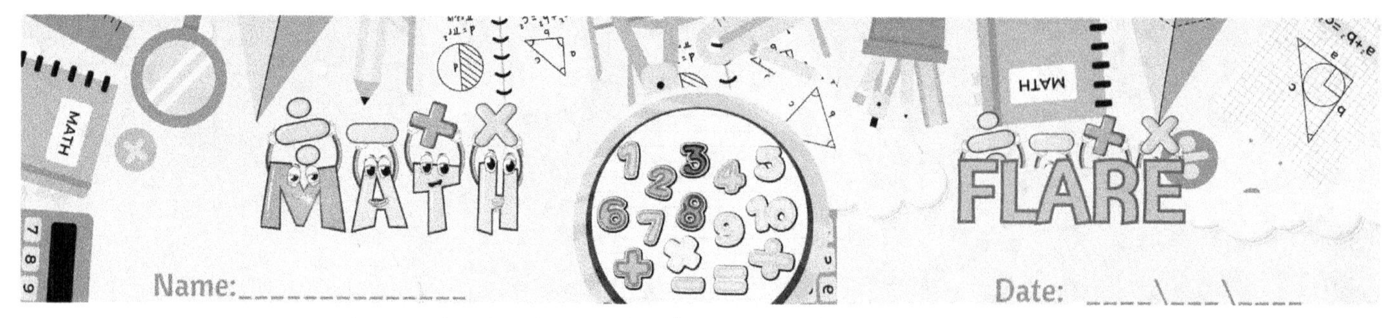

7.

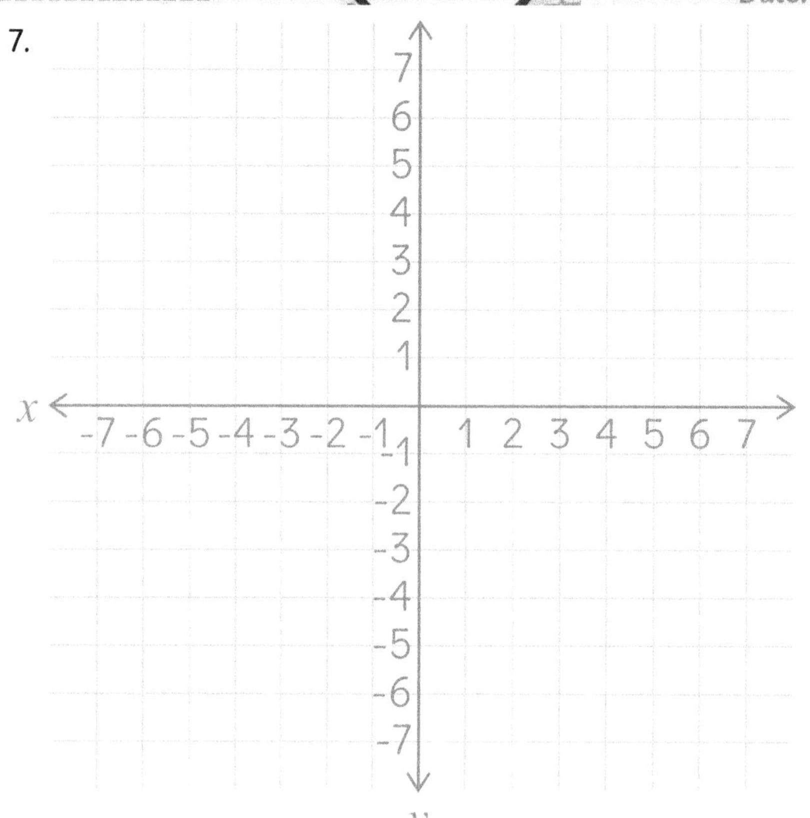

A = (-5, -3)   B = (-6, -5)

C = (0, 7)   D = (-2, 3)

E = (-3, 1)   F = (-1, 5)

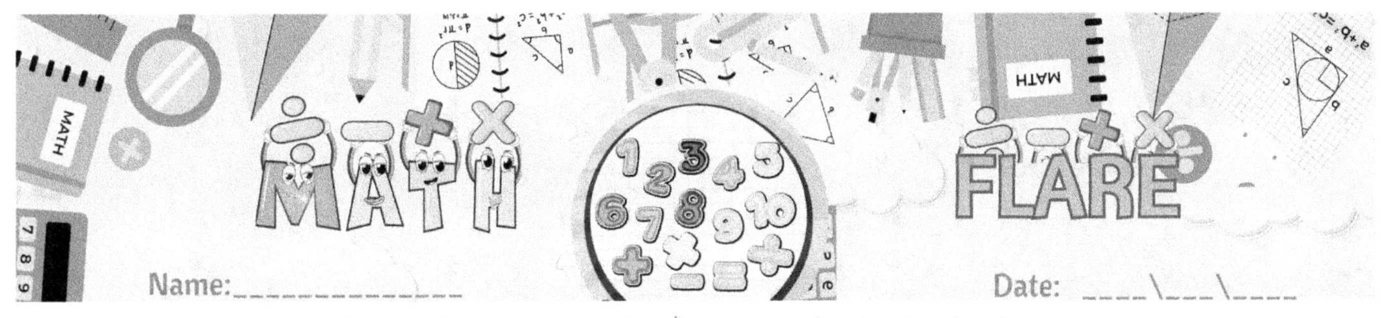

8.

A = (1, 4)   B = (5, 0)

C = (7, -2)   D = (-1, 6)

E = (6, -1)   F = (4, 1)

9.

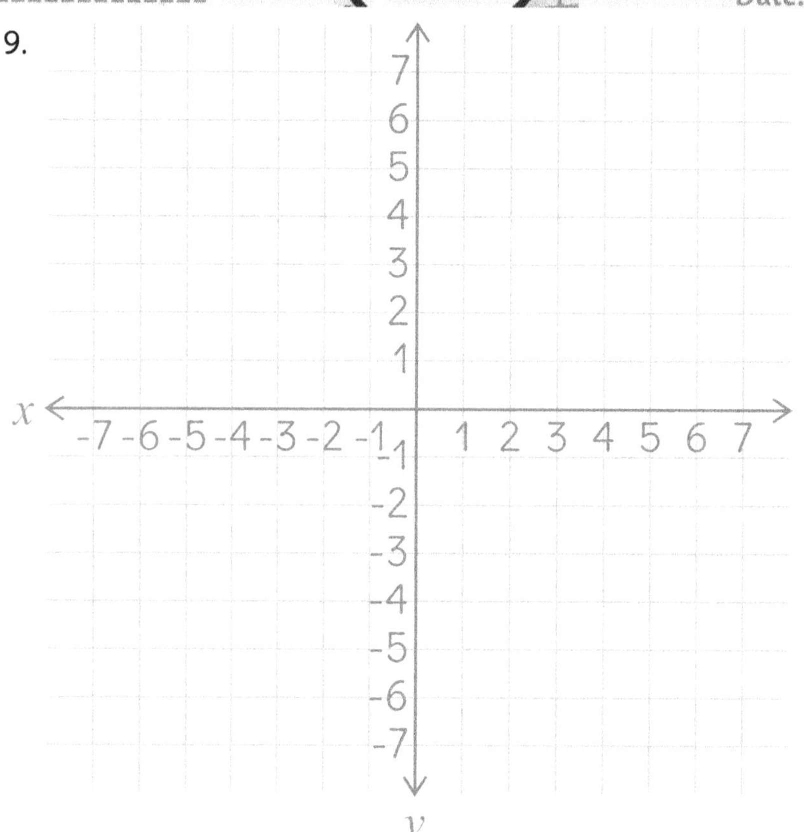

A = (-2, -3)   B = (-4, -7)

C = (-3, -5)   D = (1, 3)

E = (2, 5)   F = (3, 7)

10.

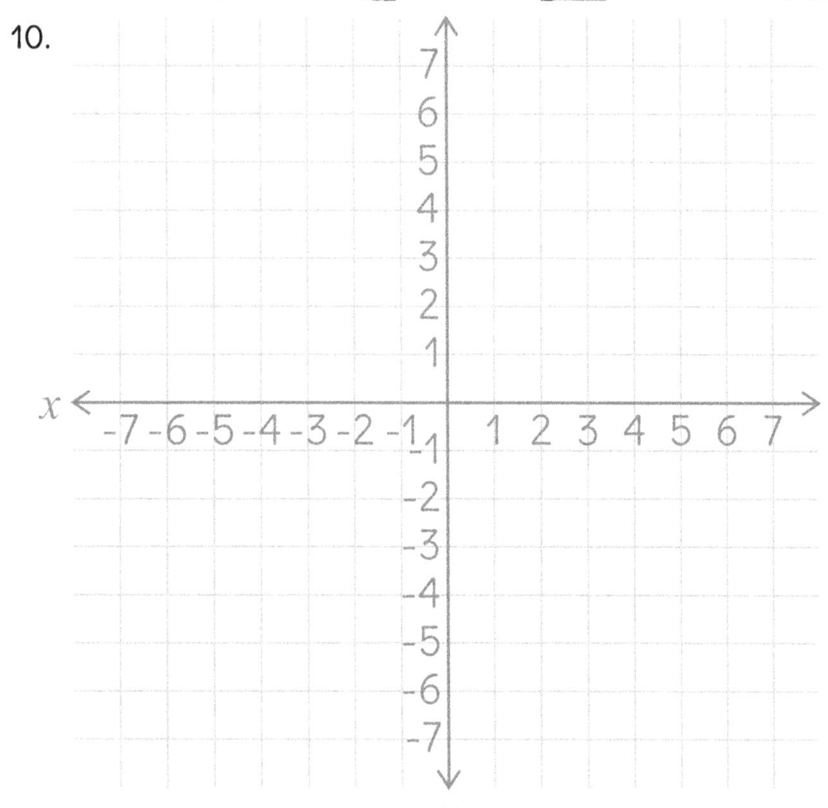

A = (3, -6)   B = (1, -6)

C = (-7, -6)   D = (-3, -6)

E = (4, -6)   F = (0, -6)

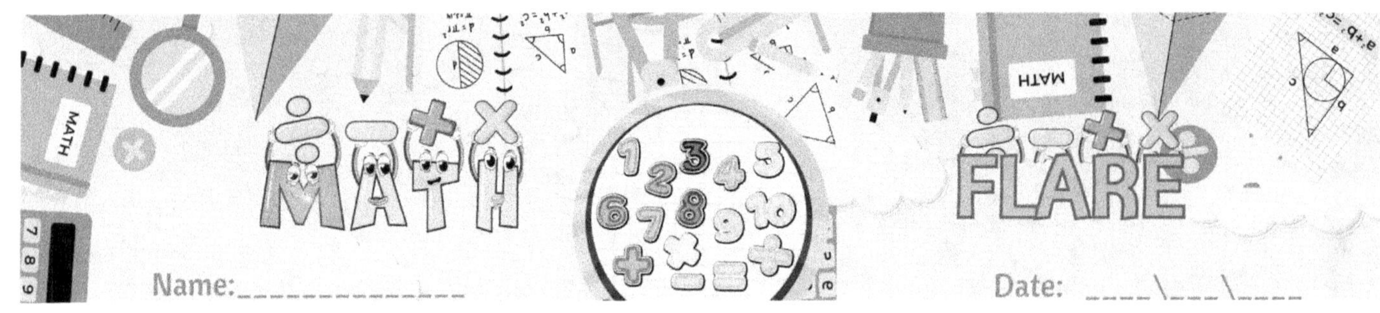

Graphing Linear Equations

1. $y = -x - 1$

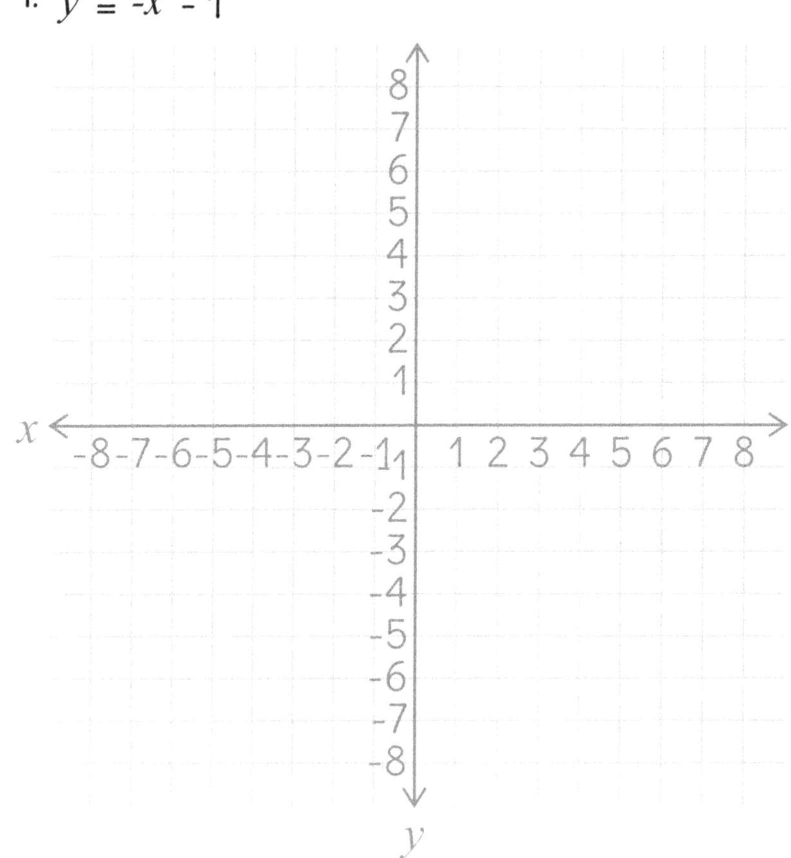

4. $y = \dfrac{-9}{4}x + 1$

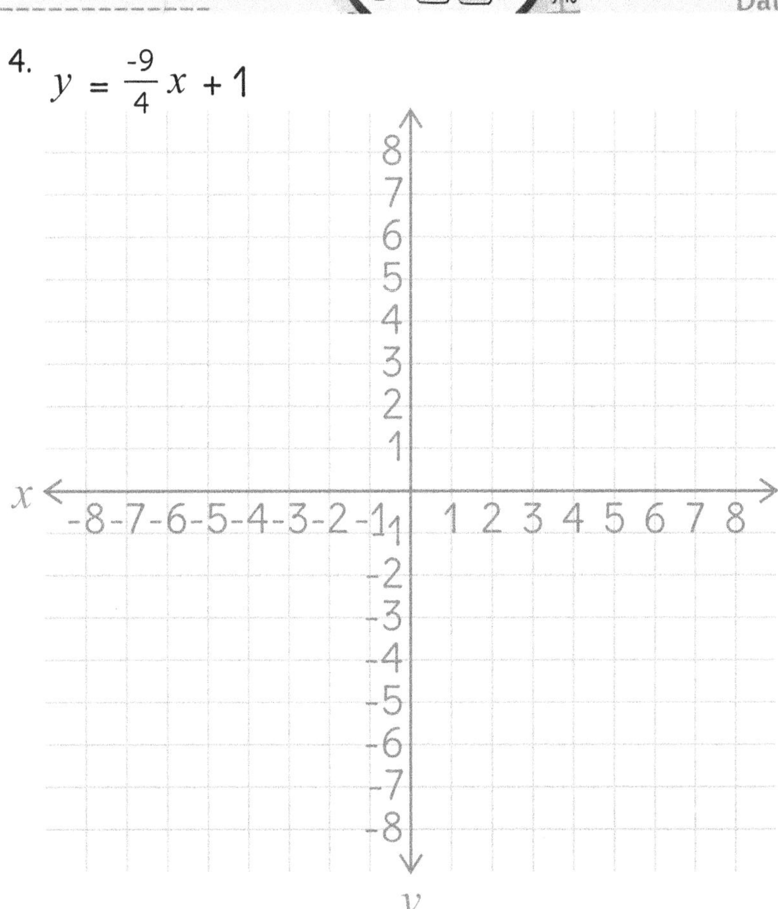

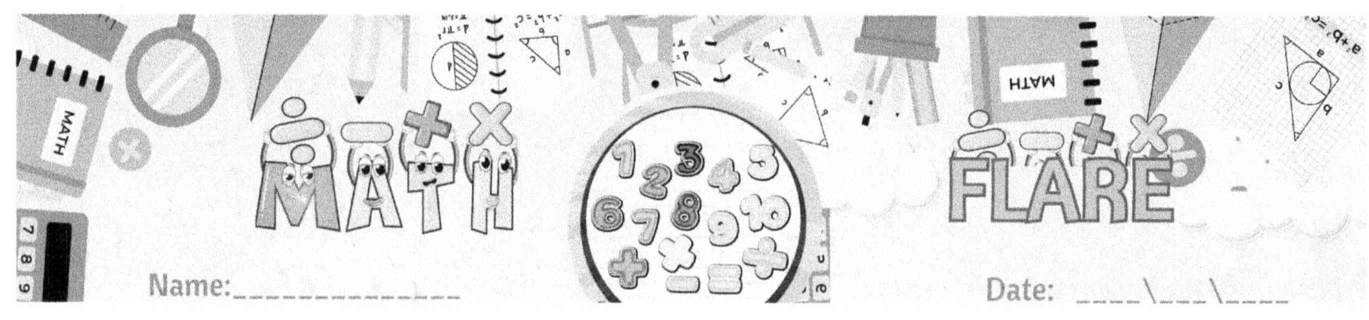

5. $y = \dfrac{-1}{2}x - 7$

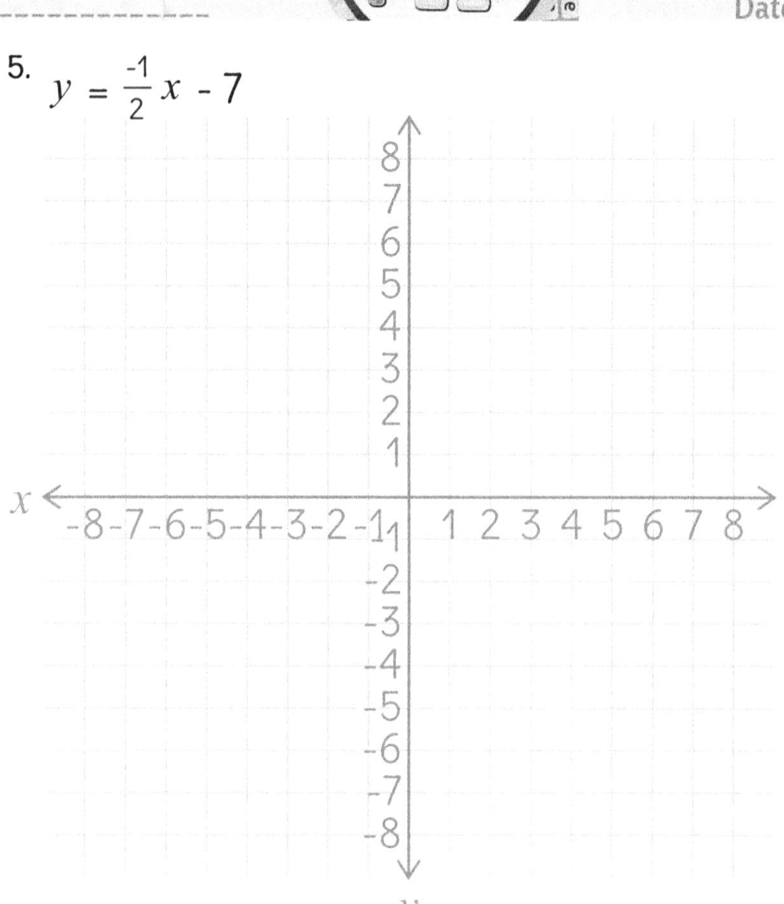

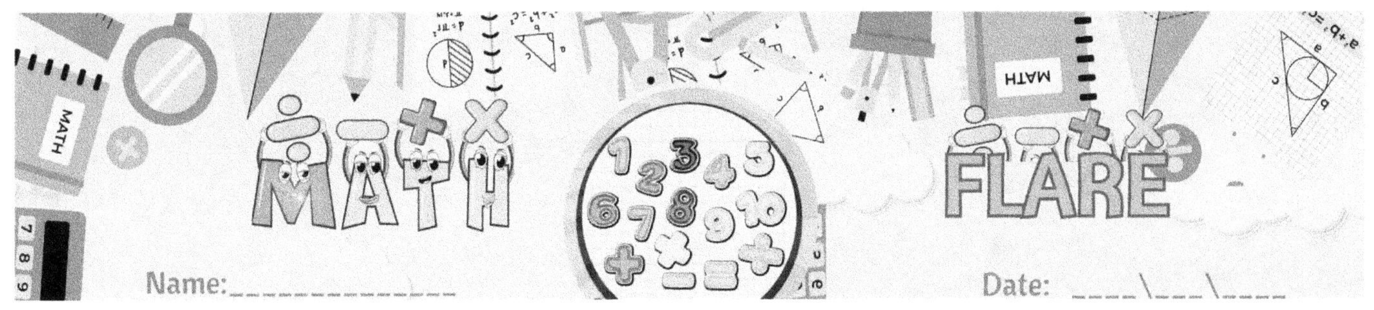

6.

$$y = \frac{5}{2}x - 6$$

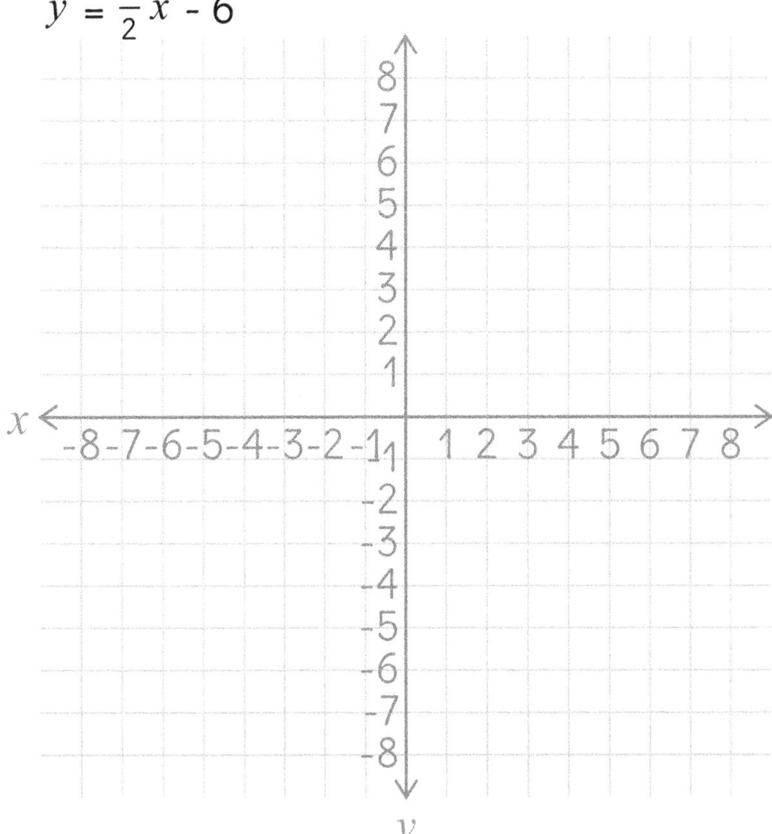

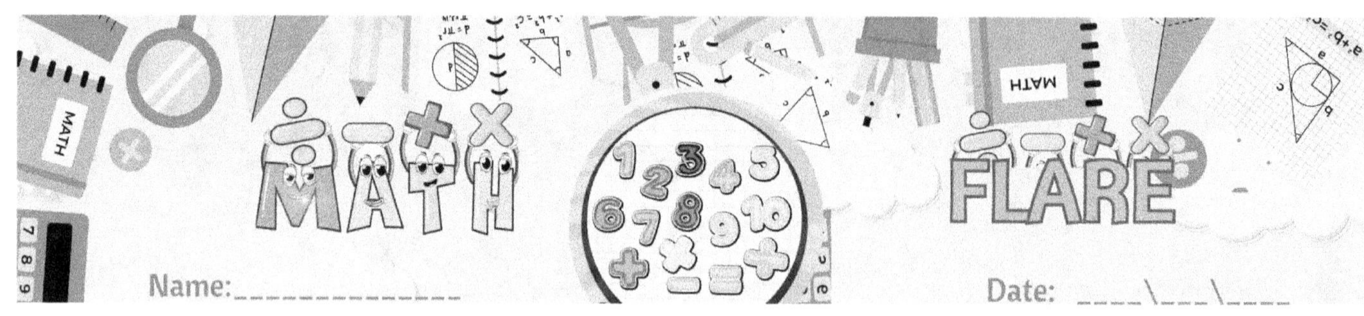

7. $y = \dfrac{3}{4}x - 3$

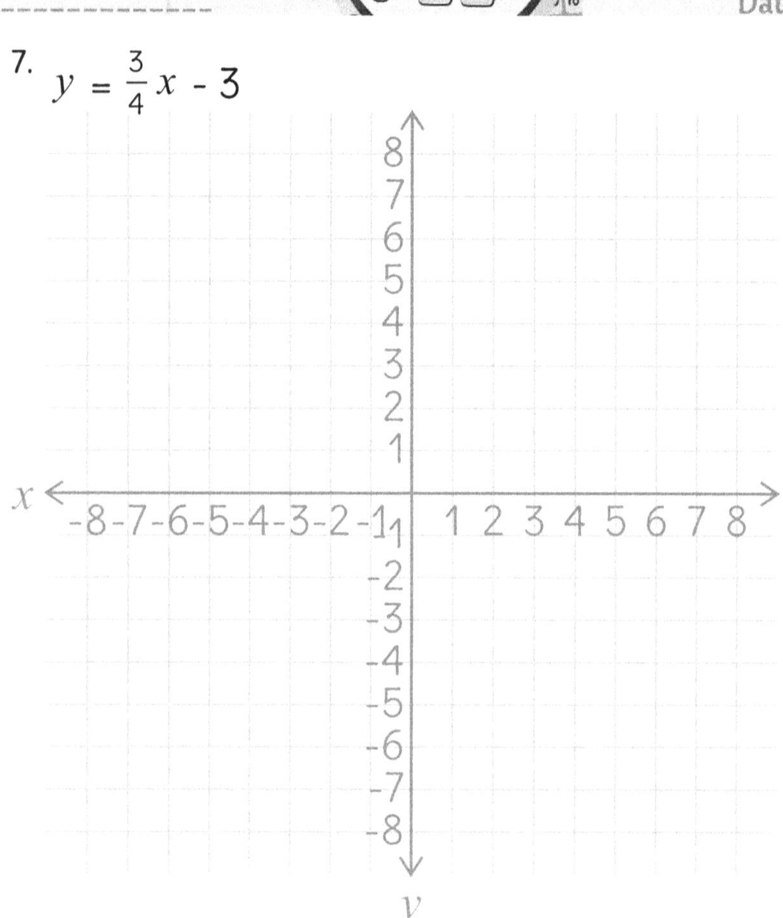

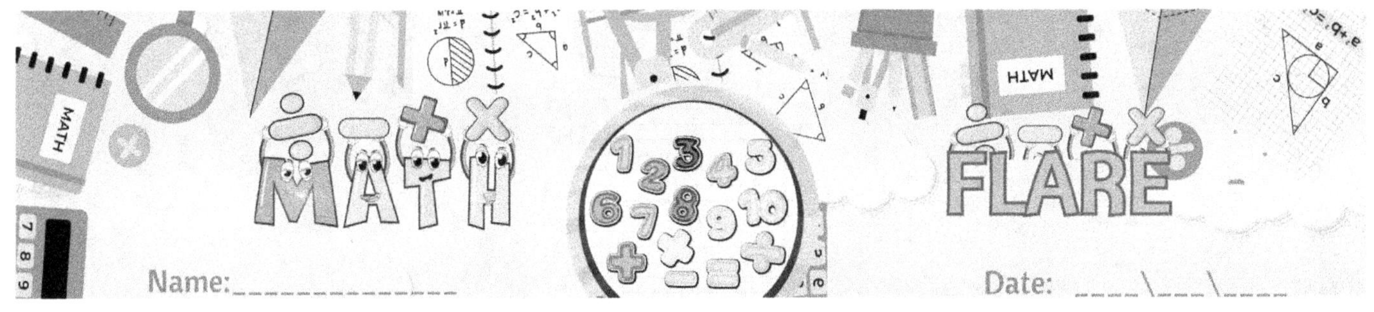

8. $y = \dfrac{-9}{4}x - 4$

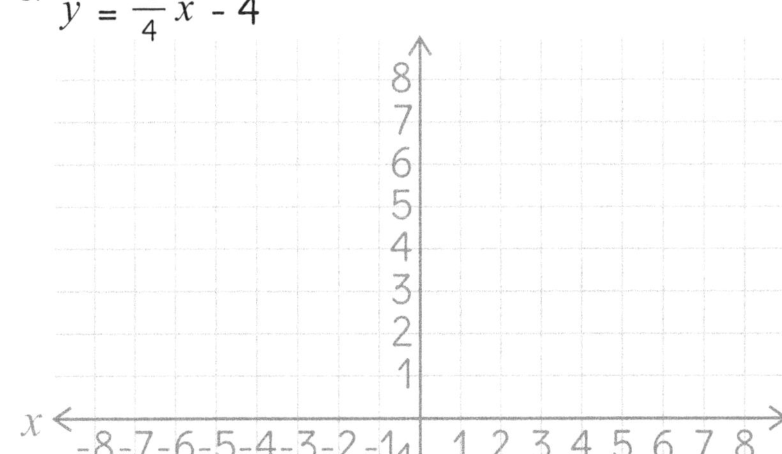

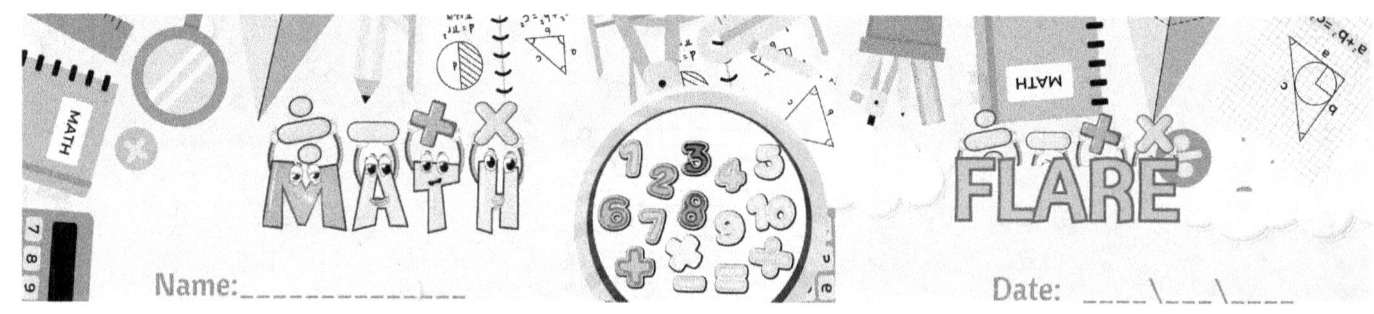

9. $y = \dfrac{-9}{4}x + 3$

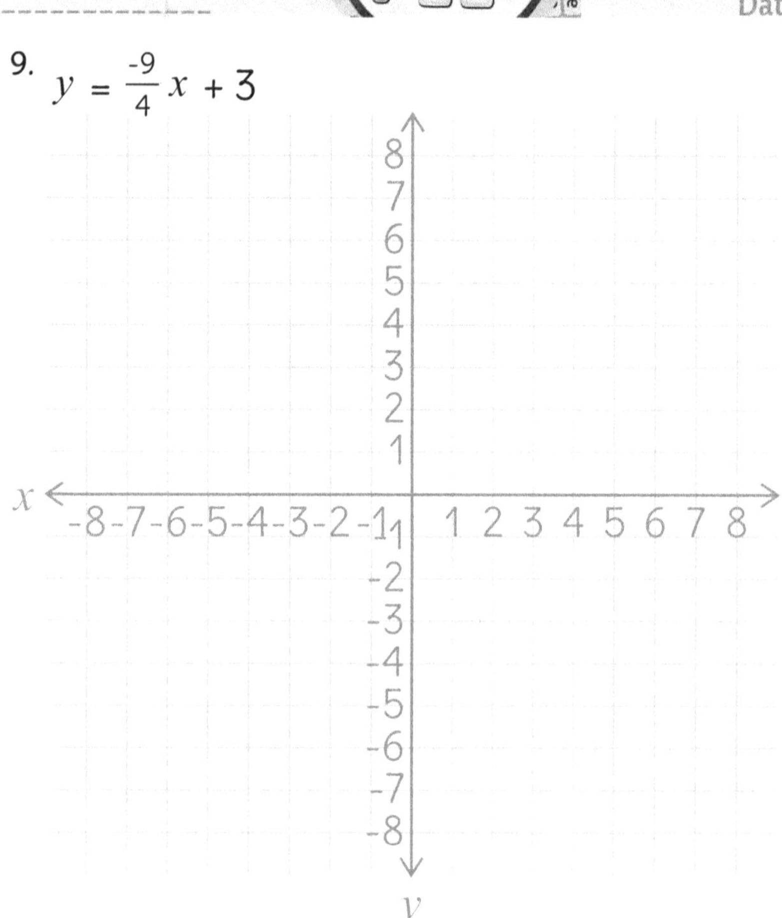

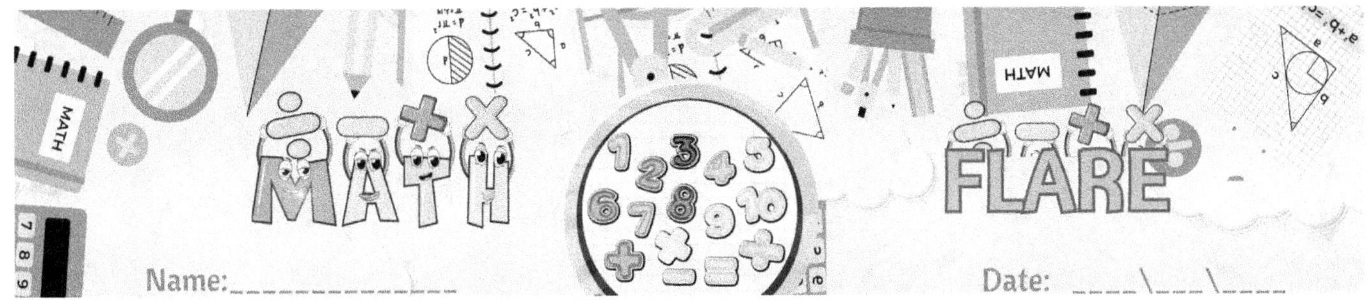

10. 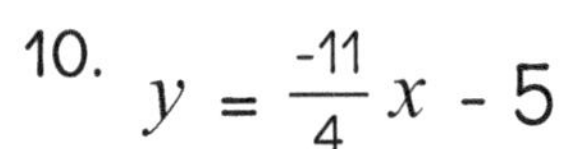

$$y = \frac{-11}{4}x - 5$$

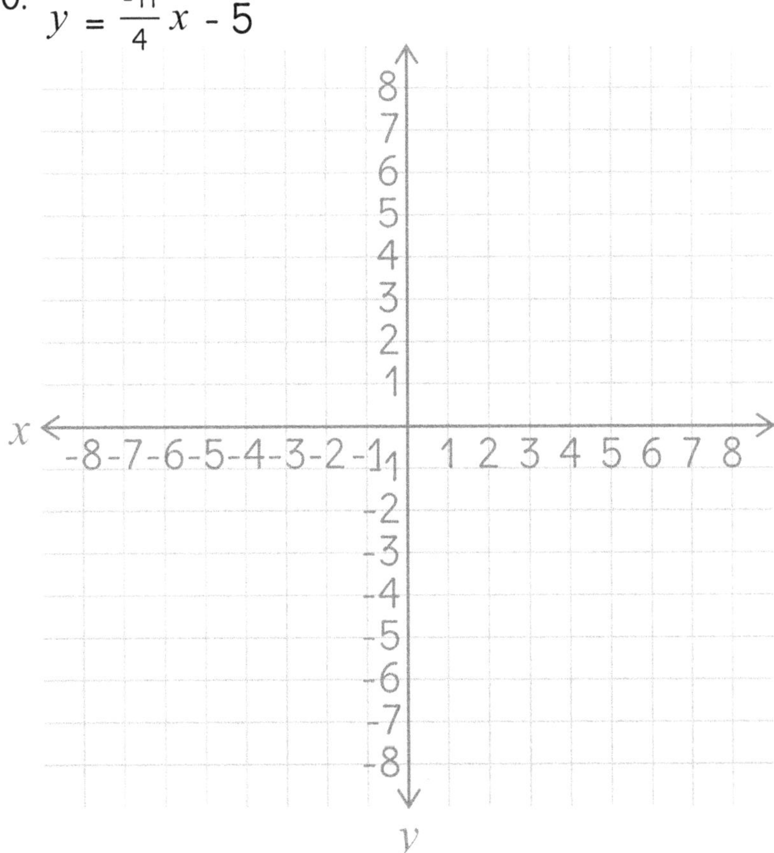

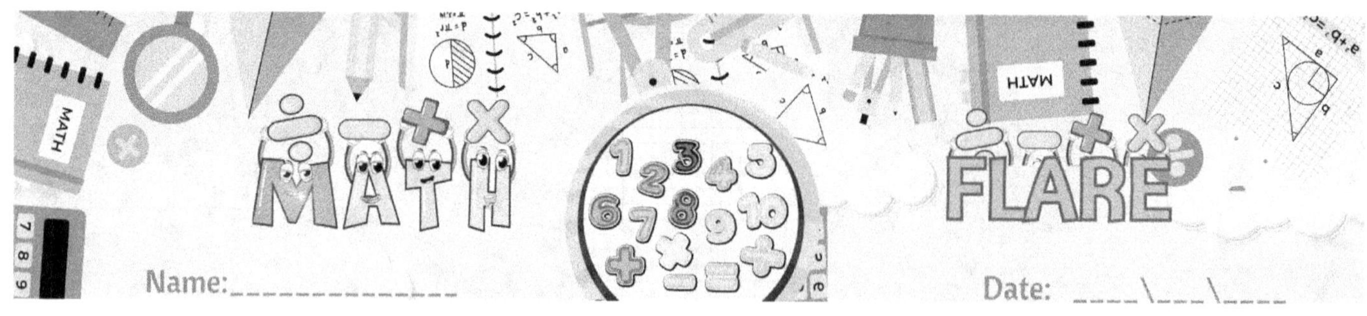

11. $y = \dfrac{-3}{4}x - 6$

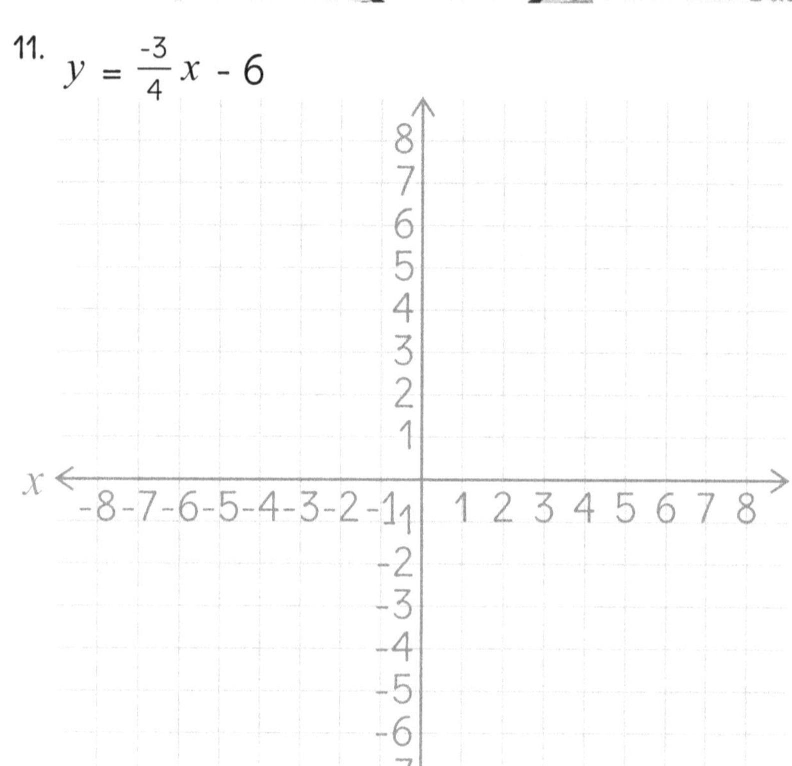

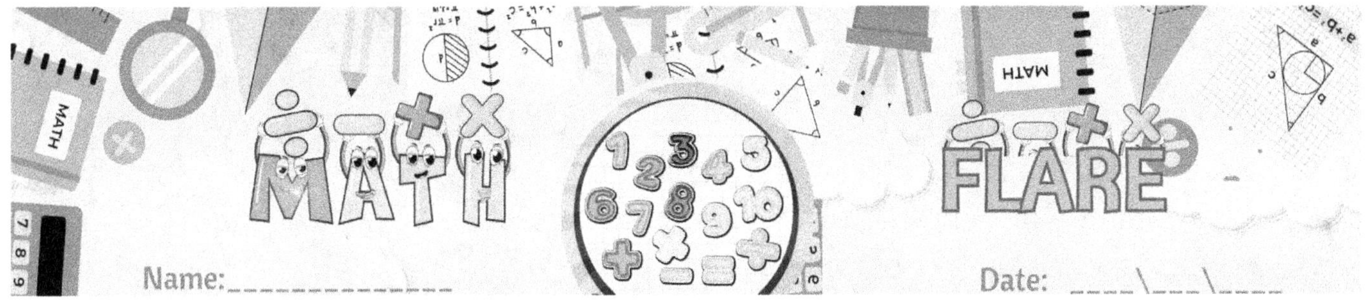

Name:_______________ Date: ____________

12. $y = x - 2$

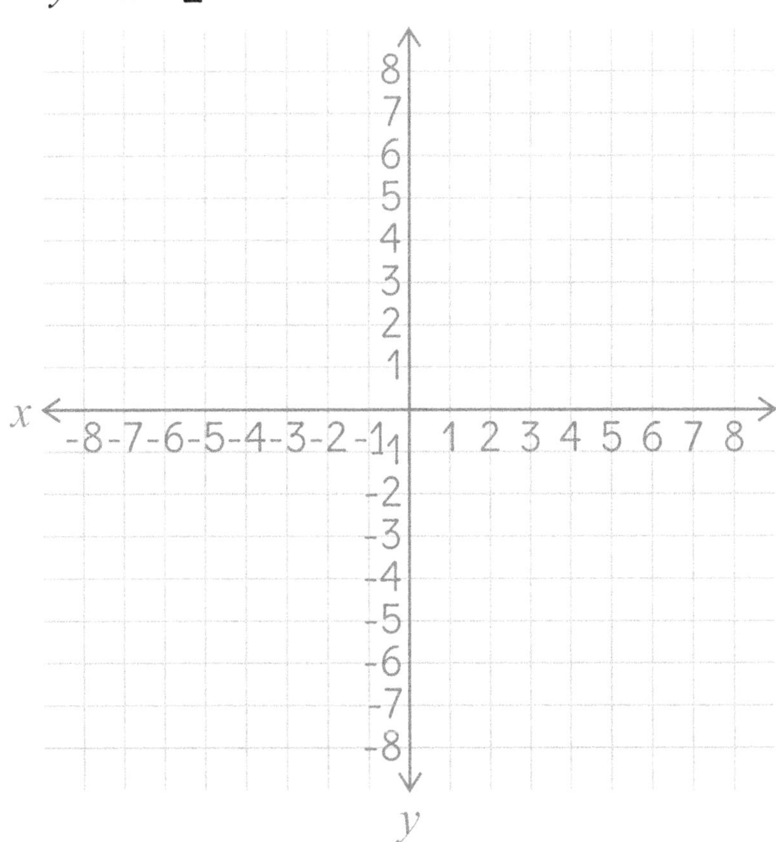

13.
$$y = 2x - 5$$

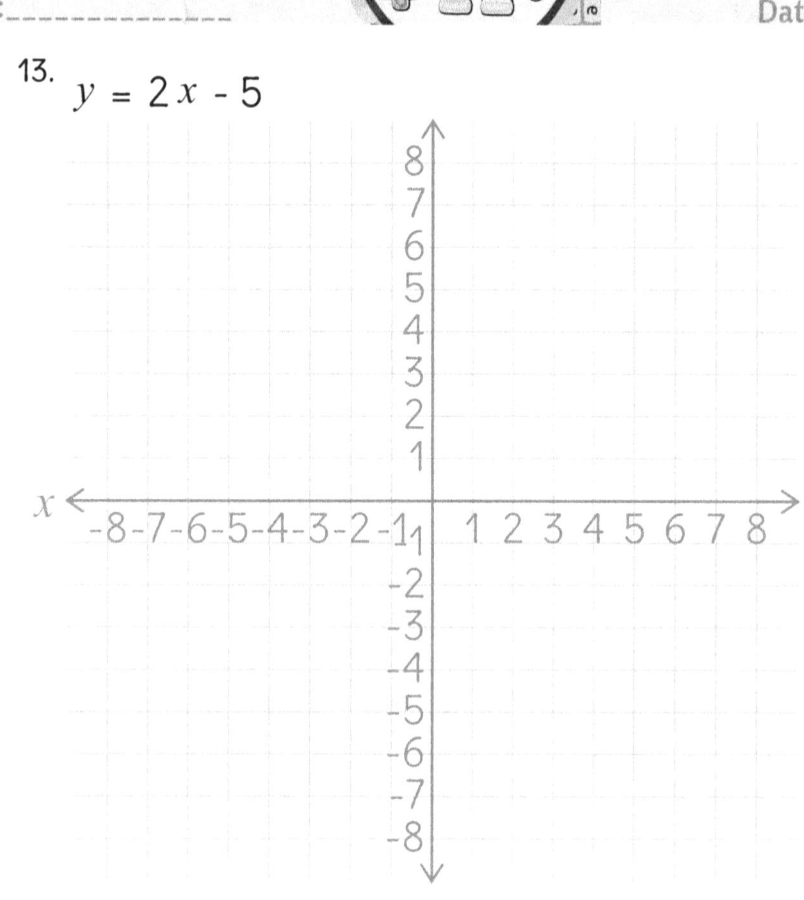

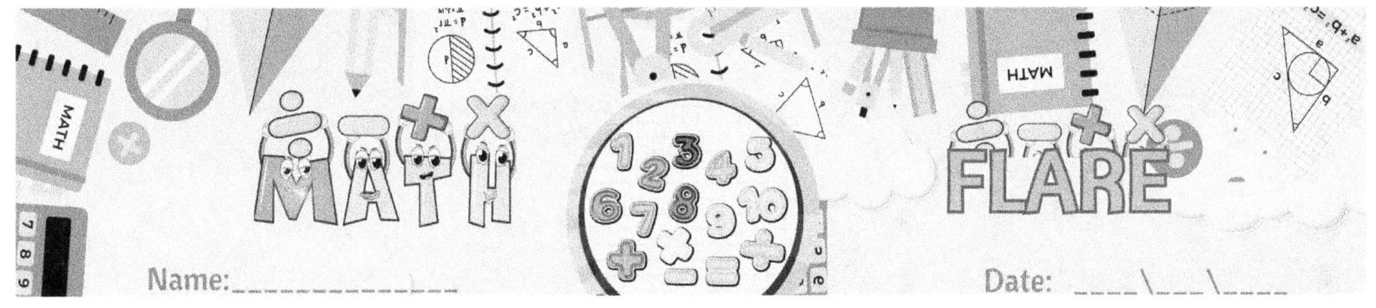

Name: _______________ Date: ___/___/___

14.
$$y = -3x + 3$$

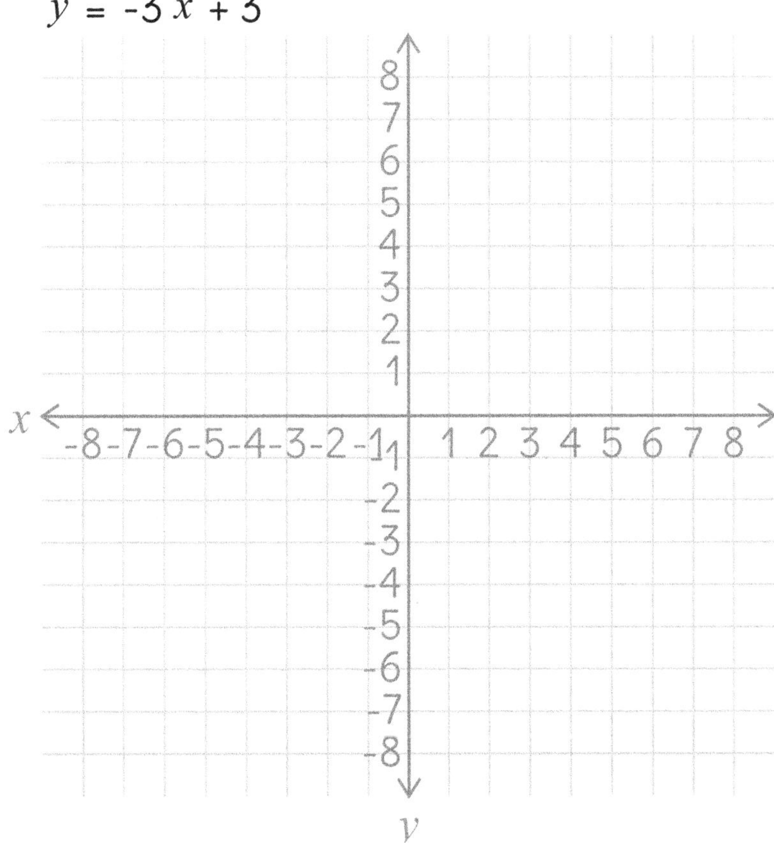

15. $y = \dfrac{3}{4}x - 2$

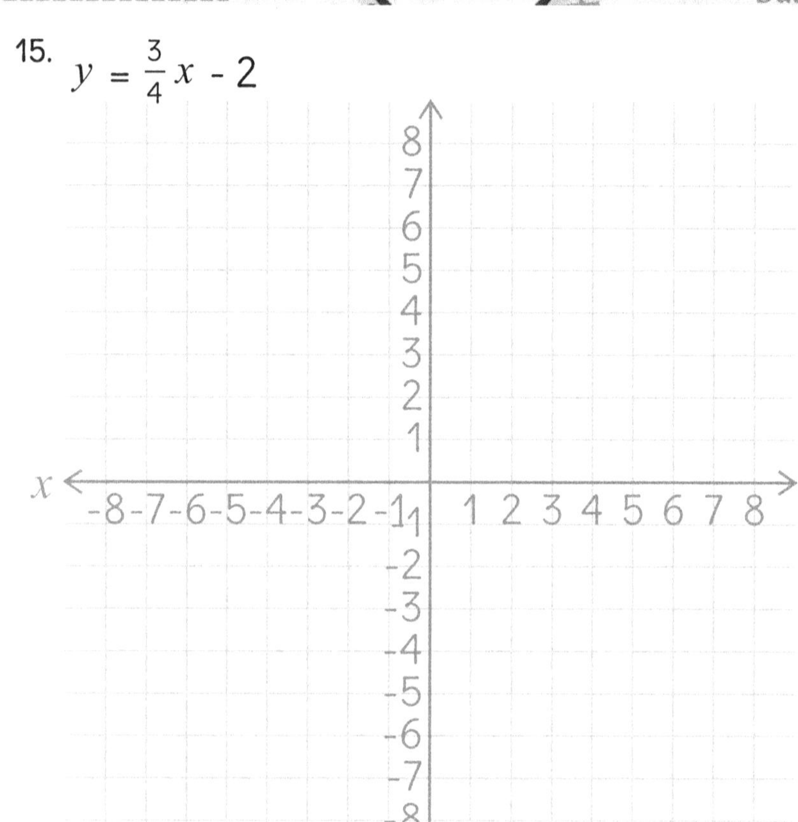

Name:________________ Date:_________

16. $y = \dfrac{-9}{4}x + 6$

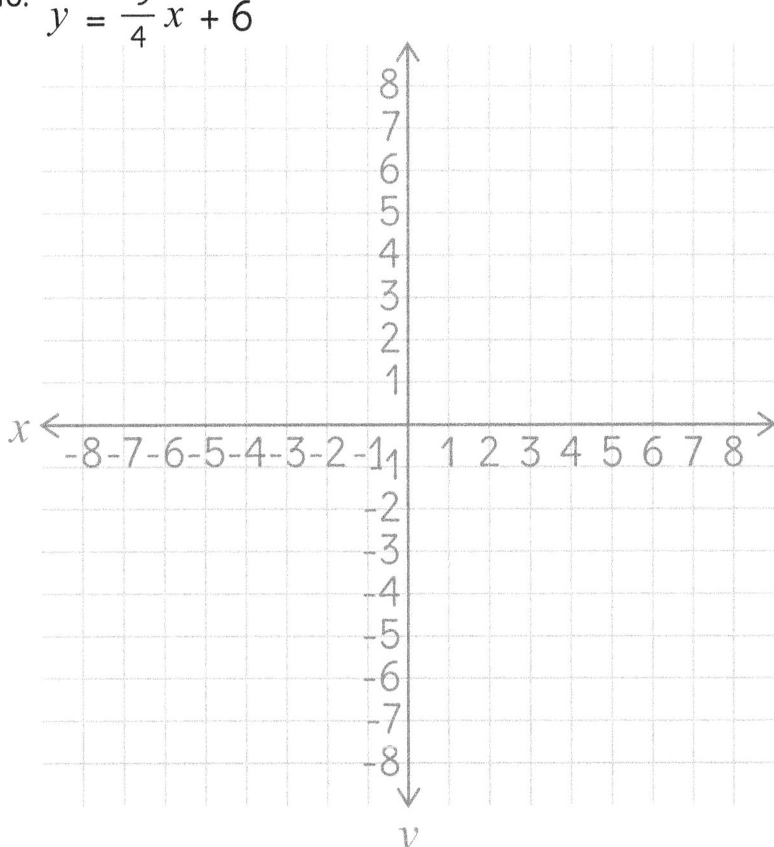

17. $x = -3$

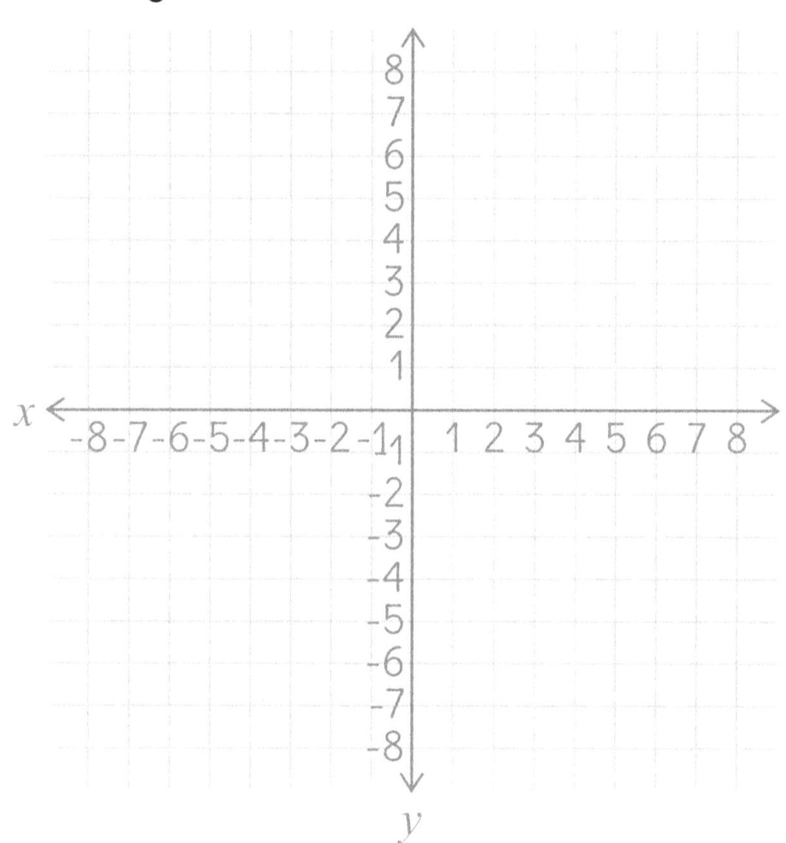

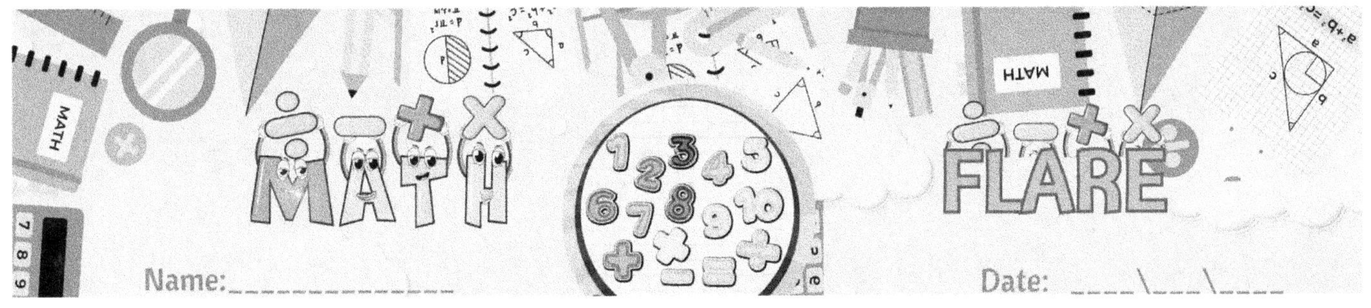

18.
$$y = \frac{3}{4}x + 4$$

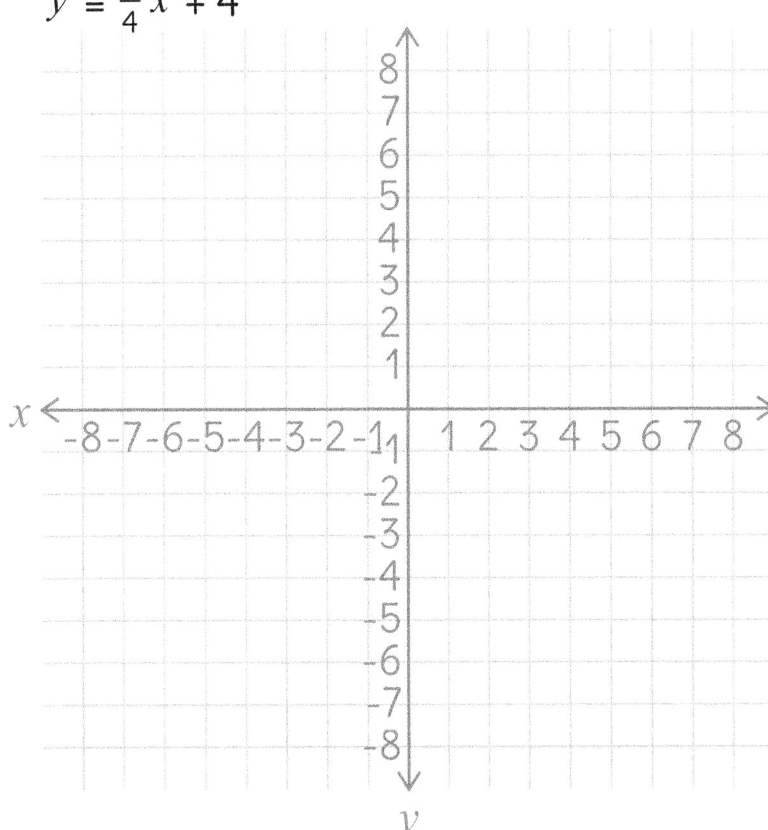

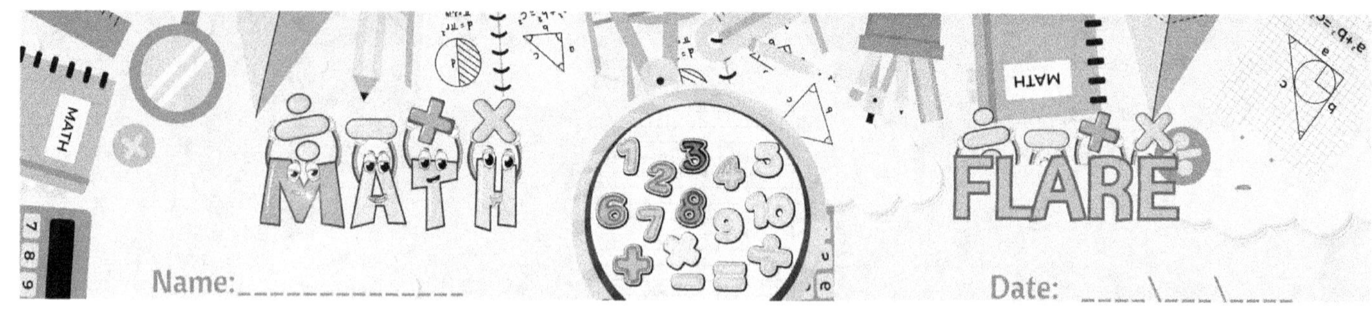

Name:_______________   Date: _____________

19.
$$y = 3x - 1$$

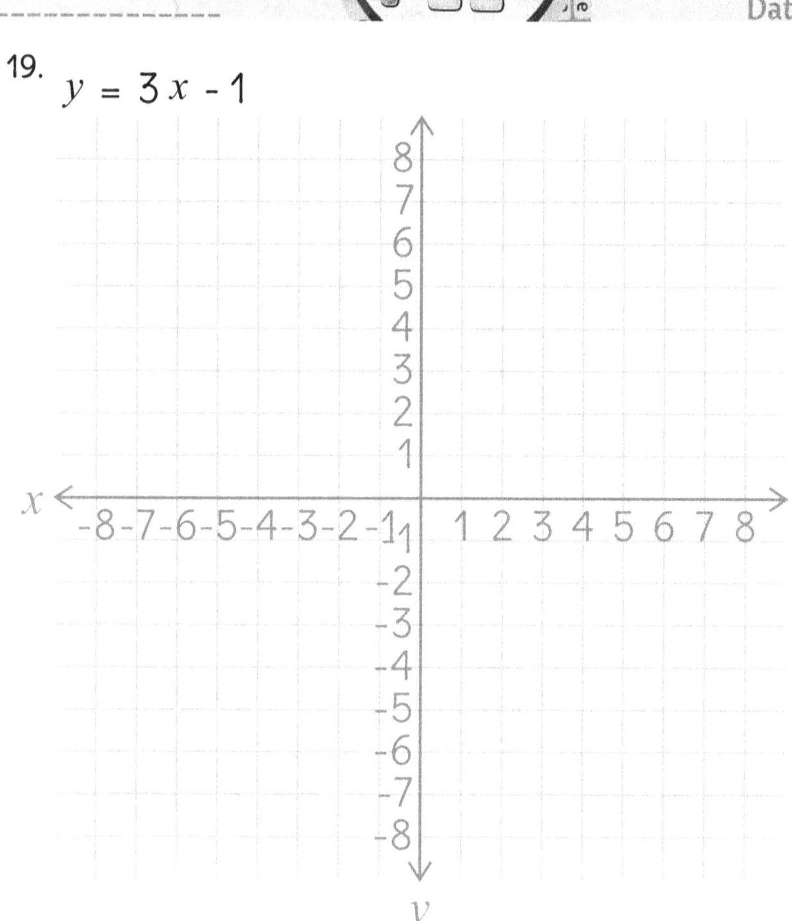

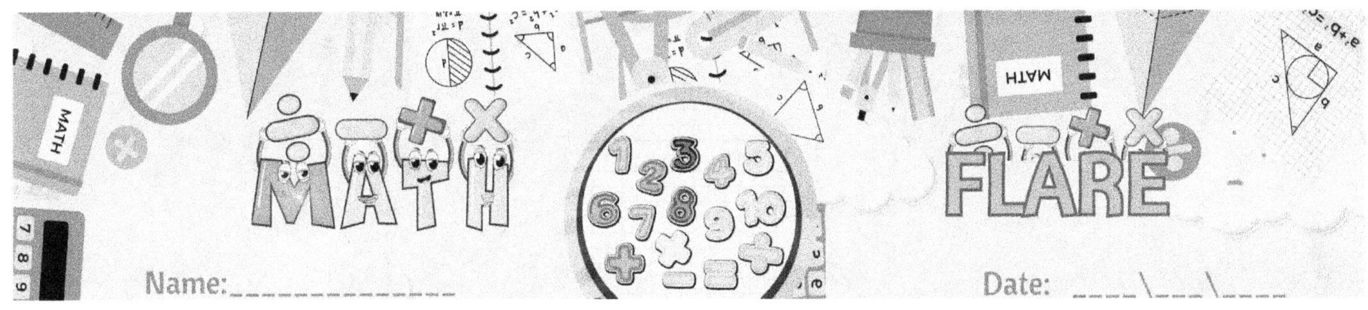

20. $y = x + 3$

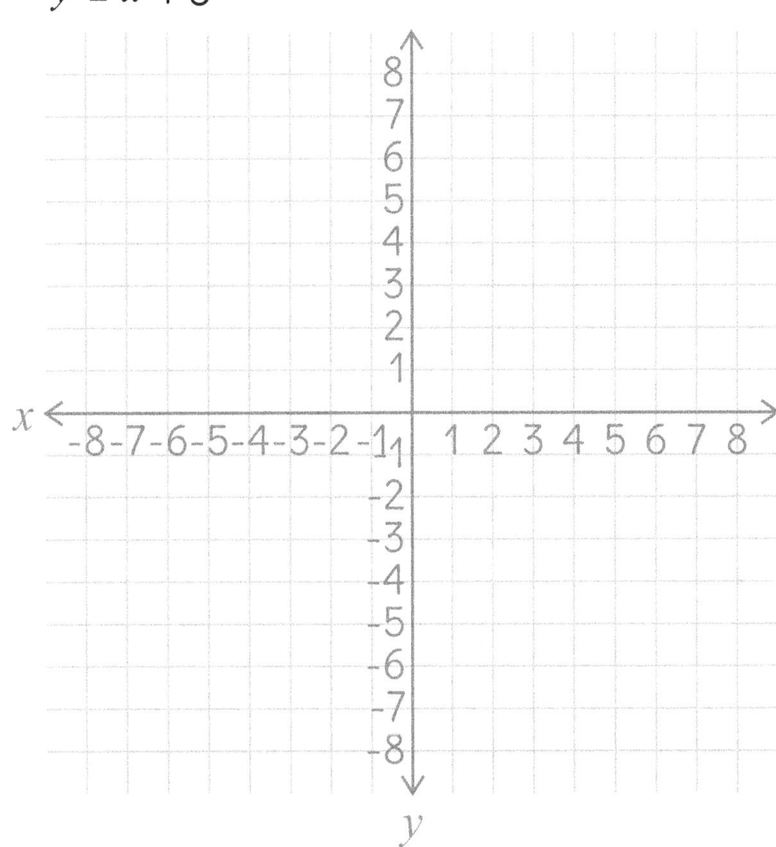

Name:________________ Date: __________

System of Equations

1. $4x + 2y = 6$

   $5x + 3y = 3$

2. $9x + 8y = 1$

   $1x + 3y = 10$

3. $3x + 7y = 2$

   $5x + 3y = 6$

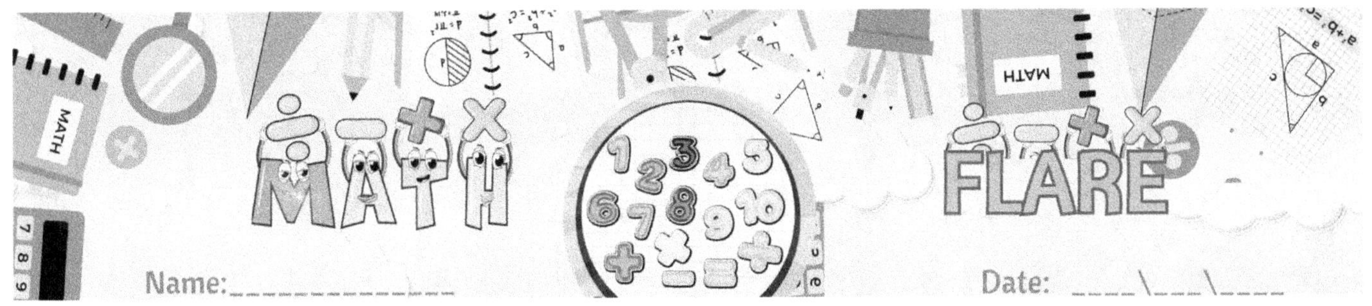

4. $10x + 9y = 8$

   $5x + 4y = 1$

5. $6x + 4y = 7$

   $6x + 6y = 8$

6. $3x + 9y = 1$

   $4x + 6y = 4$

7. 6x + 5y = 10

   9x + 10y = 7

8. 3x + 2y = 6

   1x + 7y = 2

9. 4x + 10y = 1

   9x + 6y = 9

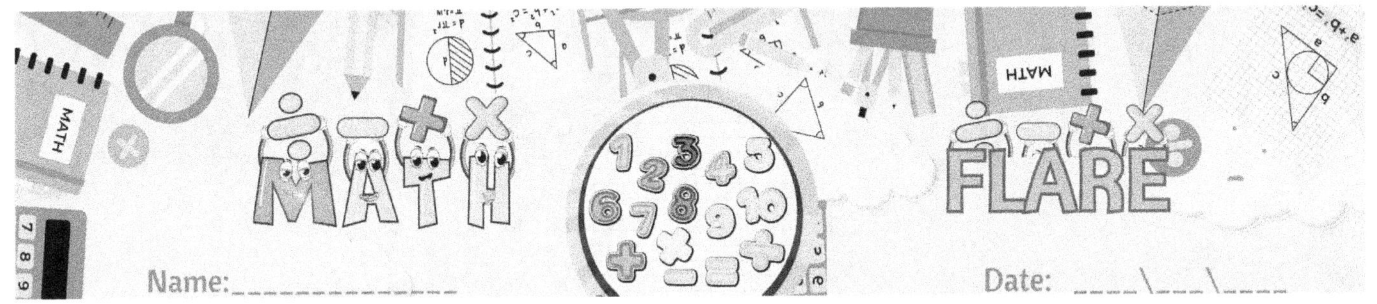

Name:___________________

Date: ______________

10. 5x + 10y = 10

9x + 4y = 10

11. 4x + 6y = 4

4x + 3y = 8

12. 1x + 10y = 7

4x + 10y = 3

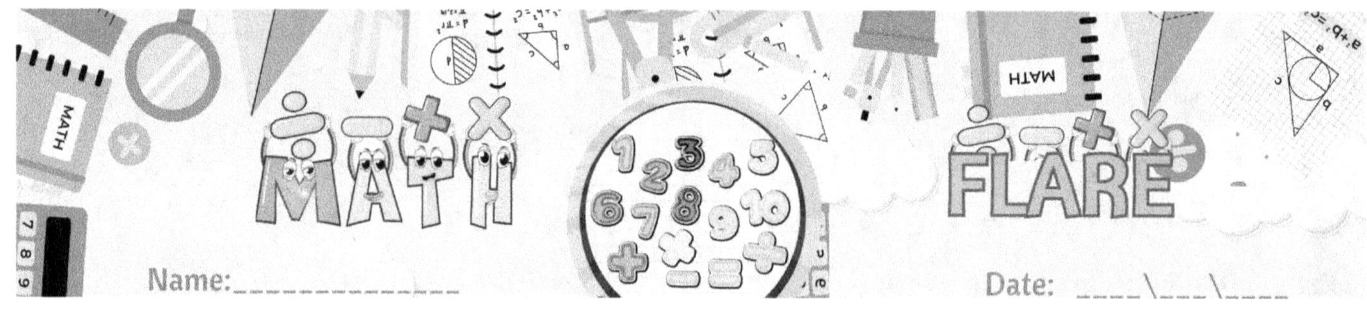

13. $5x + 8y = 8$

$8x + 10y = 3$

14. $5x + 7y = 5$

$9x + 6y = 7$

15. $1x + 1y = 2$

$2x + 4y = 5$

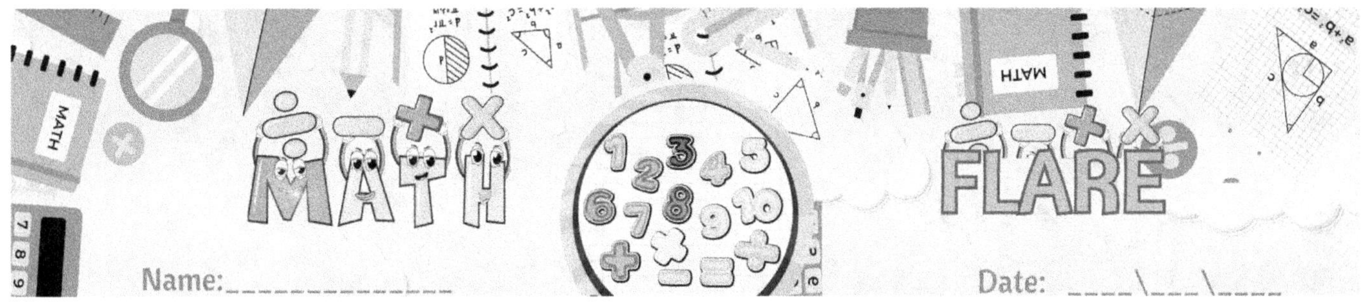

16. $7x + 2y = 4$

$2x + 3y = 3$

17. $4x + 5y = 5$

$9x + 9y = 7$

18. $5x + 2y = 3$

$7x + 9y = 8$

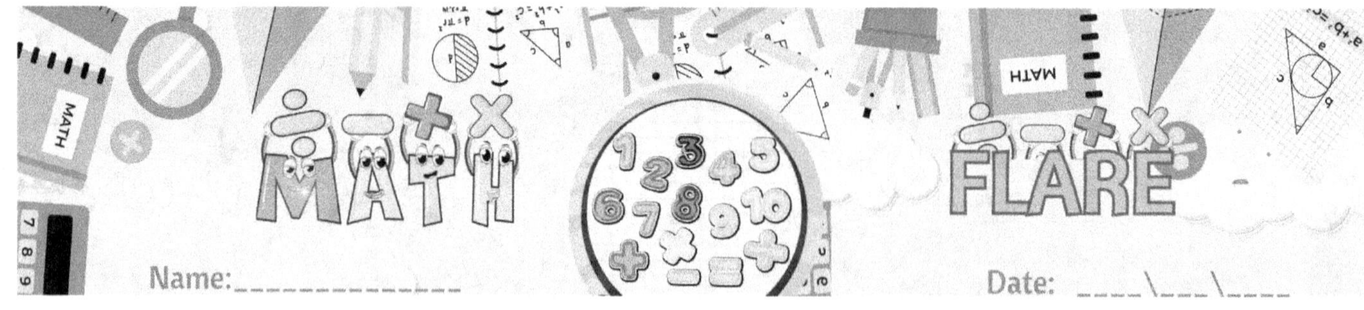

19. 10x + 8y = 6

    10x + 6y = 8

20. 9x + 1y = 5

    6x + 8y = 4

21. 10x + 1y = 10

    10x + 10y = 1

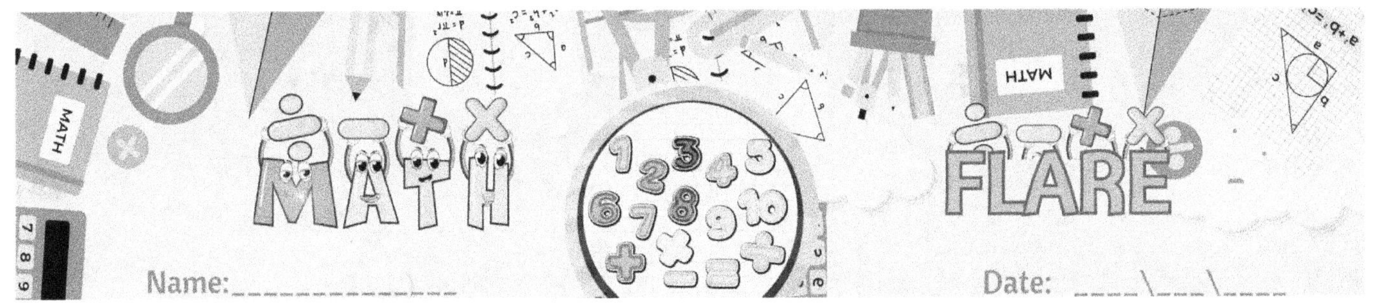

22. $3x + 1y = 7$

$5x + 8y = 8$

23. $2x + 7y = 6$

$3x + 9y = 9$

24. $8x + 7y = 3$

$2x + 3y = 3$

25. $9x + 3y = 6$

   $8x + 3y = 7$

26. $3x + 2y = 3$

   $2x + 4y = 3$

27. $8x + 9y = 2$

   $10x + 4y = 7$

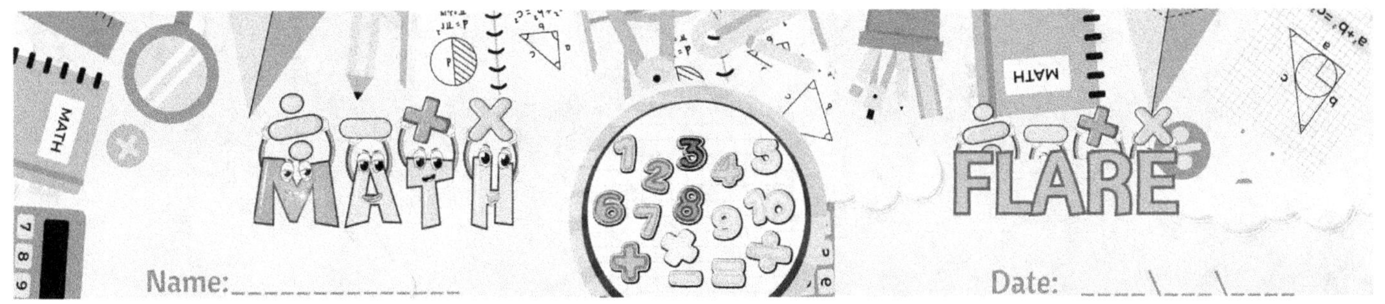

28. 8x + 4y = 7

2x + 6y = 9

29. 8x + 6y = 2

9x + 1y = 2

30. 10x + 1y = 4

2x + 8y = 4

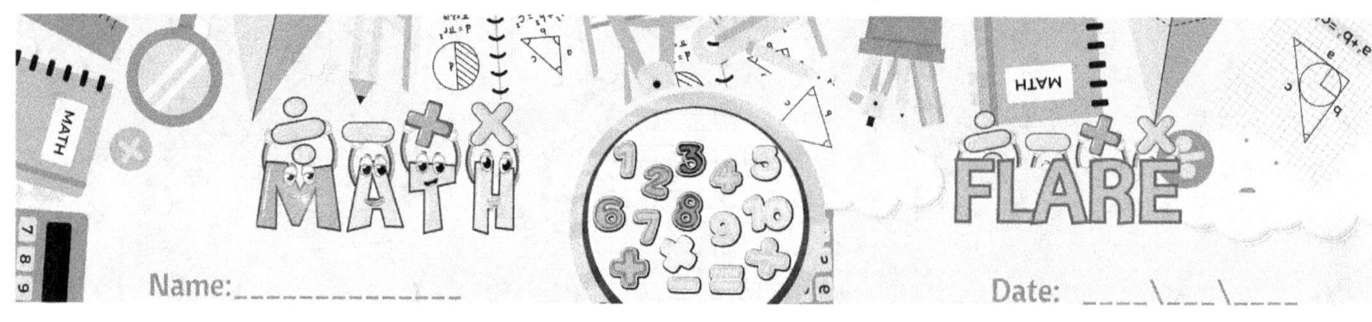

Polynomials: Addition and Subtraction

1. $(3m^2 + 6m^3) + (7m^3 - 6m^2)$

2. $(3k^4 + 5k) + (3k^4 + 8k)$

3. $(v^3 + 2v^2) + (7v^3 + 6v^2)$

4. $(4x + 4) + (8x + 3x^4)$

5. $(4n^3 + 5n^4) + (2n^4 - 5n^3)$

6. $(4p^2 + 4p^3) - (3p^3 - 7p^2)$

7. $(5b^4 + 8) - (2b^4 - 5)$

8. $(2k^3 - k^2) + (7k^3 + 6k^2)$

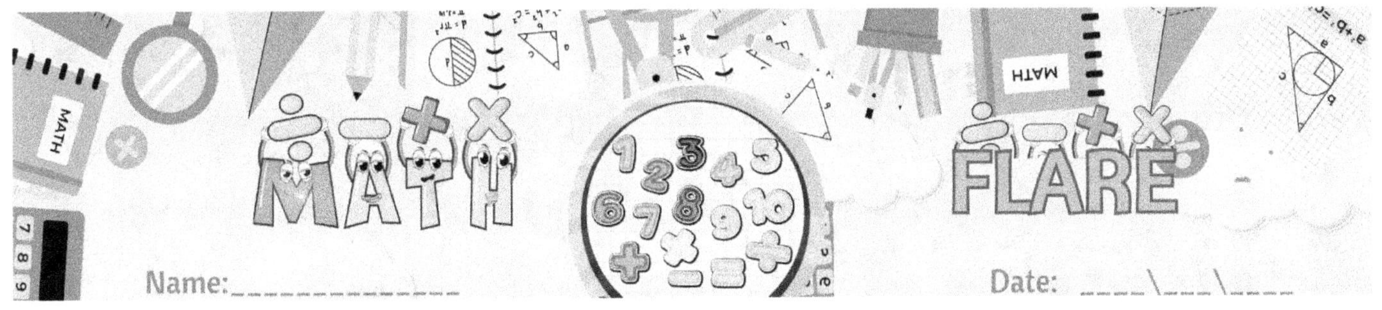

9. $(4a - 3) + (2a + 2)$

14. $(5x^2 - 6x^3) + (2x^3 - 3x^2)$

10. $(6 + 7r) + (4 + 4r^3)$

15. $(7 + 5k^2) + (8 - 2k)$

11. $(2n^4 + 8n) - (n - 7n^4)$

16. $(1 - 5n^2) + (6 + 4n^2)$

12. $(5a - 2) + (6a - 2)$

17. $(3 - 4x^4) + (1 - 3x^4)$

13. $(n^2 - 5) - (n^2 - 1)$

18. $(6a^4 + 5a^3) + (2a^4 - 4a^3)$

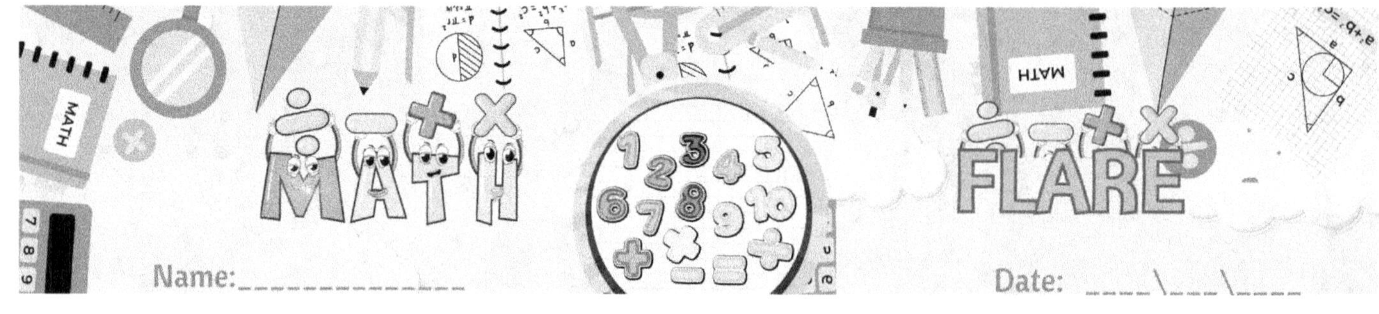

19. $(4p^4 - 4p^3) + (7p^4 - p^3)$

24. $(4 + x) - (4 + 3x)$

20. $(2n^2 - 6) + (3 + 2n^2)$

25. $(5 - 5x^3) + (8x^3 + 1)$

21. $(3a^2 - 6a^4) - (8a^4 + a^2)$

26. $(7n - n^2) - (5n + n^2)$

22. $(8n - 3n^3) + (6n^3 - n)$

27. $(p^4 + 6p) - (2p + 4p^4)$

23. $(3v^2 - 7) + (3v^2 - 2)$

28. $(2 - 2x^3) + (6x^3 - 3)$

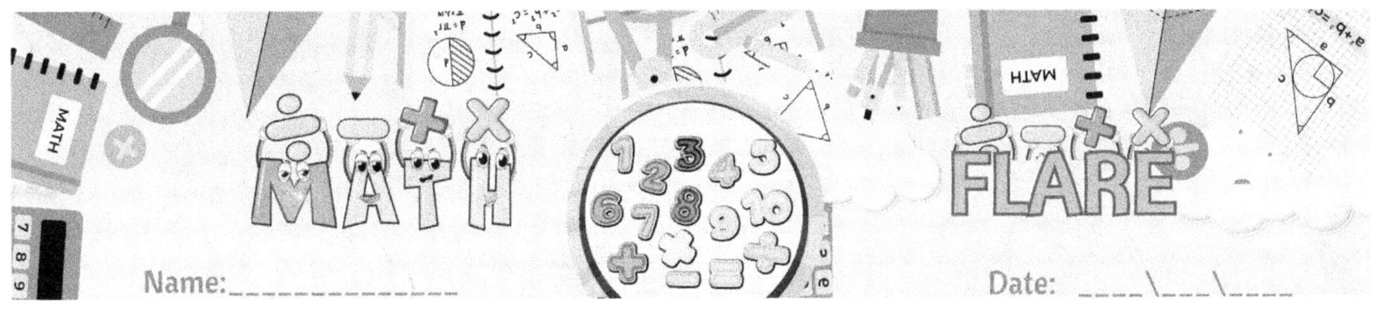

29. $(3r^2 + 8r^3) + (7r^2 + 5r^3)$

30. $(4b^4 - 3b^2) - (7b^4 + b^2)$

31. $(7 - 5x^3) + (5 + 3x^3 + x^2)$

32. $(1 - n) - (6 - 6n - 6n^4)$

33. $(6 - 6n^4) + (8 - 7n^4 - 3n^2)$

34. $(7x^3 + 6x^4) - (5x^3 + 3x^4 - x^2)$

35. $(2n^3 - 2n^4) + (6n^4 - 2n^2 + 8n^3)$

36. $(5v^3 + v) - (v^2 - 4v^3 - 7v)$

37. $(5 + 2p^2) - (3p^3 + 7p^2 + 1)$

38. $(3k^4 - 3k^2) - (4k^4 + 2k^2 - k)$

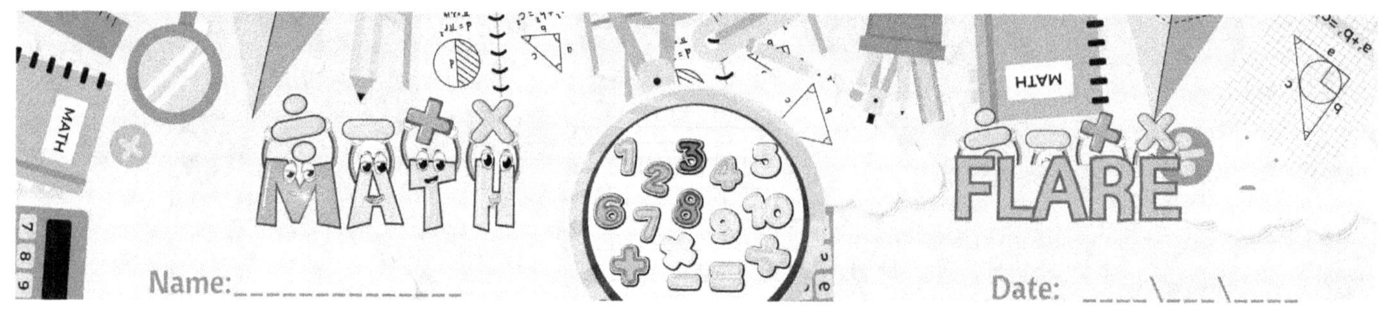

39. $(7x^2 - 7x) + (3x^2 - 4 + 4x)$

44. $(3x - 7x^2) + (8x - 2x^3 - x^2)$

40. $(6 - k^4) - (k^3 - 3 + 5k^4)$

45. $(3x^2 - 8x) + (3x - 8x^2 + 7x^3)$

41. $(2a^3 + 5a) - (a + 7a^2 + a^3)$

46. $(7 + 3x^2) + (3 - 8x^3 + 8x^2)$

42. $(2x^2 + 3x) - (8x - 7x^2 + 4x^3)$

47. $(x^3 + 8) + (6 - 6x^3 + 8x^2)$

43. $(4x^4 + 2) + (5x + 8 + 4x^4)$

48. $(5x^3 + x^4) - (8x + 7x^3 + 5x^4)$

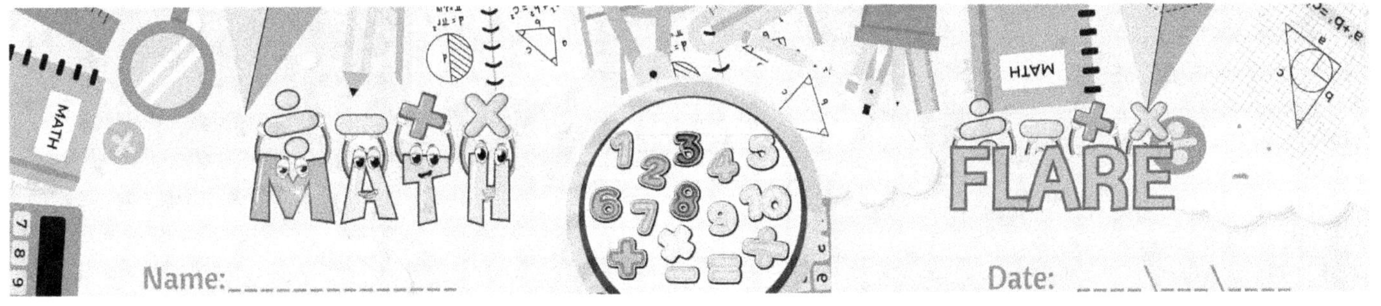

49. $(6n^3 - 5n) + (7n + 3n^3 - 2)$

54. $(4x^2 - 4x^3) + (4x^3 + 7x^2 - 8x)$

50. $(8a^2 - 4a^4) - (3a^2 - 3a^4 - 4a^3)$

55. $(5 + 2n^2) + (1 + 5n^4 - 8n^2)$

51. $(2x^3 + 5x^4) - (5 + 8x^3 - 5x^4)$

56. $(4k^2 + 8k) + (k + k^2 - 5k^3)$

52. $(7a^2 - 1) - (8a^4 - 5 - 4a^2)$

57. $(x^2 + x^3) - (7x - 6x^2 + 3x^3)$

53. $(5 - 6x^2) - (6x^2 - 7x + 7)$

58. $(6n^2 - 8n^3) + (4n^3 + 7n^2 + 5n^4)$

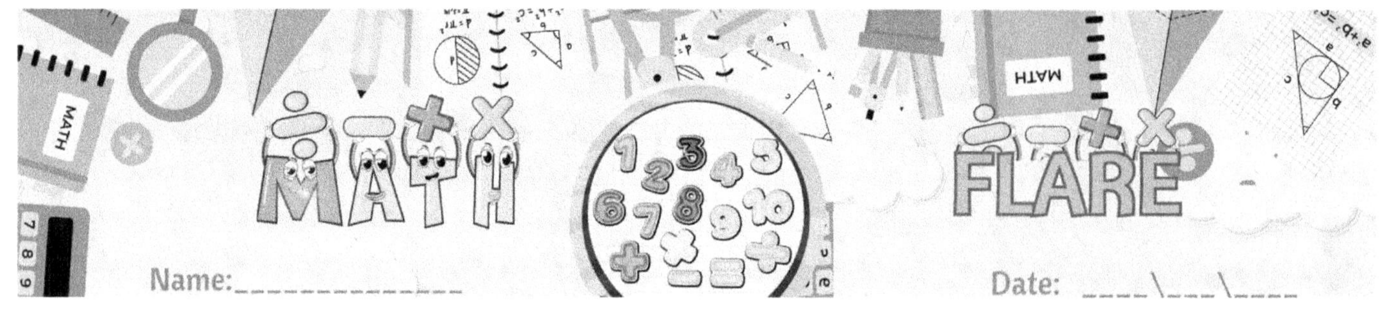

59. $(6v^2 + 8) + (2v^2 + 7 - 5v^3)$

60. $(6b^3 - b) + (4b^3 + 2b - 4b^4)$

61. $(1 - 2a^2 + a^3) - (2 - 5a^2 - a^3)$

62. $(4 - 2a^4 + 2a^3) + (6a^3 + 5a^2 - 4)$

63. $(3 + 4a^2 - 2a^3) - (7 - a^2 - 7a^3)$

64. $(5x + 6 + 6x^4) - (2x^3 - 8x^4 - 5x)$

65. $(3p^2 + 4p^4 + 3p) - (7p - 4p^2 + 2p^4)$

66. $(x^4 + 7x - 2x^2) - (7x^2 - 8x^3 + 4x^4)$

67. $(8v^3 - 3v^4 + 3) + (v - 7v^3 + 8v^4)$

68. $(5 + 7p - p^3) + (2p + 5p^3 + 7)$

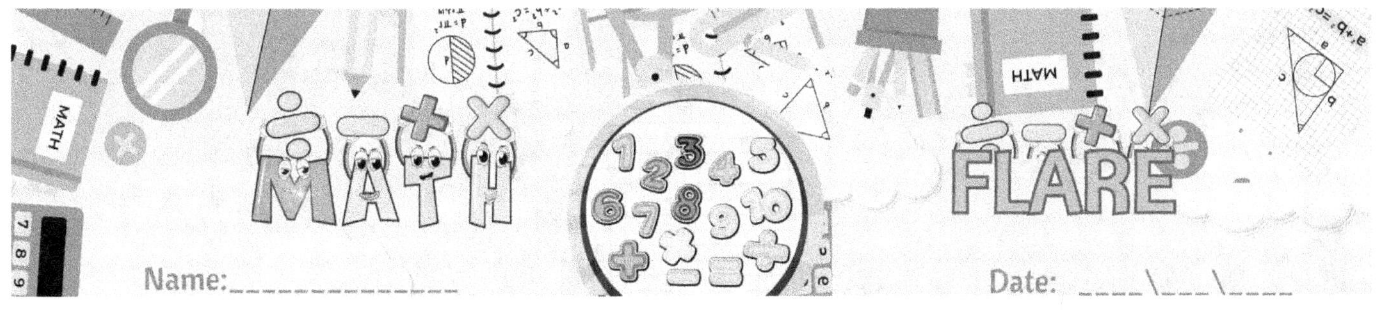

69. $(5x - 2x^4 + 2x^2) + (4x - 2x^2 + 5x^4)$

74. $(6n^3 + 6 - 3n) - (2 + 8n + 2n^3)$

70. $(2x^3 - x - 6x^2) - (7x^2 - 7 + 4x)$

75. $(7v + 3v^3 - 3) + (8v^3 - 2v^2 - 6v)$

71. $(6n^3 + 8n^4 - 5) - (6 - 7n^4 - 8n^3)$

76. $(3n^2 - 7 + 4n) + (6n - 8n^2 - 3n^3)$

72. $(3v^3 + 8v - 4v^2) + (5v + 8v^2 - 7v^3)$

77. $(5x + 2x^3 - 5) - (6x - 4x^4 - 8x^3)$

73. $(2v^3 + 5v^2 - 6v) + (v^3 - v^2 - v)$

78. $(8x^2 + 8x^4 - x) - (7x^2 - 7x^4 + 6x)$

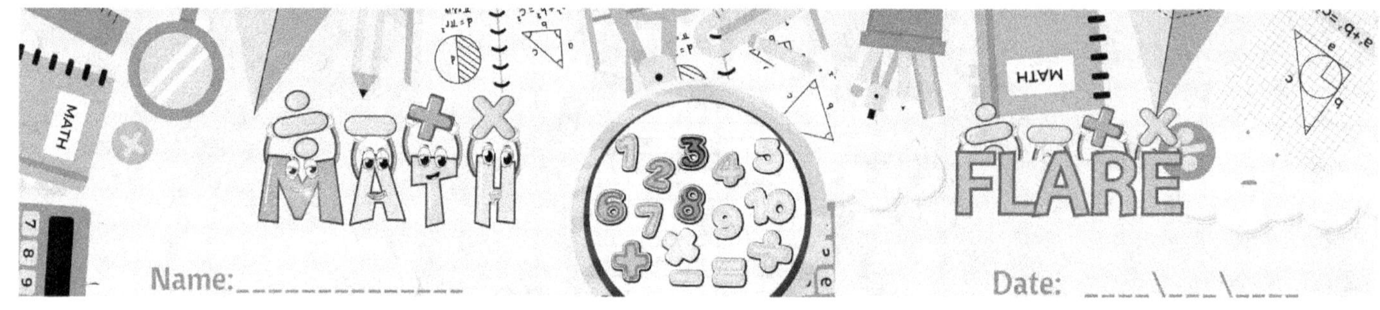

Name:________________

Date: ____________

79. $(6x - 8x^2 - 3x^4) + (x^2 - 7x + 6x^4)$

84. $(1 - n^3 + 3n^4) + (n + 4n^4 - 4n^3)$

80. $(5n^4 + 4n^3 - 5n^2) - (3n - 5n^2 + n^3)$

85. $(4 - 8v^2 - v^3) + (7v^2 + 2 + 4v^3)$

81. $(p^3 - 4 + 4p) - (5p + 4p^4 + 3p^3)$

86. $(6 + 2x + x^2) + (3x + 6x^2 + 5)$

82. $(6v^4 - 4v - 5) + (v^4 - 4 - v)$

87. $(5n + 3n^2 + 2) - (2 + 2n^2 - n)$

83. $(8p^2 - 6p^4 + 4p^3) - (8p^4 + 7 - 3p^2)$

88. $(3a + 2a^3 - 7a^4) + (3a + 2 + 8a^3)$

Name:__________________ Date: ____________

Polynomials: Multiplication

1. $(2x + 4y)(5x - 7y)$

2. $(a - 2b)(5a - 5b)$

3. $(7x + 2y)(x - 6y)$

4. $(8a - 4b)(4a - 2b)$

5. $(x - 5y)(8x - 7y)$

6. $(4u + 4v)(u + 3v)$

7. $(5x - y)(5x + 4y)$

8. $(3a - 6b)(a - 7b)$

9. (7a - 7b)(5a - 6b)

14. (6x - y)(8x + 3 y)

10. (6x - 3 y)(7x - 7 y)

15. (2x + 3 y)(6x - 3 y)

11. (7x + 8 y)(4x + y)

16. (4a + 8b)(4a + 2b)

12. (6m + 5n)(m + 8n)

17. (x - 6 y)(4x + 5 y)

13. (2a + 6b)(7a + 3b)

18. (5a + 7b)(2a - 5b)

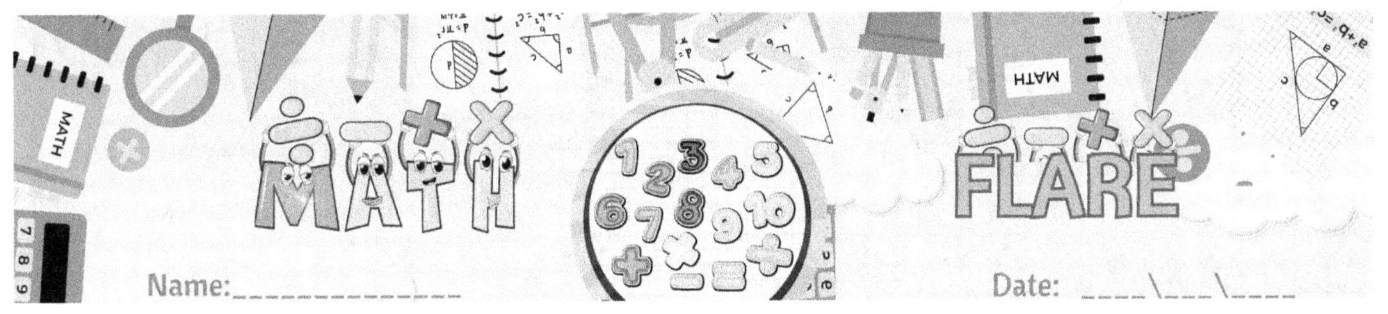

19. $(3a + b)(2a + 3b)$

24. $(8m + 7n)(5m - 5n)$

20. $(7x - 6y)(5x - 3y)$

25. $(u + 2v)(2u - 2v)$

21. $(2x + 4y)(x - 2y)$

26. $(5x + 2y)(6x + 3y)$

22. $(5a - 4b)(6a + 3b)$

27. $(3x + 7y)(5x + 7y)$

23. $(5x - 5y)(8x - 6y)$

28. $(2x - 8y)(8x - 3y)$

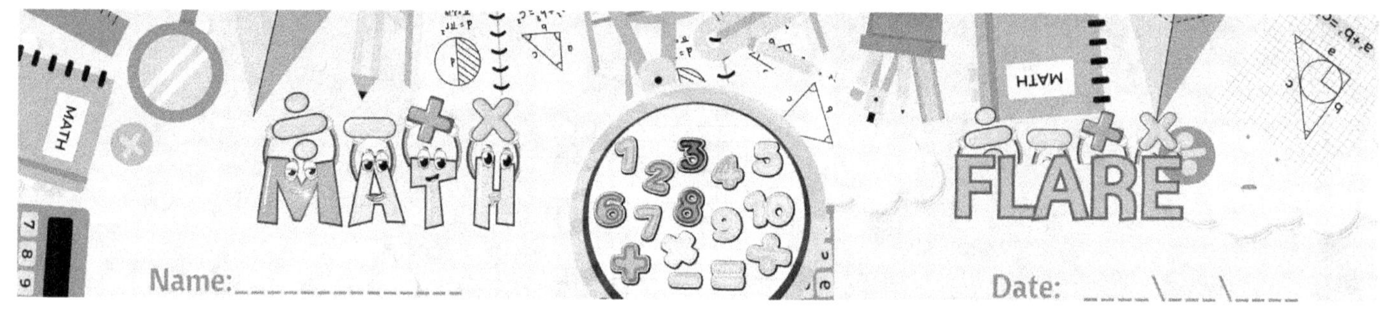

29. $(8x + 4y)(3x - 4y)$

30. $(3x - 2y)(5x + 6y)$

31. $(5u + 6v)(4u^2 - 7uv - 5v^2)$

32. $(3x - 2y)(x^2 + 7xy + 6y^2)$

33. $(7a - 8b)(7a^2 - ab + b^2)$

34. $(6a - 4b)(6a^2 - 8ab + 7b^2)$

35. $(6u - 2v)(7u^2 - 3uv - 7v^2)$

36. $(x - y)(4x^2 + 4xy + 2y^2)$

37. $(5u + v)(7u^2 - uv + 2v^2)$

38. $(8x - 7y)(3x^2 + 8xy + 6y^2)$

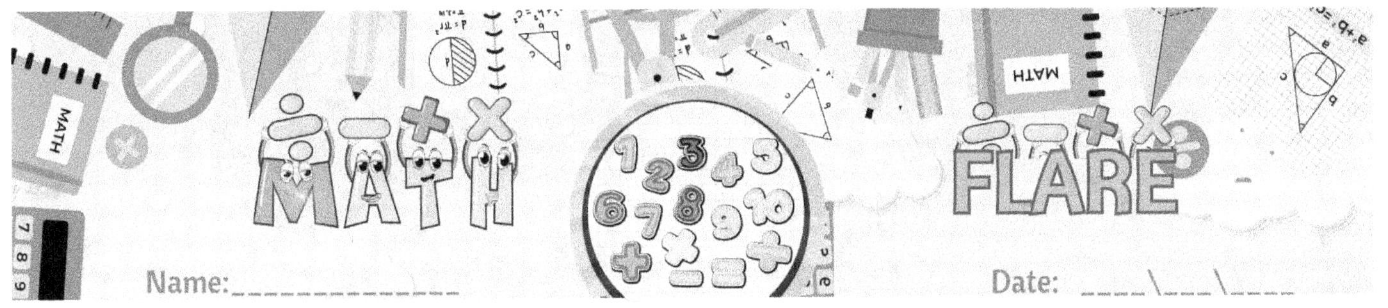

39. $(m - 4n)(m^2 + 3mn + 8n^2)$

44. $(5x - 6y)(x^2 - 7xy - 5y^2)$

40. $(4a + 6b)(a^2 + 8ab - 3b^2)$

45. $(4x - 5y)(8x^2 + 4xy + 8y^2)$

41. $(8x + 6y)(2x^2 - 4xy + 6y^2)$

46. $(6x - 6y)(7x^2 - xy + 5y^2)$

42. $(5x + 8y)(6x^2 - 6xy + 7y^2)$

47. $(3u - 5v)(2u^2 - 7uv + 5v^2)$

43. $(5m - n)(8m^2 + 5mn - n^2)$

48. $(3a + b)(7a^2 - 7ab + 4b^2)$

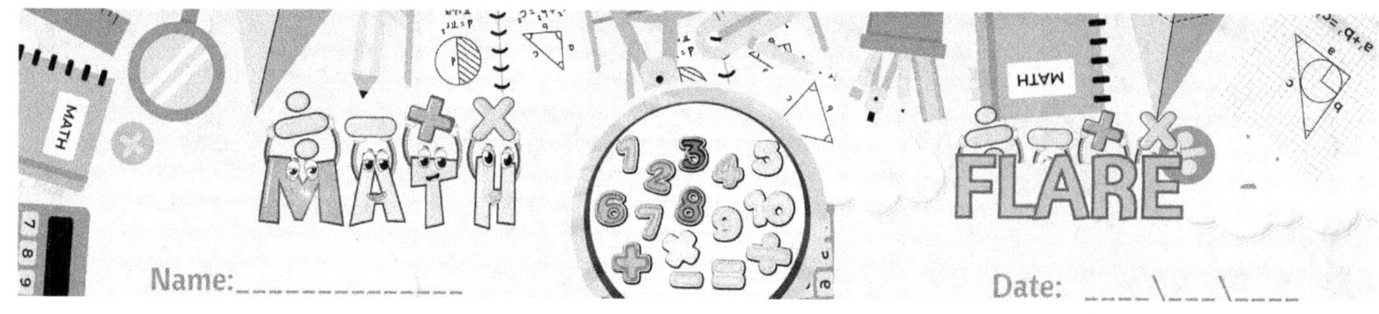

49. $(7x - 3y)(7x^2 - 4xy + 7y^2)$

54. $(5m - 2n)(7m^2 - 6mn - 7n^2)$

50. $(4x + 3y)(3x^2 + 4xy + y^2)$

55. $(5x - 5y)(4x^2 + 3xy - 2y^2)$

51. $(6m + 2n)(4m^2 - mn - n^2)$

56. $(2x - 3y)(5x^2 + 7xy + 4y^2)$

52. $(2x - 6y)(4x^2 - xy + y^2)$

57. $(2x + y)(x^2 - 4xy - 8y^2)$

53. $(x + 2y)(7x^2 + 8xy + 2y^2)$

58. $(4a - 6b)(5a^2 - 3ab + b^2)$

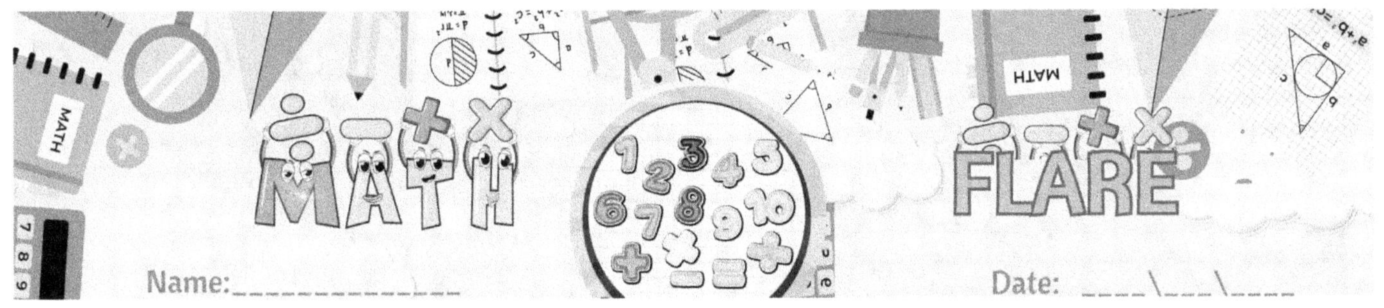

59. $(7a + 6b)(6a^2 + 6ab - 7b^2)$

60. $(4x + 6y)(4x^2 - 2xy - y^2)$

61. $(7x^2 + 5xy - 7y^2)(8x^2 + 8xy + 3y^2)$

62. $(3x^2 - 3xy - 8y^2)(8x^2 + 6xy - 2y^2)$

63. $(3a^2 + 5ab + 2b^2)(8a^2 + 6ab + 7b^2)$

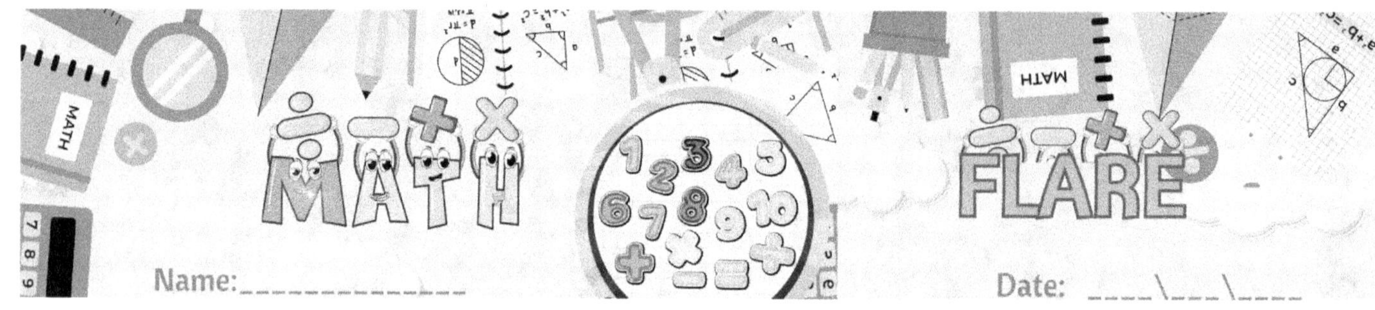

64. $(3x^2 - 7xy - 8y^2)(2x^2 - 7xy + 6y^2)$

65. $(6u^2 + 5uv + v^2)(7u^2 - 8uv - 4v^2)$

66. $(2u^2 - 2uv + 5v^2)(3u^2 + 7uv + 5v^2)$

67. $(3a^2 - 8ab - 8b^2)(7a^2 + 7ab + 4b^2)$

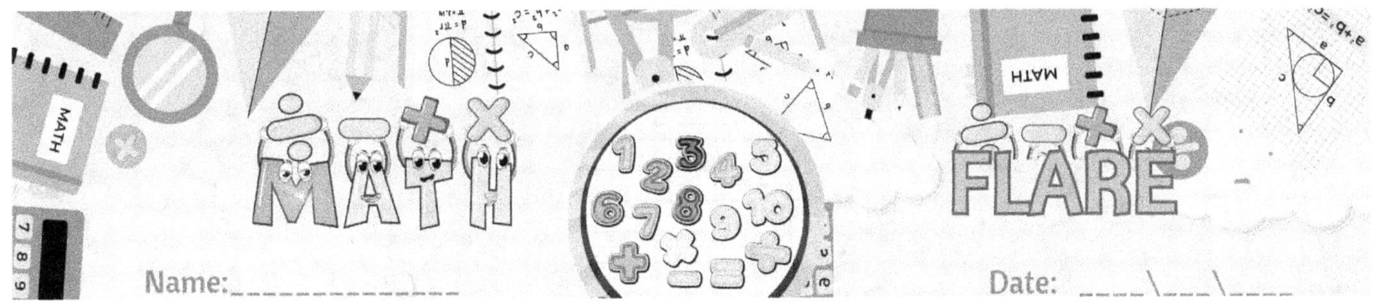

68. $(2m^2 - mn - n^2)(7m^2 + 8mn - n^2)$

69. $(7m^2 - 4mn - 3n^2)(5m^2 + 4mn - 6n^2)$

70. $(8x^2 - 8xy - 5y^2)(3x^2 + xy - 5y^2)$

71. $(5u^2 + 5uv + 6v^2)(5u^2 - 6uv - 8v^2)$

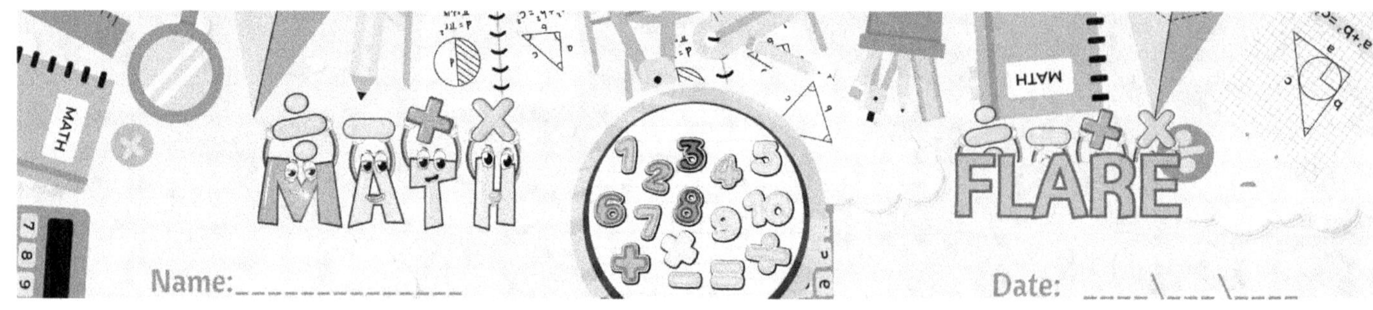

72. $(2u^2 - 8uv - 6v^2)(2u^2 - uv + v^2)$

73. $(2x^2 + xy + 5y^2)(6x^2 - 3xy - 8y^2)$

74. $(6x^2 - xy - 4y^2)(2x^2 + 8xy - 2y^2)$

75. $(6x^2 + 4xy - 2y^2)(x^2 - 7xy - 3y^2)$

76. $(6x^2 - 5xy - y^2)(6x^2 + xy + 3y^2)$

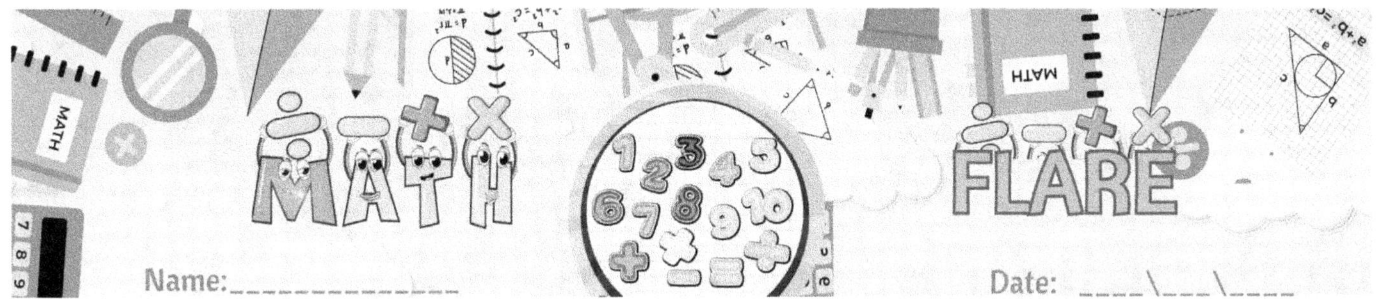

77. $(x^2 - 6xy - 2y^2)(3x^2 - xy + 3y^2)$

78. $(3x^2 + 3xy + 8y^2)(5x^2 - 5xy + 7y^2)$

79. $(3u^2 - 4uv + 7v^2)(4u^2 - 7uv - 7v^2)$

80. $(3x^2 + 5xy + 6y^2)(7x^2 - 2xy - 3y^2)$

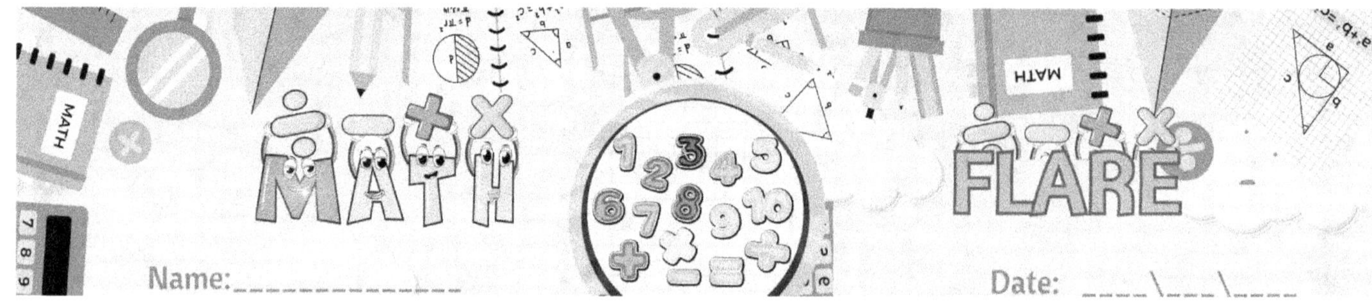

81. $(6x^2 - xy + 6y^2)(x^2 - 4xy - 7y^2)$

82. $(2a^2 - 2ab - 2b^2)(4a^2 + 4ab + 5b^2)$

83. $(a^2 - 5ab - 3b^2)(5a^2 - 2ab + 5b^2)$

84. $(2m^2 + mn + n^2)(4m^2 - 7mn + 2n^2)$

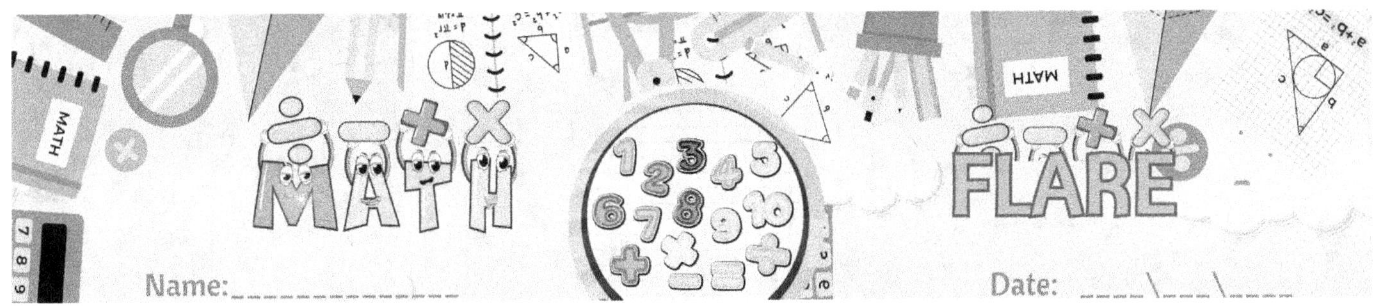

85. $(6x^2 - 2xy + 7y^2)(5x^2 + 6xy - y^2)$

86. $(7m^2 - 7mn - 7n^2)(8m^2 + 6mn - 8n^2)$

87. $(2x^2 - 6xy - 5y^2)(x^2 - 2xy + y^2)$

88. $(8x^2 - xy + 7y^2)(8x^2 - 8xy + 2y^2)$

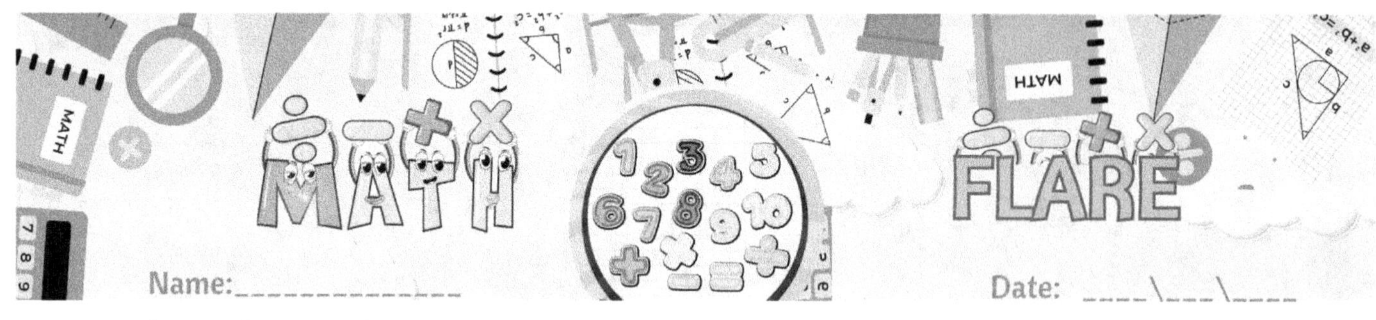

Quadratic Equations

1. $-5r^2 - 9r + 24 = 0$

2. $-4v^2 - 4v + 48 = 0$

3. $5p^2 - 2p - 115 = 0$

4. $2r^2 + 8r - 13 = 0$

5. $2n^2 - 10n + 12 = 0$

6. $-4b^2 + 121 = 0$

7. $v^2 + 7v + 4 = 0$

8. $6n^2 + 8n - 22 = 0$

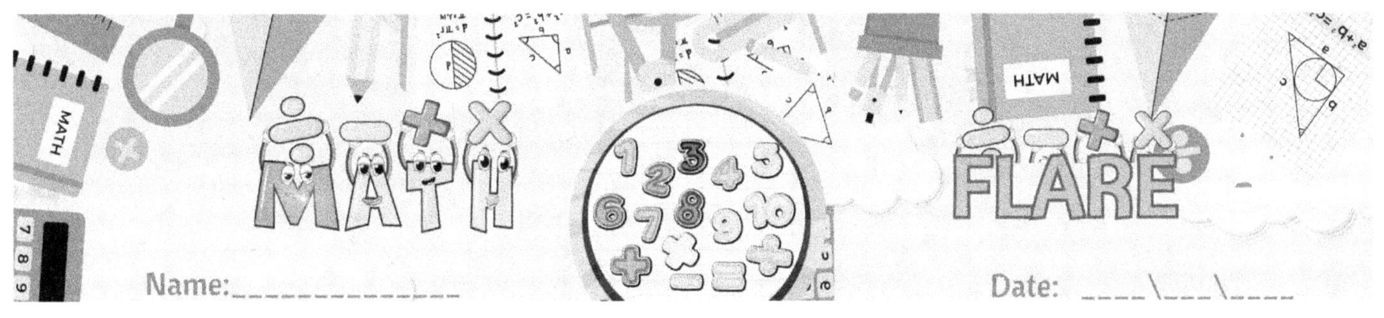

9. $4n^2 - 9n + 2 = 0$

13. $-9r^2 - 11r + 1 = 0$

10. $4b^2 + 11b - 108 = 0$

14. $4x^2 - 9x - 14 = 0$

11. $4v^2 - 21 = 0$

15. $11n^2 + 11n - 6 = 0$

12. $5b^2 - b - 48 = 0$

16. $-x^2 - 11x - 24 = 0$

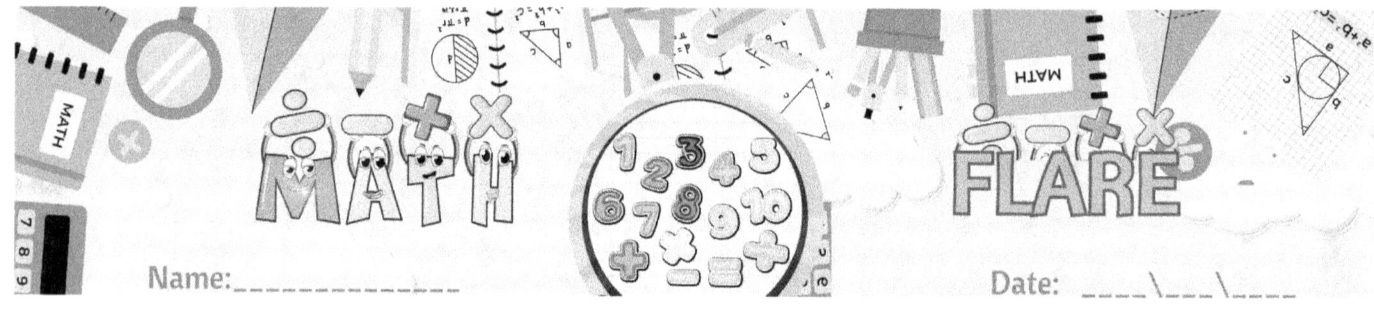

17. $-12p^2 + 11p + 18 = 0$

21. $12k^2 - 8k + 9 = 0$

18. $7n^2 + 3n - 16 = 0$

22. $-2k^2 + 2 = 0$

19. $4r^2 + 3r - 45 = 0$

23. $-x^2 - 10x + 75 = 0$

20. $7v^2 - 20 = 0$

24. $10r^2 - 7 = 0$

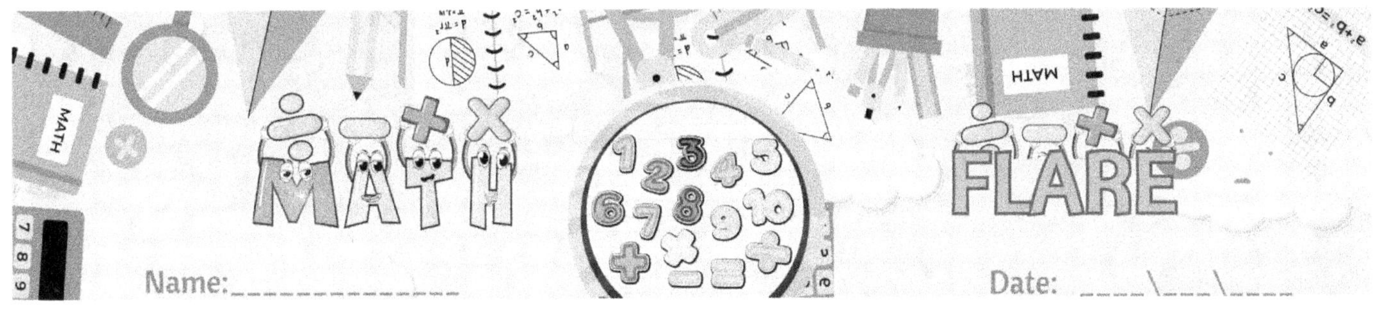

25. $6v^2 - 12v + 1 = 0$

26. $6x^2 + 5x + 9 = 0$

27. $6b^2 + 9b - 14 = 0$

28. $7x^2 - 10x - 13 = 0$

29. $-4p^2 + 100 = 0$

30. $12x^2 - 2x - 8 = 0$

31. $-4m^2 + 9 = -7$

32. $-5x^2 - 7x + 10 = 4$

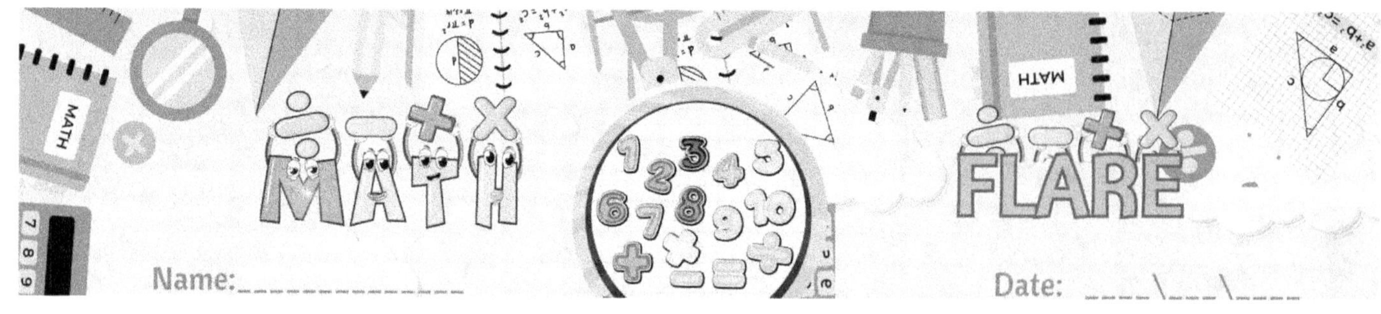

33. $3a^2 + 17 = 6$

37. $4x^2 + 4x - 18 = -3$

34. $4a^2 + 4a - 38 = 10$

38. $4x^2 - 11x - 109 = 10$

35. $3x^2 - 1 = 11$

39. $9n^2 - 6n - 18 = 2$

36. $-4b^2 + 136 = -8$

40. $x^2 - 70 = -6$

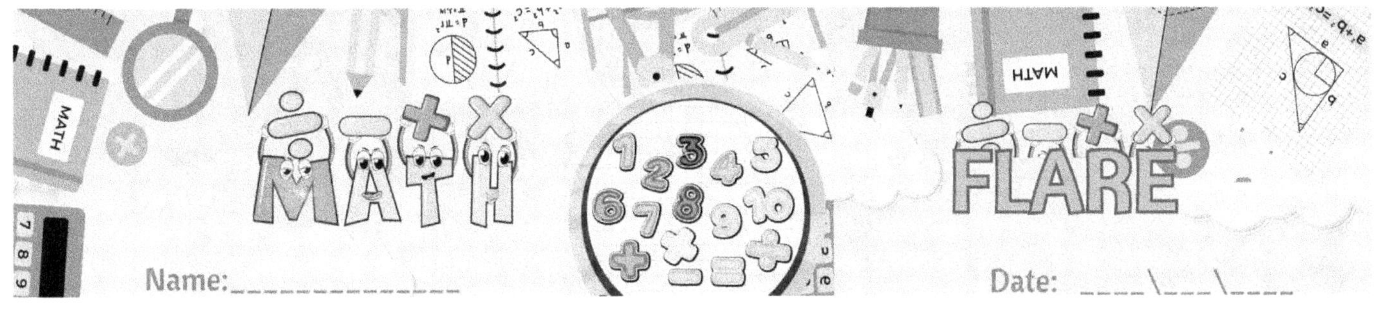

Name:________________   Date: _______________

41. $-9a^2 - 12a + 15 = -3$

45. $12x^2 - 3x + 8 = 7$

42. $-n^2 + 12 = -4$

46. $-2b^2 + 12 = -6$

43. $n^2 - 11n + 9 = -3$

47. $4v^2 - 71 = -7$

44. $6m^2 - 3m + 6 = -2$

48. $-k^2 + 8k + 10 = 7$

Name:_________________   Date: _______________

49. $8b^2 - 23 = -12$

50. $2x^2 + x - 52 = 3$

51. $-5k^2 - 7k + 18 = -3$

52. $-12k^2 - 3k - 4 = -9$

53. $-3r^2 - 12r + 2 = -2$

54. $r^2 - 86 = -5$

55. $6b^2 + 7b - 13 = -10$

56. $4r^2 - 4r - 116 = 4$

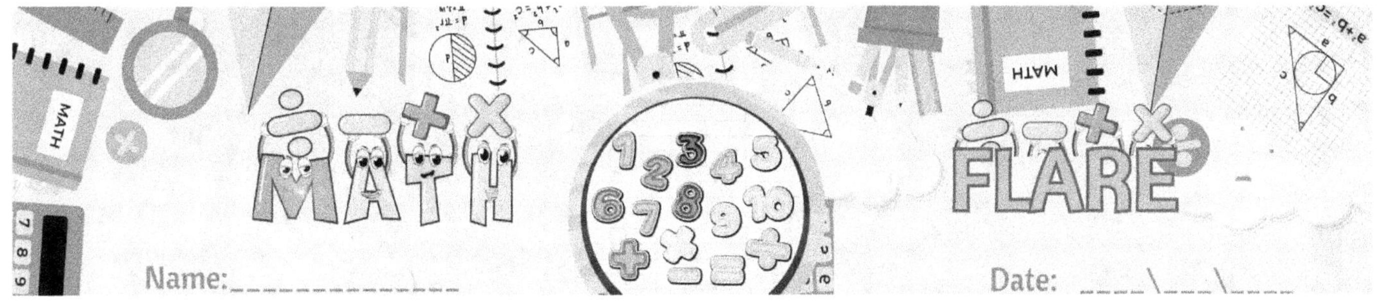

57. $2m^2 + m + 2 = 12$

61. $-5x^2 + 10x = 5$

58. $2x^2 - 11x + 14 = 7$

62. $8x^2 = x + 18$

59. $-7n^2 + 10n + 24 = 10$

63. $5x^2 - 3x = 2$

60. $7v^2 - 15 = -9$

64. $-9n^2 = 8n + 8$

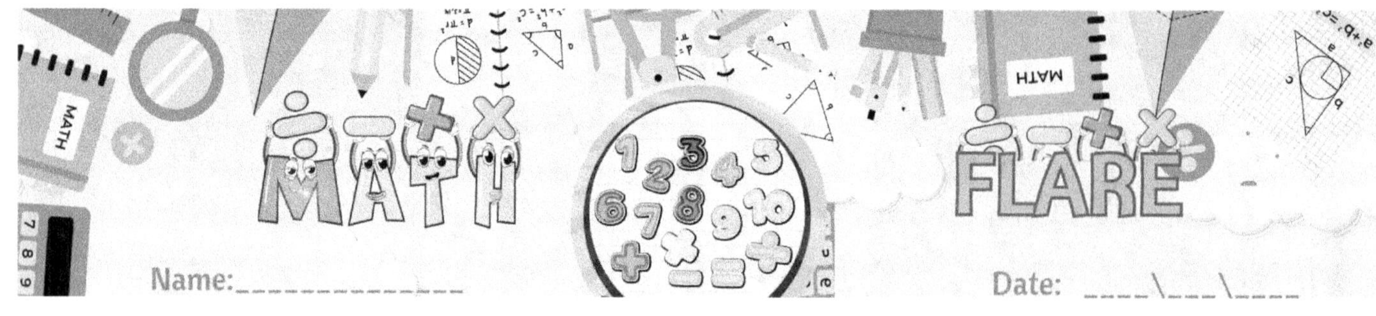

65. $-3x^2 - 4x = -20$

69. $3a^2 + 4 = -8a$

66. $-12m^2 + 9 = -10m$

70. $-11x^2 - 9 = -9x$

67. $6v^2 = 6$

71. $10x^2 - 12x = 21$

68. $12m^2 - 6m = 20$

72. $n^2 = 17$

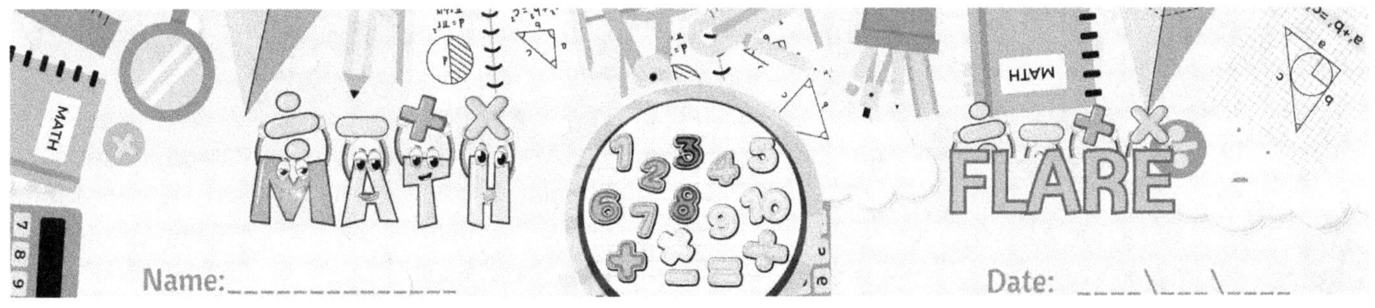

Name:______________________   Date: _______________

73. $3x^2 + 9 = 4x$

77. $-7m^2 - 3 = 0$

74. $2n^2 = 72$

78. $-2x^2 = -72$

75. $4n^2 = -7n + 18$

79. $4v^2 = 10 + 5v$

76. $-a^2 = 4a + 2$

80. $3x^2 - 22 = -5x$

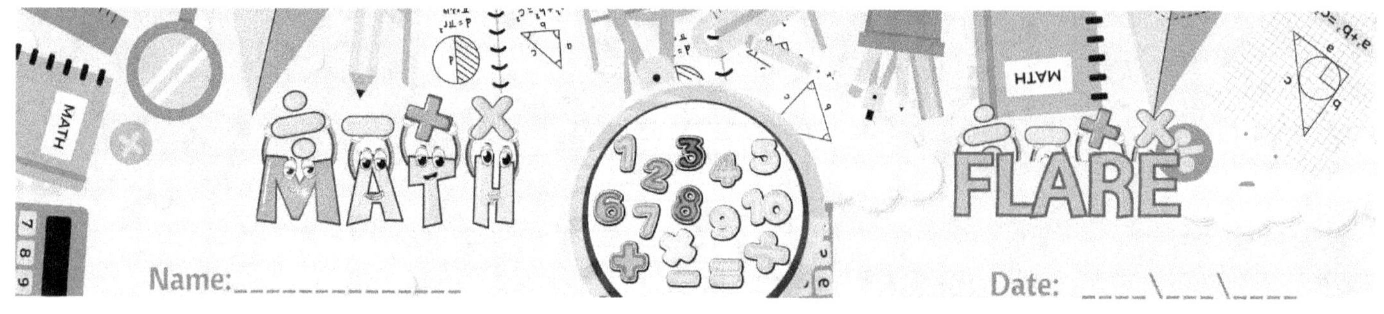

81. $-n^2 = -119 + 10n$

85. $4a^2 + 8a = -4$

82. $-6x^2 = -9 + 9x$

86. $-2a^2 = -18 + 9a$

83. $-x^2 = -8$

87. $10n^2 + 7 = -11n$

84. $-x^2 + 25 = 0$

88. $7n^2 - 3 = -10n$

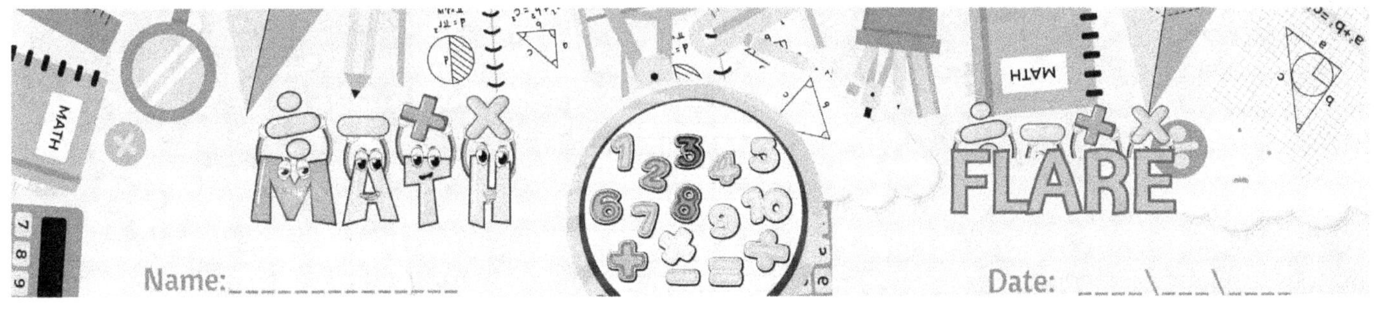

89. $-5a^2 = -17 - a$

93. $7x^2 = 9 + 3x$

90. $x^2 - 19 = 7x$

94. $3x^2 = 17$

91. $-5x^2 = -6$

95. $-2x^2 = -128$

92. $3x^2 = 48$

96. $8p^2 + 7p = 14$

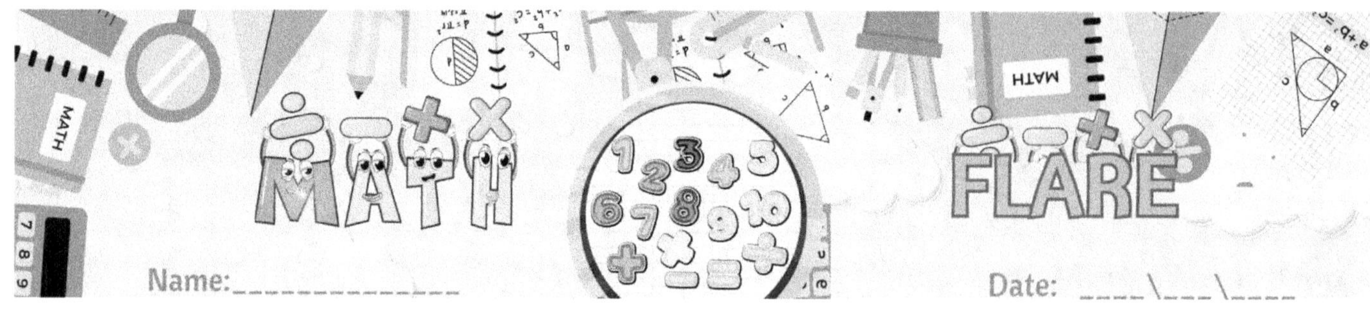

Exponents

Convert the values.

1. $16^3 =$ _______________

2. $6^{-2} =$ _______________

3. $7^4 =$ _______________

4. $5^{-2} =$ _______________

5. $18^2 =$ _______________

6. $4^{-2} =$ _______________

7. $20^4 =$ _______________

8. $14^{-2} =$ _______________

9. $10^4 =$ _______________

10. $18^{-3} =$ _______________

11. $7^2 =$ _______________

12. $7^3 =$ _______________

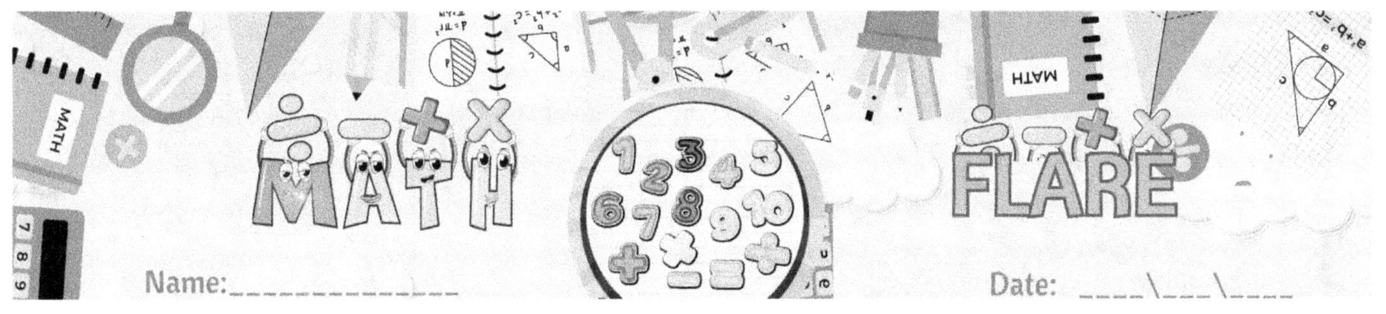

13. $12^2 =$ ______________________

14. $1^{-2} =$ ______________________

15. $9^{-3} =$ ______________________

16. $16^{-3} =$ ______________________

17. $7^{-3} =$ ______________________

18. $10^{-3} =$ ______________________

19. $5^3 =$ ______________________

20. $15^4 =$ ______________________

21. $11^2 =$ ______________________

22. $16^{-2} =$ ______________________

23. $19^{-3} =$ ______________________

24. $5^{-3} =$ ______________________

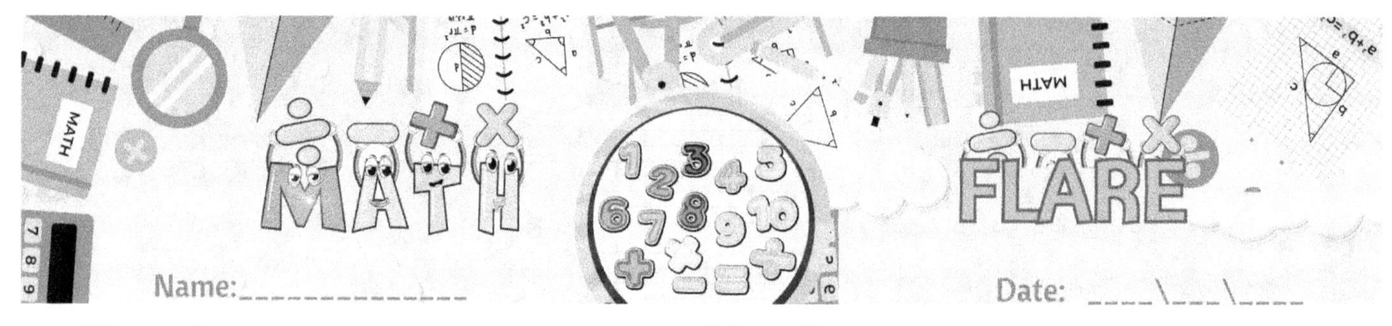

25. $19^3 = $ ______________________

26. $3^3 = $ ______________________

27. $14^2 = $ ______________________

28. $11^{-2} = $ ______________________

29. $15^{-3} = $ ______________________

30. $12^{-3} = $ ______________________

31. $10^2 = $ ______________________

32. $12^{-2} = $ ______________________

33. $19^{-2} = $ ______________________

34. $13^2 = $ ______________________

35. $12^4 = $ ______________________

36. $4^3 = $ ______________________

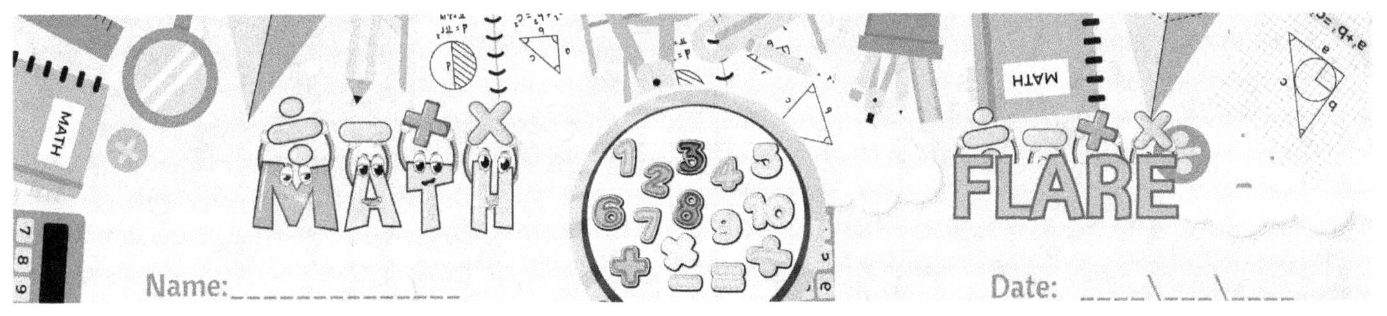

37. $16^2 =$ _______________

38. $18^3 =$ _______________

39. $18^{-2} =$ _______________

40. $8^{-2} =$ _______________

41. $20^{-2} =$ _______________

42. $2^3 =$ _______________

43. $1^{-3} =$ _______________

44. $1^4 =$ _______________

45. $3^2 =$ _______________

46. $15^3 =$ _______________

47. $13^4 =$ _______________

48. $2^2 =$ _______________

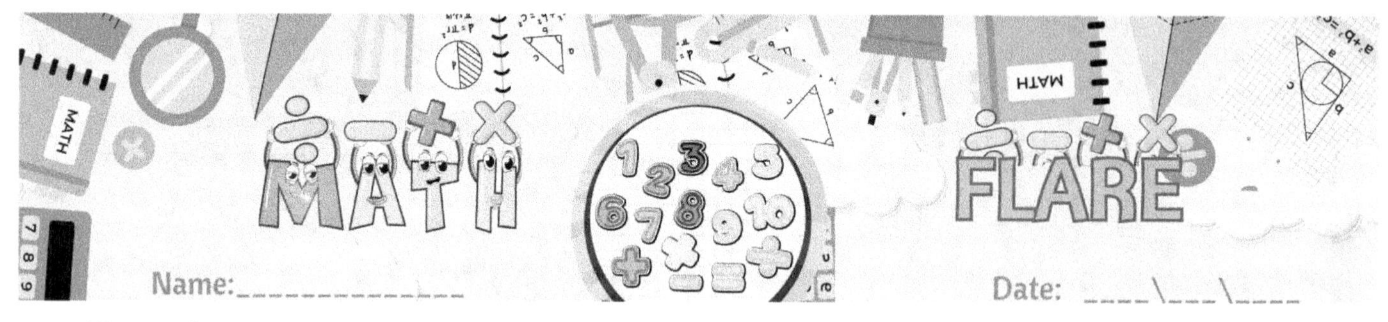

49. $17^2 =$ _______________

50. $1^2 =$ _______________

51. $7^{-2} =$ _______________

52. $8^4 =$ _______________

53. $2^{-3} =$ _______________

54. $13^{-2} =$ _______________

55. $8^{-3} =$ _______________

56. $3^{-3} =$ _______________

57. $20^{-3} =$ _______________

58. $13^3 =$ _______________

59. $4^2 =$ _______________

60. $20^2 =$ _______________

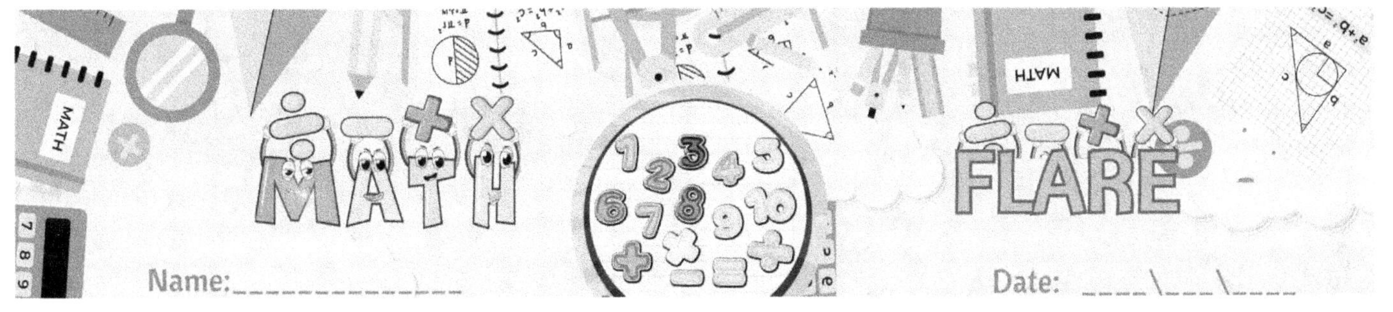

Name:____________________   Date: ____________

61. $8^2 =$ _______________

62. $17^{-3} =$ _______________

63. $10^3 =$ _______________

64. $3^4 =$ _______________

65. $20^3 =$ _______________

66. $19^4 =$ _______________

67. $16^4 =$ _______________

68. $6^{-3} =$ _______________

69. $13^{-3} =$ _______________

70. $10^{-2} =$ _______________

71. $6^2 =$ _______________

72. $4^{-3} =$ _______________

MathFlare - Algebra 1 7th to 10th Grade

209

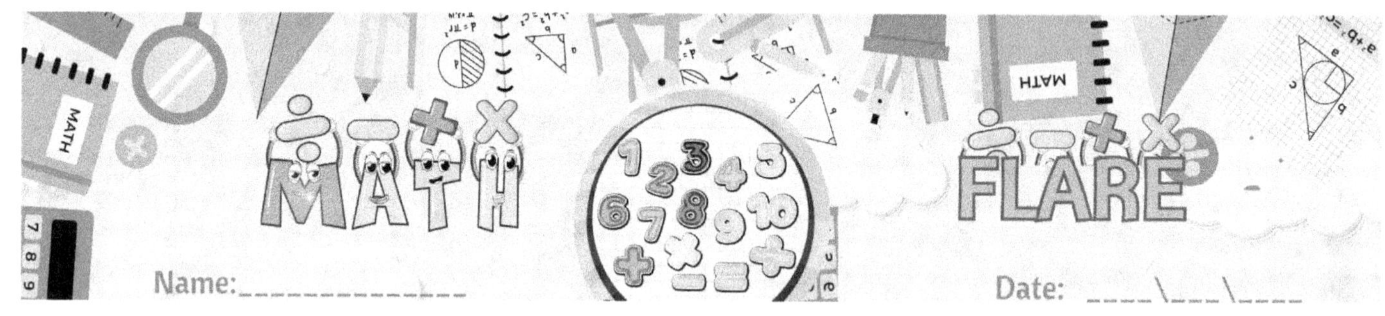

73. $19^2 =$ ___________________

74. $1^3 =$ ___________________

75. $17^4 =$ ___________________

76. $12^3 =$ ___________________

77. $3^{-2} =$ ___________________

78. $9^3 =$ ___________________

79. $6^4 =$ ___________________

80. $17^{-2} =$ ___________________

81. $15^2 =$ ___________________

82. $4^4 =$ ___________________

83. $9^2 =$ ___________________

84. $6^3 =$ ___________________

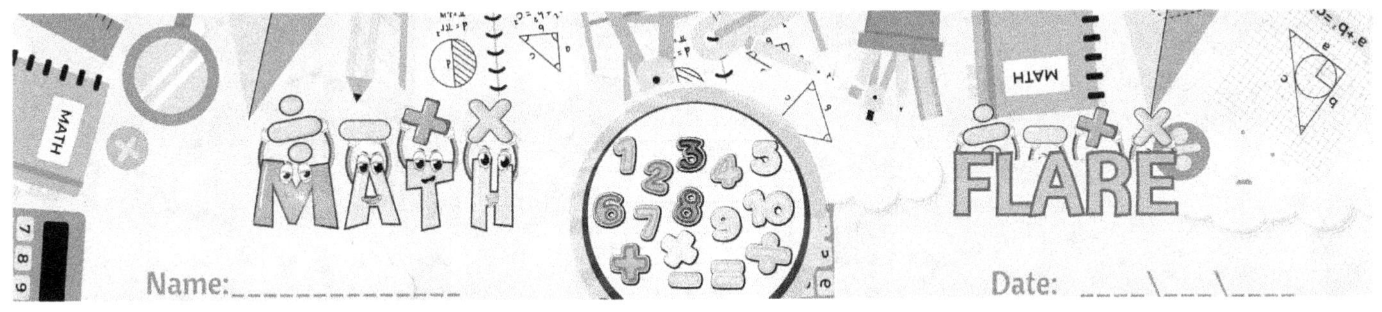

Scientific Notation
Provide the scientific notation for each value.

1. $241{,}000 =$ ______________

2. $6 \times 10^{4} =$ ______________

3. $3.3 \times 10^{3} =$ ______________

4. $56{,}000 =$ ______________

5. $8.7 \times 10^{4} =$ ______________

6. $87 =$ ______________

7. $1.5 \times 10^{2} =$ ______________

8. $2.5 \times 10^{3} =$ ______________

9. $2.7 \times 10^{5} =$ ______________

10. $1.938 \times 10^{6} =$ ______________

11. $1{,}100 =$ ______________

12. $58 =$ ______________

13. $2{,}274{,}000 =$ ______________

14. $3 \times 10^{6} =$ ______________

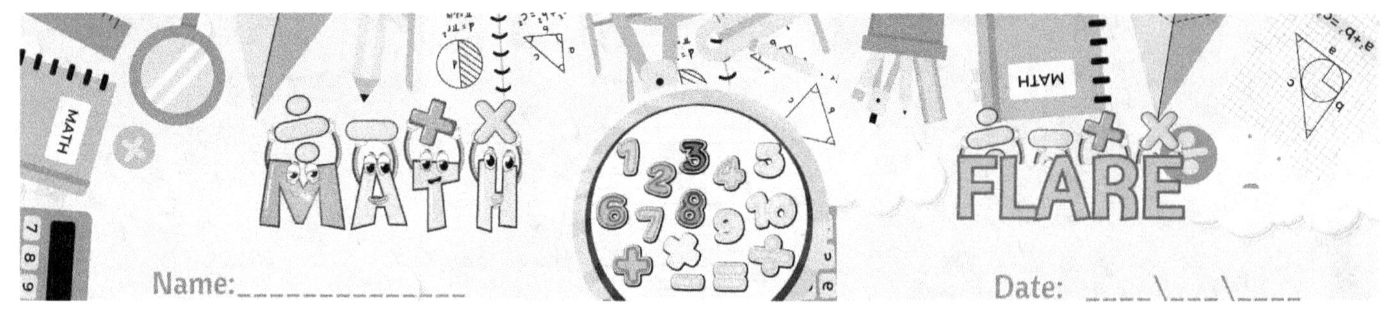

Name:_______________   Date: _______________

15. $7.7 \times 10^1 =$ _______________

16. $580,000 =$ _______________

17. $89 =$ _______________

18. $7.6 \times 10^2 =$ _______________

19. $3.4 \times 10^2 =$ _______________

20. $790,000 =$ _______________

21. $4,600 =$ _______________

22. $2,400 =$ _______________

23. $4.8 \times 10^1 =$ _______________

24. $23,000 =$ _______________

25. $3,900 =$ _______________

26. $3.5 \times 10^5 =$ _______________

27. $1,220,000 =$ _______________

28. $9.1 \times 10^2 =$ _______________

MathFlare - Algebra 1 7th to 10th Grade

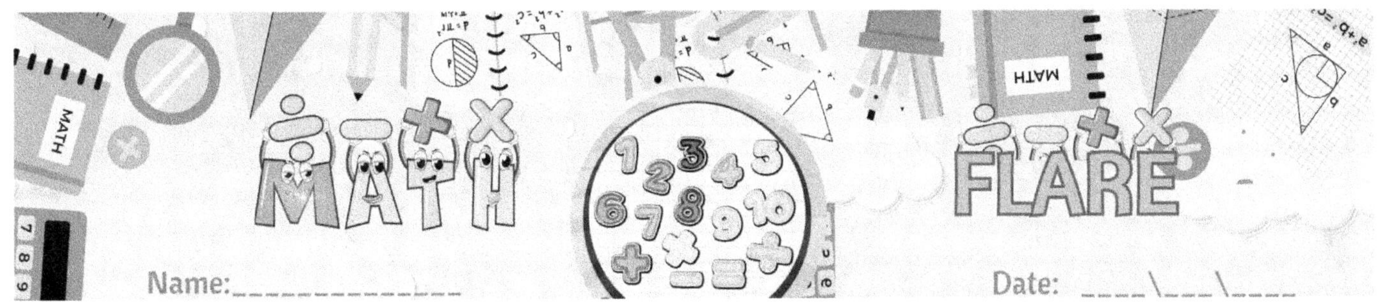

29. 250,000 = _____________

30. 9,500,000 = _____________

31. 2,670,000 = _____________

32. 64,000 = _____________

33. 780 = _____________

34. 660,000 = _____________

35. 4.489×10^6 = _____________

36. 7.8×10^3 = _____________

37. 55,000 = _____________

38. 9×10^4 = _____________

39. 180,000 = _____________

40. 6.183×10^6 = _____________

41. 280 = _____________

42. 7.3×10^1 = _____________

43. $9 \times 10^{3} =$ _______________

44. $55 =$ _______________

45. $2{,}530{,}000 =$ _______________

46. $50{,}000 =$ _______________

47. $4 \times 10^{3} =$ _______________

48. $4{,}460{,}000 =$ _______________

49. $4.3 \times 10^{2} =$ _______________

50. $82{,}000 =$ _______________

51. $300 =$ _______________

52. $5.2 \times 10^{4} =$ _______________

53. $2.01 \times 10^{5} =$ _______________

54. $556{,}000 =$ _______________

55. $7{,}600 =$ _______________

56. $5 \times 10^{6} =$ _______________

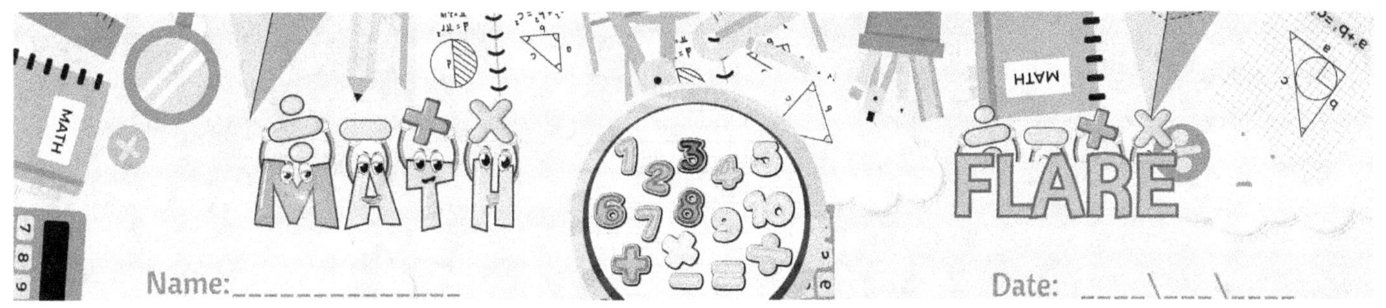

57. $4.4 \times 10^4 =$ _______________

58. $7.6 \times 10^5 =$ _______________

59. $7.1 \times 10^2 =$ _______________

60. $3.1 \times 10^3 =$ _______________

61. $9{,}170{,}000 =$ _______________

62. $7.4 \times 10^6 =$ _______________

63. $8.5 \times 10^3 =$ _______________

64. $33{,}000 =$ _______________

65. $4.128 \times 10^6 =$ _______________

66. $1{,}200{,}000 =$ _______________

67. $1{,}800 =$ _______________

68. $554{,}000 =$ _______________

69. $190{,}000 =$ _______________

70. $46 =$ _______________

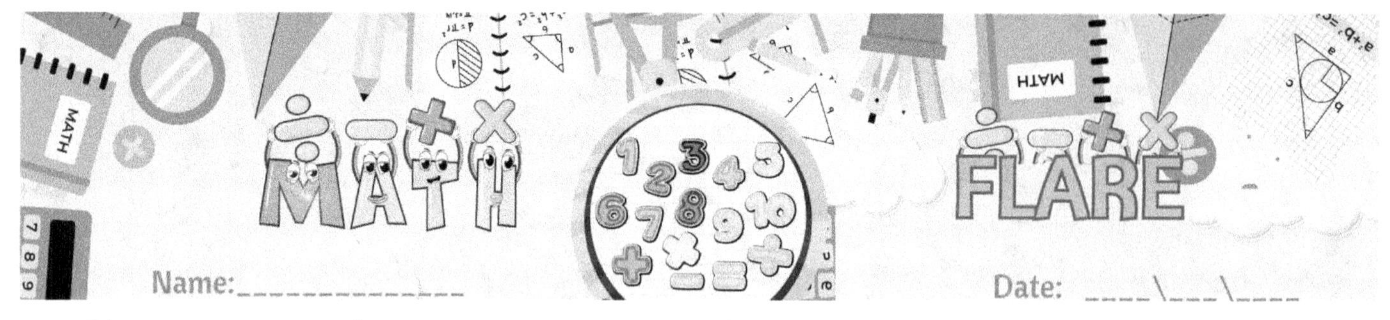

71. $2.301 \times 10^6 =$ ___________

72. $12 =$ ___________

73. $6.307 \times 10^6 =$ ___________

74. $200,000 =$ ___________

75. $4.1 \times 10^4 =$ ___________

76. $54,000 =$ ___________

77. $7.83 \times 10^6 =$ ___________

78. $74 =$ ___________

79. $56 =$ ___________

80. $8,900 =$ ___________

81. $92 =$ ___________

82. $7 \times 10^6 =$ ___________

83. $66 =$ ___________

84. $4,000,000 =$ ___________

ANSWERS

Page 1: Rational Numbers: Operations

1. 9	2. 5	3. 8	4. 11	5. -56	6. 0.6
7. 8	8. 49	9. -1	10. 14	11. 4	12. 12
13. 2	14. 11	15. 19	16. 6	17. 15	18. -4
19. 8	20. 15	21. -1	22. 6	23. 0.1	24. 180
25. -1	26. 3	27. 80	28. -2	29. -2	30. 10
31. 4	32. 1	33. 400	34. -72	35. -2	36. 600
37. -11	38. -252	39. 1	40. 2	41. 8	42. -1
43. 7	44. -54	45. -16	46. 5	47. 19	48. 80
49. 90	50. 23	51. 9	52. -7	53. -360	54. -42
55. 9	56. -3.3	57. 7	58. -2	59. -168	60. -252

61. 14	62. 56	63. -6	64. 72	65. 2.3	66. -81
67. -18	68. 1	69. 1	70. 160	71. 1.1	72. 18
73. 6	74. -45	75. 2	76. -144	77. -2.5	78. 0
79. 90	80. -15	81. -12	82. -10	83. 6	84. 16
85. -8	86. 15	87. -6	88. -1	89. -36	90. -7
91. -64	92. -36	93. 0.7	94. -7	95. 22	96. -10
97. -7	98. 5				

Page 11: Order of Operations (PEMDAS)

1. 27	2. 80	3. 104	4. 17	5. 31	6. 33	7. 70
8. 224	9. 55	10. 26	11. 79	12. 4	13. 16	14. 5
15. 187	16. 50	17. 4	18. 9	19. 6	20. 32	21. 22
22. 72	23. 24	24. 62	25. 14	26. 39	27. 15	28. 313
29. -5	30. 44	31. 444	32. 1.6	33. 72	34. 4	35. 90
36. 30	37. 8	38. 613	39. 353	40. 3	41. 44	42. 9
43. 63	44. 60	45. 12	46. 11	47. 21	48. 105	49. 24
50. 1.7	51. 94	52. 185	53. 21	54. 7	55. 90	56. 9
57. 135	58. 21	59. 20	60. 577	61. 40	62. 81	63. 126
64. 48	65. 189	66. 57	67. 3	68. 100	69. 27	70. 2.2
71. 4	72. 290	73. 17	74. 16	75. 162	76. 5	77. 22
78. 365	79. -11	80. 18	81. 13	82. 25	83. 377	84. 19
85. 156	86. 13	87. 56	88. 12	89. -3	90. 11	91. 169
92. 6	93. 125	94. 55	95. 32	96. 1.4	97. 60	98. 5

Page 21: Combining and Distributing Terms

1. 0
2. 3n
3. 6a - 1
4. -8m - 4
5. 1
6. 1 + 7x
7. -5x
8. 11x - 7
9. 1 + 8n
10. 9a + 9
11. n - 1
12. 1 - 6x
13. 12a
14. 9 + 15n
15. -2x
16. -b
17. 7n + 5
18. -1 + 12v
19. 1 - n
20. 4n
21. -2r
22. 7r
23. -a
24. -7 + 6r
25. n
26. 6 + 8 p
27. -3x - 6
28. 2n - 5
29. -10n
30. -4x - 5

31. 2 + 6x
32. 4 p
33. 8 + 3r
34. 2m - 8
35. -3 p
36. 8m + 16
37. 12k
38. -12v
39. -12a
40. 4 - m
41. -6 p - 30
42. -2 p - 14
43. -8x - 7
44. -x + 6
45. -36x + 36
46. -7n + 5
47. 12x + 21
48. -7 - 42n
49. -20 + 28n
50. -4r - 1
51. -8 + 64n
52. 7 + 3 p
53. -a + 4
54. -6 p + 12
55. -20x - 28
56. 16 + 16a
57. -20n - 24
58. -35 + 35x
59. -2 p - 8
60. -48b + 48

61. -25 - 18a
62. -12 + 25b
63. -28 + 9k
64. -43 - 12x
65. -1
66. -38b - 21
67. -29 + 32a
68. 45 + 36v
69. 29 + 56x
70. -3 + 18 p
71. -29 - 24n
72. -6 + 46x
73. 23 - 15a
74. -22b + 35
75. -11x - 20
76. -14x - 24
77. -9r - 1
78. -k + 4
79. -12 + 3x
80. - p + 5
81. -35x - 55
82. 49 + 8a
83. 15 - 43n
84. 19 - 7n
85. 86 + 32b
86. -23 + 43r
87. -10 p + 18
88. -13m + 22
89. -43n + 55
90. -29 + 18x

91. -9a - 57
92. 3 p - 16
93. -32x + 44
94. -7 - 5r
95. -9b - 9
96. -11 - 39m
97. -53 - 44 p
98. -46b + 16

Page 31: Solving One-Step Equations

1. 10   2. 7   3. 9   4. 6   5. 1   6. 2   7. 6   8. 2
9. 8   10. 9   11. 10   12. 1   13. 6   14. 6   15. 6   16. 5
17. 3   18. 9   19. 9   20. 9   21. 6   22. 8   23. 10   24. 8
25. 4   26. 6   27. 6   28. 1   29. 8   30. 10   31. 6   32. 5
33. 6   34. 3   35. 2   36. 6   37. 5   38. 6   39. 4   40. 9
41. 9   42. 7   43. 6   44. 8   45. 4   46. 4   47. 2   48. 7
49. 4   50. 8   51. 10   52. 4   53. 4   54. 2   55. 7   56. 8

Page 38: Solving Two-Step Equations

1. 1   2. 9   3. 6   4. 10   5. 9   6. 4   7. 3   8. 10   9. 6
10. 4   11. 10   12. 10   13. 4   14. 6   15. 6   16. 6   17. 4   18. 5
19. 2   20. 6   21. 4   22. 4   23. 4   24. 9   25. 8   26. 2   27. 9
28. 9   29. 1   30. 3   31. 6   32. 10   33. 10   34. 5   35. 6   36. 7
37. 4   38. 3   39. 8   40. 2   41. 4   42. 6   43. 8   44. 3   45. 8
46. 7   47. 4   48. 8   49. 8   50. 7   51. 7   52. 1   53. 1   54. 6
55. 4   56. 9

Page 45: Solving Multi-Step Equations

1. 3   2. 1   3. 3   4. 3   5. 5   6. 4   7. 5   8. 6   9. 3
10. 10   11. 9   12. 10   13. 2   14. 4   15. 4   16. 8   17. 9   18. 9
19. 5   20. 8   21. 1   22. 5   23. 8   24. 2   25. 3   26. 3   27. 7
28. 1   29. 2   30. 7   31. 3   32. 4   33. 8   34. 1   35. 2   36. 5
37. 6   38. 9   39. 5   40. 5   41. 5   42. 7   43. 10   44. 8   45. 8
46. 3   47. 7   48. 10   49. 8   50. 7   51. 2   52. 7   53. 6   54. 8
55. 1   56. 8

Page 52: Equations One Side

1. m = 5	2. k = 12	3. k = 2	4. y = 6	5. y = 6
6. k = -6	7. m = 16	8. m = 20	9. m = 14	10. k = 1
11. y = 0	12. y = 13	13. z = 169	14. y = -5	15. k = 6
16. x = 10	17. z = -9	18. y = 1	19. k = -9	20. m = -5
21. x = -2	22. x = -6	23. m = -8	24. z = -7	25. z = 8
26. z = -3	27. y = 17	28. m = 19	29. x = 20	30. k = -3
31. m = 1	32. k = 5	33. z = 3	34. x = 13	35. z = 19
36. x = -10	37. k = 20	38. m = -3	39. x = -10	40. y = -90
41. z = -48	42. z = -5	43. z = 3	44. y = 11	45. m = -3
46. x = 18	47. m = 1	48. k = 12	49. m = -7	50. y = 15
51. z = -4	52. k = 18	53. k = -7	54. k = 19	55. k = 1
56. y = 1				

Page 59: Equations Two Side

1. s = 5	2. a = 1	3. b = 2	4. s = 2	5. z = 4
6. k = -8	7. s = 6	8. s = 9	9. z = 6	10. k = -5
11. k = 3	12. y = 4	13. k = 5	14. a = -9	15. m = 6
16. a = -2	17. x = 3	18. z = 3	19. m = 7	20. m = -9
21. b = -5	22. z = 4	23. s = 8	24. z = -7	25. s = 2
26. y = 1	27. k = -4	28. s = -10	29. m = 7	30. m = -1
31. b = -3	32. b = 5	33. m = 3	34. s = -2	35. y = -4
36. b = 7	37. y = 8	38. k = 7	39. b = -4	40. a = -9
41. s = -8	42. z = -3	43. z = 10	44. b = 1	45. b = -8
46. z = -8	47. k = 1	48. y = 9	49. y = -4	50. y = -3
51. x = 3	52. b = 1	53. x = -10	54. z = -2	55. y = 5
56. s = -8				

Page 66: Simplify Expressions

1. −9y + 16	2. 16y	3. −4y + 15	4. 11x
5. 27	6. 18	7. −33m + 19	8. −32k + 31
9. 14k + 6	10. −3y − 32	11. 8k + 20	12. 20y
13. −12k − 26	14. 15y + 1	15. 3z	16. 30k − 18
17. −13z − 7	18. 5z	19. −6y	20. −6m − 8
21. 10	22. −28z − 6	23. 11y − 12	24. 19y + 4
25. −13x + 23	26. −6x − 5	27. −5z	28. −9x
29. 9m	30. −14y	31. 12y + 14	32. −10k − 7
33. 14z + 14	34. −17y − 15	35. 16z − 20	36. −5k + 4
37. 26k + 13	38. 21m	39. −21z + 5	40. 10k − 2
41. k + 5	42. k	43. 8m	44. 12y − 1
45. 17z + 20	46. −27y + 11	47. m + 19	48. 3y − 19
49. 20k + 5	50. 13m − 20	51. 13x	52. 30z − 1
53. 9k − 12	54. 23y − 20	55. 13z	56. 3z − 34
57. 12z − 7	58. 11z + 36	59. −5z − 18	60. 10x
61. 4m	62. 30y + 29	63. 34y − 8	64. 9m − 8
65. 23z − 19	66. 20k + 18	67. 26y − 7	68. 6m
69. 0	70. −19z + 11	71. 28k − 1	72. −24y + 17
73. 11z − 25	74. 8x − 15	75. −30m	76. 8k − 1
77. 2x + 2	78. 7z	79. 25z + 12	80. 32y + 16

81. 32m + 28   82. 2m - 11   83. 2x   84. 30k + 33

85. -19k   86. 3y + 7   87. 0   88. 24k + 28

89. -4z + 18   90. -13k - 22   91. -6k - 11   92. 22m - 33

93. -3m + 5   94. -6x   95. -z + 7   96. 6m + 18

97. -23m - 4   98. 20k + 12   99. -19z + 22   100. -12z

101. 18z   102. 27z + 19   103. 8z + 34   104. -2m

Page 79: Simplify Equations

1. -21   2. -16   3. 14   4. 2   5. 8   6. -22   7. 0   8. 96

Page 80: Simplify Equations

1. -20   2. 74   3. 110   4. -43   5. 14   6. -2.5   7. -180   8. -40

Page 81: Simplify Equations

1. -12   2. 24   3. -40   4. 4   5. 0.5   6. 41   7. -4   8. 7

Page 82: Simplify Equations

1. 16   2. -522   3. -7   4. 1   5. -26   6. -18   7. -76

8. 32

Page 83: Simplify Equations

1. -22   2. 400   3. -44   4. 44   5. 120   6. 0   7. -0.7   8. -4

Page 84: Simplify Equations

1. -84   2. -48   3. -23   4. 62   5. -78   6. -3   7. -11   8. 7

Page 85: Simplify Equations

1. 1   2. 1.6   3. 32   4. 49   5. 15   6. -37   7. 0

8. -100

Page 86: Simplify Equations

1. -20   2. -17   3. -108   4. 4.2   5. 0   6. 2   7. -48

8. -16

Page 87: Simplify Equations

1. -13   2. -4   3. 1   4. -11   5. -14.5   6. -6   7. 9

8. -8

Page 88: Simplify Equations

1. -20   2. -11   3. 0   4. -9   5. 9   6. 195   7. -27   8. 30

Page 89: Verbal Algebra Expressions

1. 5   2. 8   3. 3   4. 1   5. 6, 68

6. 1, 2, 3, 4   7. 2   8. 32   9. 2, 6   10. 6, 8

11. 3   12. 9, 3   13. 5, 12, 35   14. 4   15. 20, 9

16. 7   17. 8   18. 9   19. 2, 3, 4   20. 8, 9, 10

21. 9   22. 2   23. 3   24. 4   25. 6

26. 15   27. 7, 5   28. 24   29. 9   30. 11

31. 10   32. 5   33. 2   34. 2, 9   35. 9

36. 8, 9, 10   37. 3, 15   38. 6, 2   39. 3   40. 11

41. 3, 1   42. 6, 8   43. 3   44. 2   45. 5

46. 5   47. 4   48. 3   49. 6   50. 18, 9

51. 8   52. 11   53. 6, 8, 10   54. 1   55. 9, 2

56. 3, 5   57. 4, 20   58. 8   59. 5, 6, 7, 8   60. 5, 1

Page 103: Solving Inequalities

1. x > -2
2. b < 6/5
3. k ≥ -11
4. z ≥ 5
5. z ≤ 3/5
6. m ≥ -5
7. s < -5
8. s < -15
9. s > -14
10. x ≥ -36
11. b ≥ 3
12. x > 2
13. y ≤ -2/3
14. b > 56
15. y ≥ -7
16. x > -3
17. s ≤ -1/3
18. y ≤ 0
19. b < 36
20. s ≤ -1
21. x ≥ 4
22. x ≥ -2/3
23. a < 9
24. m > 16
25. s ≥ -2
26. y < 1/3
27. k ≤ 14
28. k ≤ 10
29. k < 10
30. y ≥ -4
31. y ≤ 16
32. b ≤ 6/5
33. a ≤ 2
34. m ≤ -18
35. a > -3
36. m > 1
37. z ≤ 12
38. b ≤ 2/3
39. b ≥ -9
40. k < 6
41. x ≥ 32
42. b ≤ -2
43. y ≤ 3
44. x ≤ -15
45. a ≥ 18
46. k ≤ 48
47. z < -4
48. m ≥ 4
49. s ≥ 5
50. k ≤ -3
51. y ≥ -16
52. y ≤ -7
53. z ≤ 2/3
54. a < 25
55. x > 10
56. z > -1
57. a > 6
58. y ≥ -3
59. k > -11
60. a ≥ 12
61. b < 4
62. b > -2
63. b ≥ -16
64. y ≥ 4/3
65. z > -2
66. z > 14
67. x > 0
68. m ≤ 17
69. a < 3
70. m > -3
71. x < 8
72. k > 1
73. x > 5
74. z < 40
75. y ≤ -6
76. s < 2/3
77. z > -13
78. m ≥ 30
79. k ≥ -2/7
80. b > -5
81. y ≤ -9
82. y ≥ -3
83. y < 2
84. a > 4
85. z > 3
86. a ≤ -1
87. k ≥ 24
88. z > 3
89. x ≥ -3/2
90. b ≥ -35
91. k ≤ 10
92. a ≥ 3
93. y ≤ -1
94. a ≤ -2
95. a ≤ -2
96. s ≤ 7
97. z ≥ -9
98. z < 12
99. y < 9
100. a < 5/4
101. x ≤ -16
102. m > -3

Page 120: Standard Linear Equations

1. 8	11. 9	21. 8	31. -10	41. -9
2. 10	12. 6	22. 2	32. 3	42. -3
3. -3	13. -5	23. -6	33. 7	43. -6
4. -5	14. -8	24. -7	34. 4	44. 10
5. -7	15. 1	25. -1	35. 7	45. -9
6. 9	16. 3	26. 0	36. -9	46. -6
7. -6	17. 5	27. 7	37. 9	47. -9
8. -6	18. -8	28. -3	38. 8	48. 9
9. -9	19. -9	29. -3	39. 1	
10. 4	20. 8	30. 6	40. -7	

Page 125: Find Slope from Two Points

1. -1	11. -7	21. -10	31. 7	41. 8
2. 2	12. -7	22. 5	32. -2	42. -8
3. 2	13. 2	23. 1	33. 0	43. 10
4. 0	14. 0	24. 2	34. 2	44. -5
5. -1	15. -8	25. -3	35. -1	45. -1
6. 1	16. -4	26. -8	36. 0	46. -3
7. 10	17. 1	27. -2	37. -5	47. 7
8. -5	18. -6	28. -3	38. -6	48. -5
9. 6	19. -7	29. 2	39. -6	
10. 7	20. 5	30. -9	40. 4	

Page 130: Plotting Lines

1.

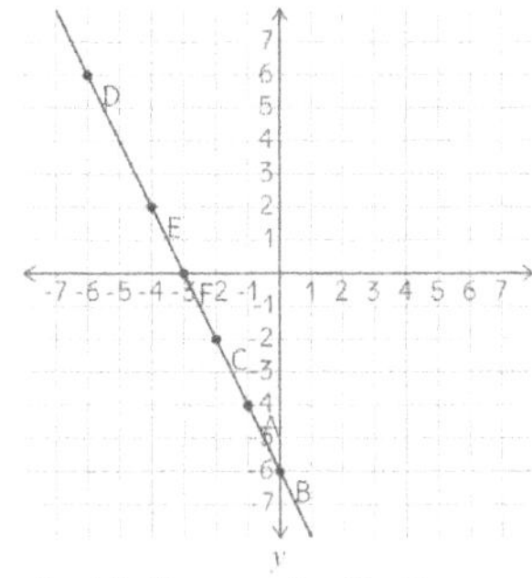

A = (-1, -4)	B = (0, -6)
C = (-2, -2)	D = (-6, 6)
E = (-4, 2)	F = (-3, 0)

2.

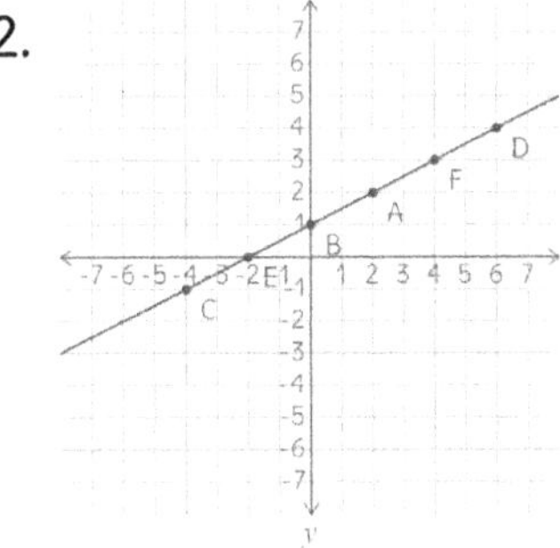

A = (2, 2)	B = (0, 1)
C = (-4, -1)	D = (6, 4)
E = (-2, 0)	F = (4, 3)

3.

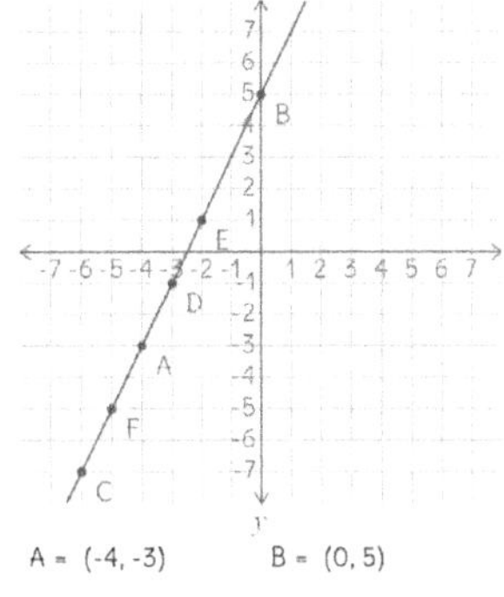

A = (-4, -3)	B = (0, 5)
C = (-6, -7)	D = (-3, -1)
E = (-2, 1)	F = (-5, -5)

4.

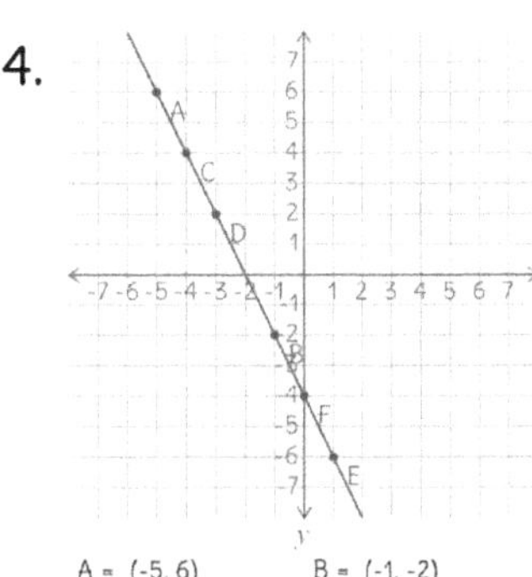

A = (-5, 6)	B = (-1, -2)
C = (-4, 4)	D = (-3, 2)
E = (1, -6)	F = (0, -4)

5.

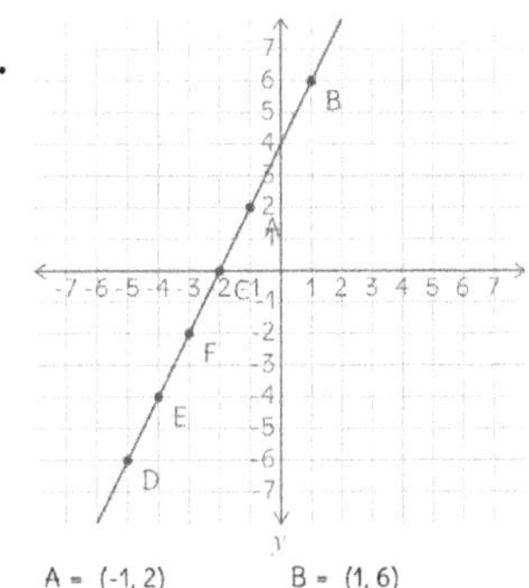

A = (-1, 2)	B = (1, 6)
C = (-2, 0)	D = (-5, -6)
E = (-4, -4)	F = (-3, -2)

6.

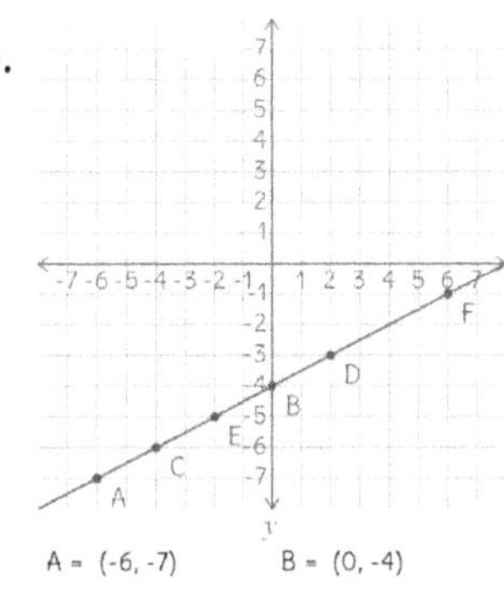

A = (-6, -7)	B = (0, -4)
C = (-4, -6)	D = (2, -3)
E = (-2, -5)	F = (6, -1)

7.

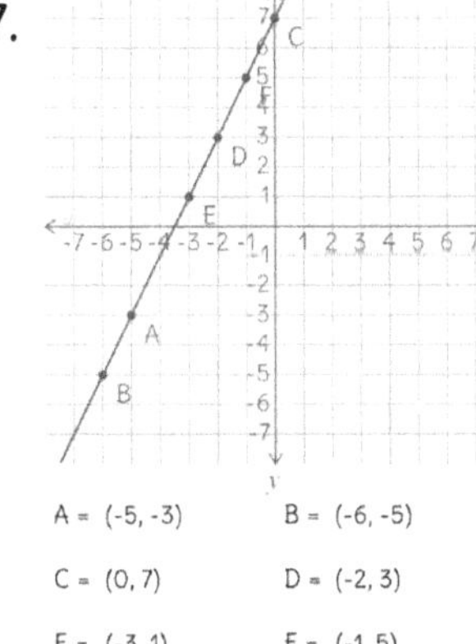

A = (-5, -3)	B = (-6, -5)
C = (0, 7)	D = (-2, 3)
E = (-3, 1)	F = (-1, 5)

8.

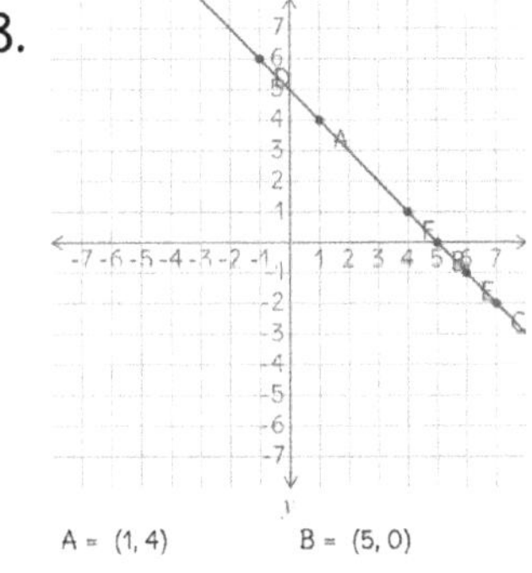

A = (1, 4)	B = (5, 0)
C = (7, -2)	D = (-1, 6)
E = (6, -1)	F = (4, 1)

9.

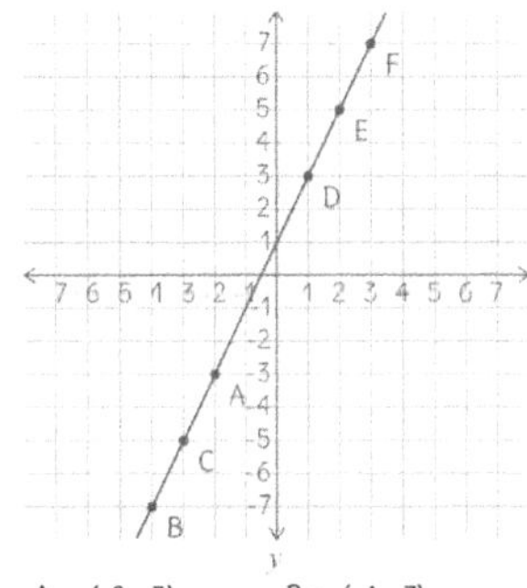

A = (-2, -3)	B = (-4, -7)
C = (-3, -5)	D = (1, 3)
E = (2, 5)	F = (3, 7)

10.

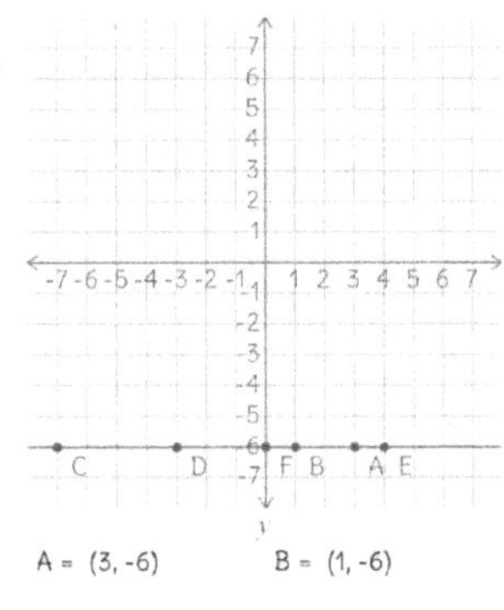

A = (3, -6)	B = (1, -6)
C = (-7, -6)	D = (-3, -6)
E = (4, -6)	F = (0, -6)

Page 140: Graphing Linear Equations

1. $y = -x - 1$
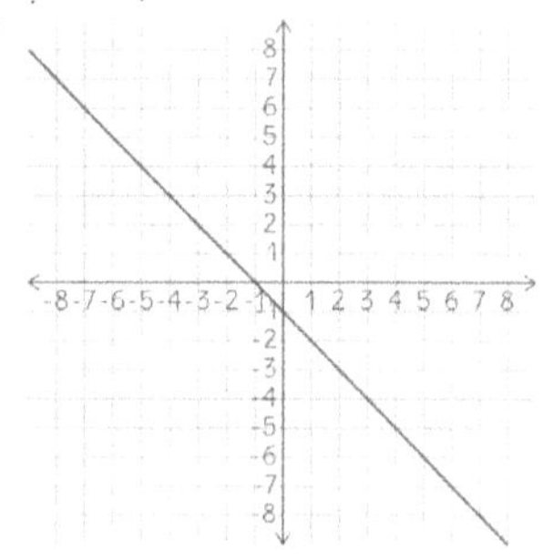

2. $y = \frac{3}{4}x + 8$
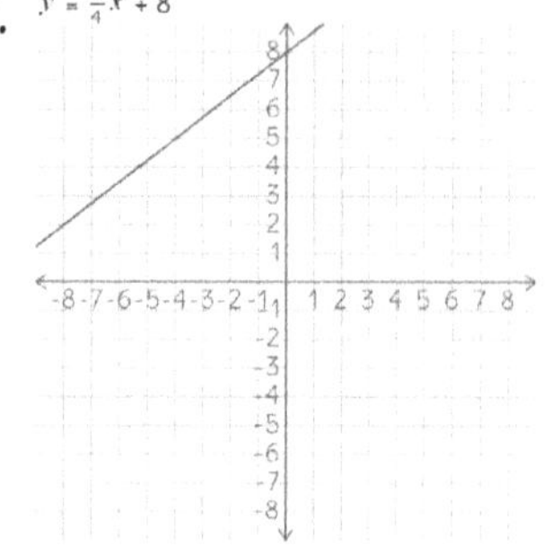

3. $y = 3x + 6$
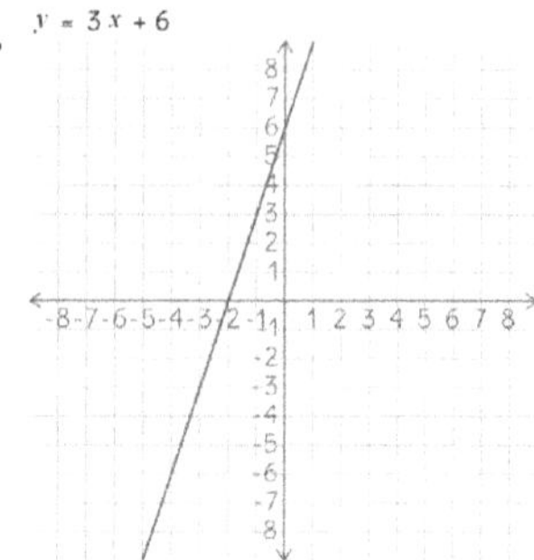

4. $y = \frac{9}{4}x + 1$
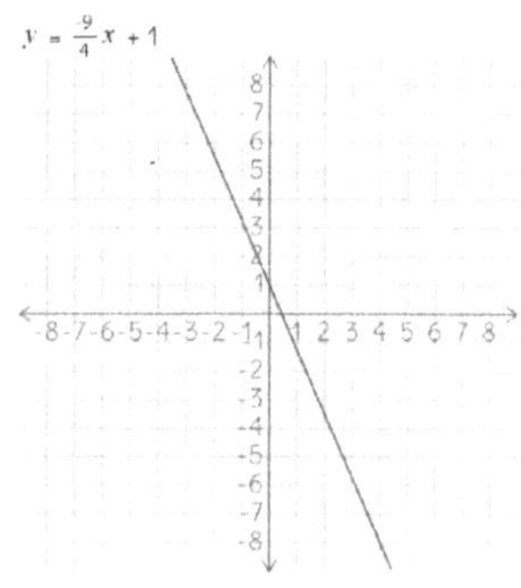

5. $y = \frac{-1}{2}x - 7$
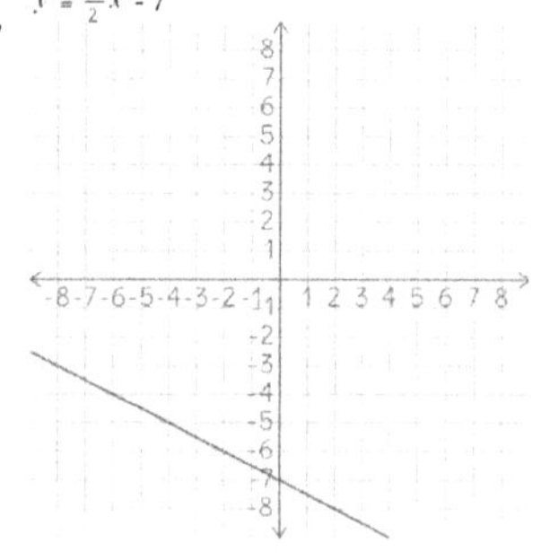

6. $y = \frac{5}{2}x - 6$
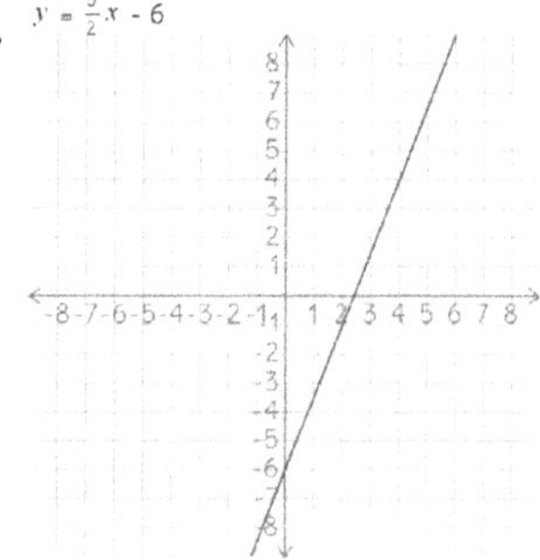

7. $y = \frac{3}{4}x - 3$
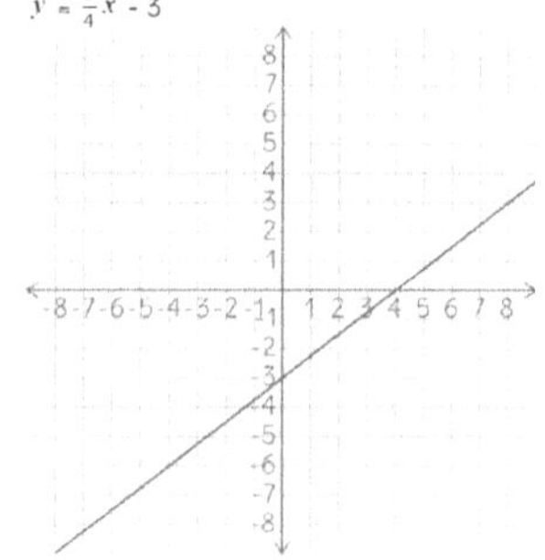

8. $y = \frac{9}{4}x - 4$
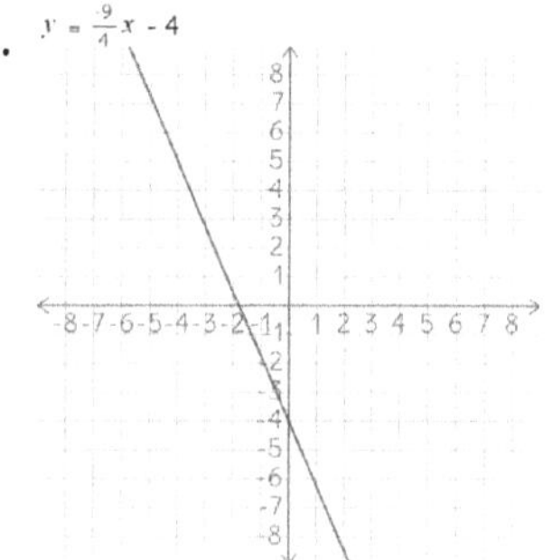

9. $y = \frac{9}{4}x + 3$
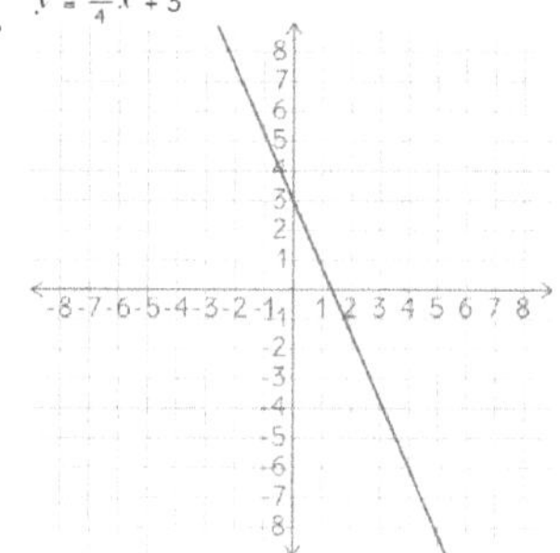

10. $y = \frac{-11}{4}x - 5$
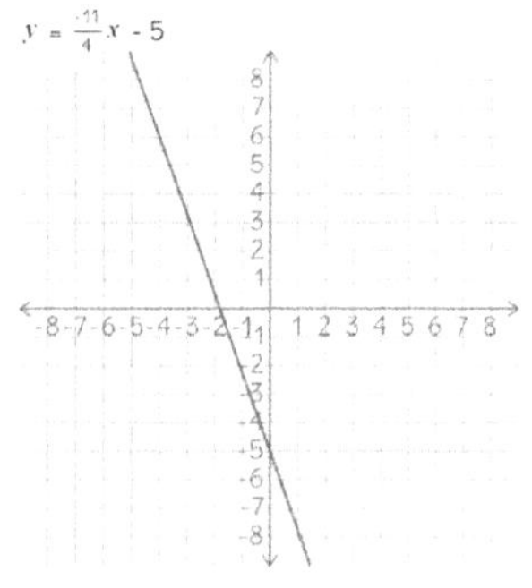

11. $y = \frac{5}{4}x - 6$
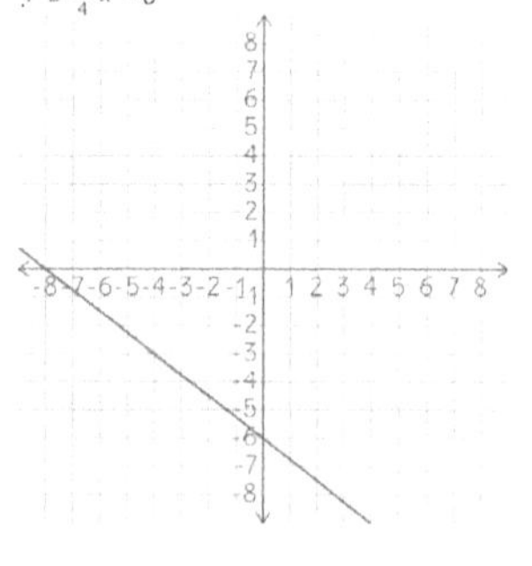

12. $y = x - 2$
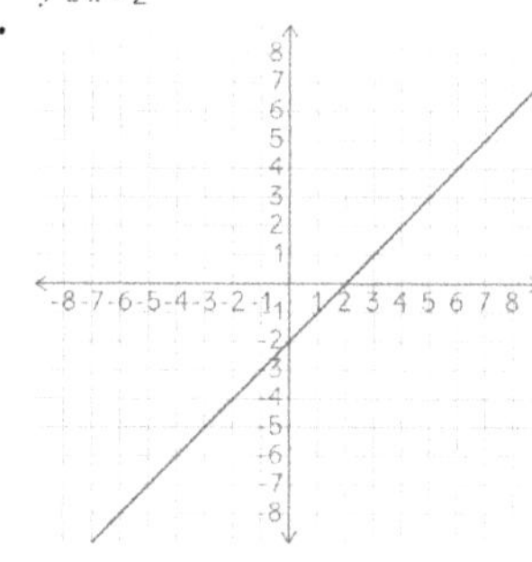

13. $y = 2x - 5$
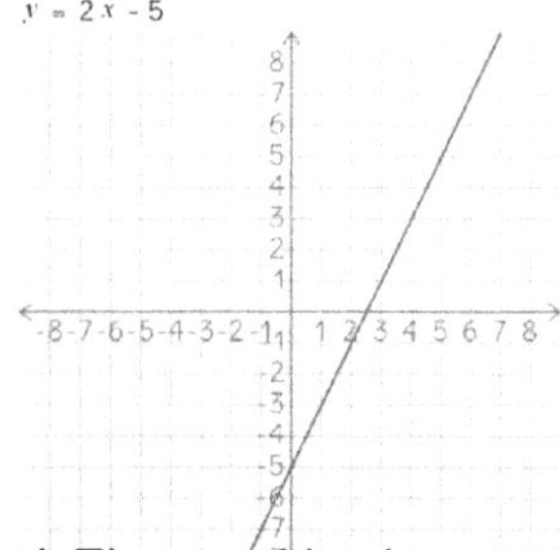

14. $y = -3x + 3$
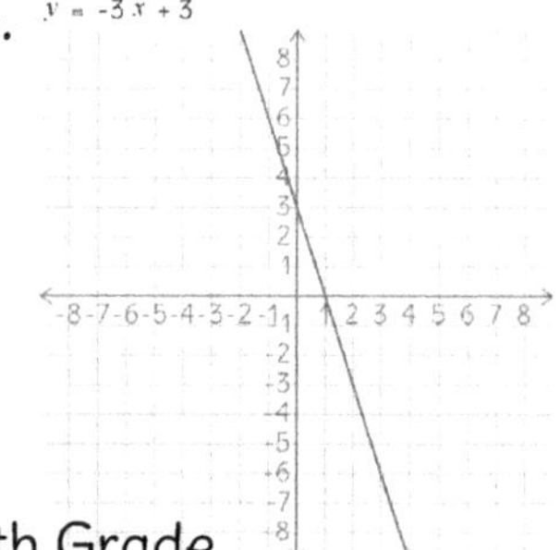

15. $y = \frac{5}{4}x - 2$
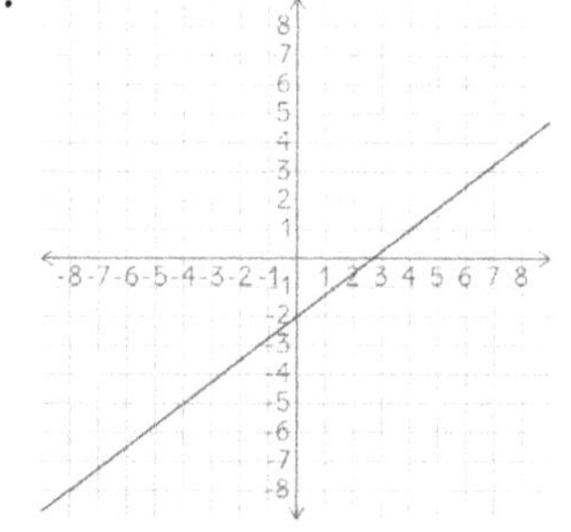

228

16. $y = \frac{-9}{4}x + 6$ 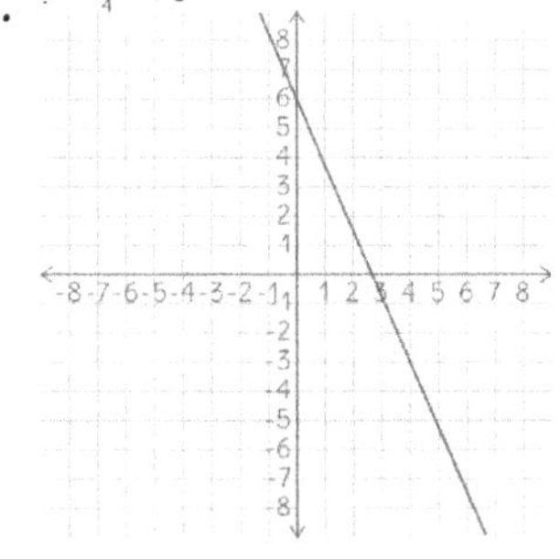

17. $x = -3$ 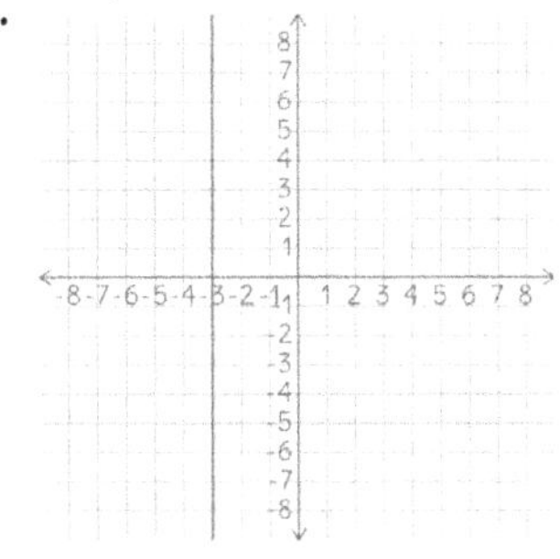

18. $y = \frac{3}{4}x + 4$ 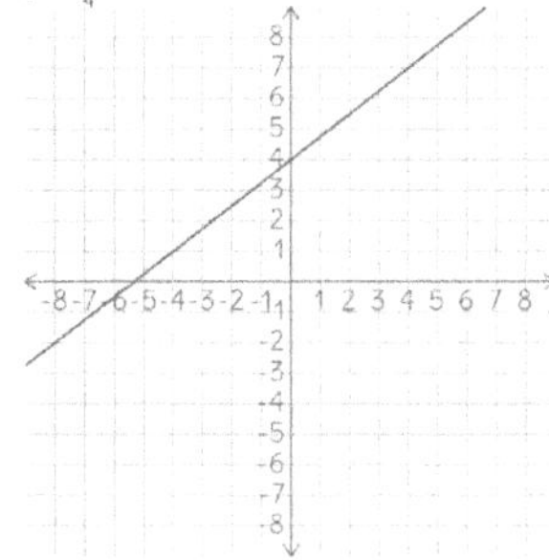

19. $y = 3x - 1$ 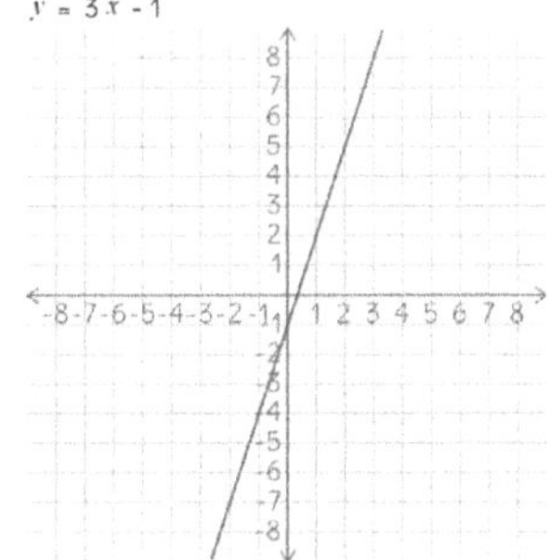

20. $y = x + 3$ 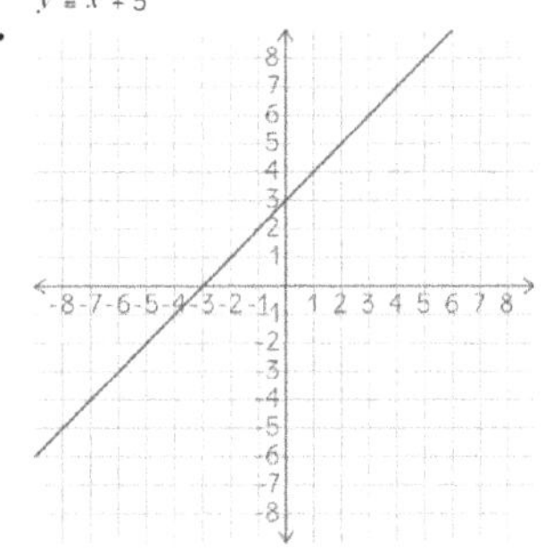

Page 160: System of Equations

1. 1. x = 6.0, y = -9.0
2. 2. x = -4.05, y = 4.68
3. 3. x = 1.38, y = -0.31
4. 4. x = -4.6, y = 6.0
5. 5. x = 0.83, y = 0.5
6. 6. x = 1.67, y = -0.44
7. 7. x = 4.33, y = -3.2
8. 8. x = 2.0, y = 0.0
9. 9. x = 1.27, y = -0.41
10. 10. x = 0.86, y = 0.57
11. 11. x = 3.0, y = -1.33
12. 12. x = -1.33, y = 0.83
13. 13. x = -4.0, y = 3.5
14. 14. x = 0.58, y = 0.3
15. 15. x = 1.5, y = 0.5

16. 16. x = 0.35, y = 0.76
17. 17. x = -1.11, y = 1.89
18. 18. x = 0.35, y = 0.61
19. 19. x = 1.4, y = -1.0
20. 20. x = 0.55, y = 0.09
21. 21. x = 1.1, y = -1.0
22. 22. x = 2.53, y = -0.58
23. 23. x = 3.0, y = -0.0
24. 24. x = -1.2, y = 1.8
25. 25. x = -1.0, y = 5.0
26. 26. x = 0.75, y = 0.38
27. 27. x = 0.95, y = -0.62
28. 28. x = 0.15, y = 1.45
29. 29. x = 0.22, y = 0.04
30. 30. x = 0.36, y = 0.41

Page 170: Polynomials: Addition and Subtraction

1. $13m^3 - 3m^2$
2. $6k^4 + 13k$
3. $8v^3 + 8v^2$
4. $3x^4 + 12x + 4$
5. $7n^4 - n^3$
6. $p^3 + 11p^2$
7. $3b^4 + 13$
8. $9k^3 + 5k^2$
9. $6a - 1$
10. $4r^3 + 7r + 10$
11. $9n^4 + 7n$
12. $11a - 4$
13. -4
14. $-4x^3 + 2x^2$
15. $5k^2 - 2k + 15$
16. $-n^2 + 7$
17. $-7x^4 + 4$
18. $8a^4 + a^3$
19. $11p^4 - 5p^3$
20. $4n^2 - 3$
21. $-14a^4 + 2a^2$
22. $3n^3 + 7n$
23. $6v^2 - 9$
24. $-2x$
25. $3x^3 + 6$
26. $-2n^2 + 2n$
27. $-3p^4 + 4p$
28. $4x^3 - 1$
29. $13r^3 + 10r^2$

30. $-3b^4 - 4b^2$
31. $-2x^3 + x^2 + 12$
32. $6n^4 + 5n - 5$
33. $-13n^4 - 3n^2 + 14$
34. $3x^4 + 2x^3 + x^2$
35. $4n^4 + 10n^3 - 2n^2$
36. $9v^3 - v^2 + 8v$
37. $-3p^3 - 5p^2 + 4$
38. $-k^4 - 5k^2 + k$
39. $10x^2 - 3x - 4$
40. $-6k^4 - k^3 + 9$
41. $a^3 - 7a^2 + 4a$
42. $-4x^3 + 9x^2 - 5x$
43. $8x^4 + 5x + 10$
44. $-2x^3 - 8x^2 + 11x$
45. $7x^3 - 5x^2 - 5x$
46. $-8x^3 + 11x^2 + 10$
47. $-5x^3 + 8x^2 + 14$
48. $-4x^4 - 2x^3 - 8x$
49. $9n^3 + 2n - 2$
50. $-a^4 + 4a^3 + 5a^2$
51. $10x^4 - 6x^3 - 5$
52. $-8a^4 + 11a^2 + 4$
53. $-12x^2 + 7x - 2$
54. $11x^2 - 8x$
55. $5n^4 - 6n^2 + 6$
56. $-5k^3 + 5k^2 + 9k$
57. $-2x^3 + 7x^2 - 7x$
58. $5n^4 - 4n^3 + 13n^2$

59. $-5v^3 + 8v^2 + 15$
60. $-4b^4 + 10b^3 + b$
61. $2a^3 + 3a^2 - 1$
62. $-2a^4 + 8a^3 + 5a^2$
63. $5a^3 + 5a^2 - 4$
64. $14x^4 - 2x^3 + 10x + 6$
65. $2p^4 + 7p^2 - 4p$
66. $-3x^4 + 8x^3 - 9x^2 + 7x$
67. $5v^4 + v^3 + v + 3$
68. $4p^3 + 9p + 12$
69. $3x^4 + 9x$
70. $2x^3 - 13x^2 - 5x + 7$
71. $15n^4 + 14n^3 - 11$
72. $-4v^3 + 4v^2 + 13v$
73. $3v^3 + 4v^2 - 7v$
74. $4n^3 - 11n + 4$
75. $11v^3 - 2v^2 + v - 3$
76. $-3n^3 - 5n^2 + 10n - 7$
77. $4x^4 + 10x^3 - x - 5$
78. $15x^4 + x^2 - 7x$
79. $3x^4 - 7x^2 - x$
80. $5n^4 + 3n^3 - 3n$
81. $-4p^4 - 2p^3 - p - 4$
82. $7v^4 - 5v - 9$
83. $-14p^4 + 4p^3 + 11p^2 - 7$
84. $7n^4 - 5n^3 + n + 1$
85. $3v^3 - v^2 + 6$
86. $7x^2 + 5x + 11$
87. $n^2 + 6n$
88. $-7a^4 + 10a^3 + 6a + 2$

Page 179: Polynomials: Multiplication

1. $10x^2 + 6xy - 28y^2$
2. $5a^2 - 15ab + 10b^2$
3. $7x^2 - 40xy - 12y^2$
4. $32a^2 - 32ab + 8b^2$
5. $8x^2 - 47xy + 35y^2$
6. $4u^2 + 16uv + 12v^2$
7. $25x^2 + 15xy - 4y^2$
8. $3a^2 - 27ab + 42b^2$
9. $35a^2 - 77ab + 42b^2$
10. $42x^2 - 63xy + 21y^2$
11. $28x^2 + 39xy + 8y^2$
12. $6m^2 + 53mn + 40n^2$
13. $14a^2 + 48ab + 18b^2$
14. $48x^2 + 10xy - 3y^2$
15. $12x^2 + 12xy - 9y^2$
16. $16a^2 + 40ab + 16b^2$
17. $4x^2 - 19xy - 30y^2$
18. $10a^2 - 11ab - 35b^2$
19. $6a^2 + 11ab + 3b^2$
20. $35x^2 - 51xy + 18y^2$
21. $2x^2 - 8y^2$
22. $30a^2 - 9ab - 12b^2$
23. $40x^2 - 70xy + 30y^2$
24. $40m^2 - 5mn - 35n^2$
25. $2u^2 + 2uv - 4v^2$
26. $30x^2 + 27xy + 6y^2$
27. $15x^2 + 56xy + 49y^2$
28. $16x^2 - 70xy + 24y^2$
29. $24x^2 - 20xy - 16y^2$
30. $15x^2 + 8xy - 12y^2$
31. $20u^3 - 11u^2v - 67uv^2 - 30v^3$
32. $3x^3 + 19x^2y + 4xy^2 - 12y^3$
33. $49a^3 - 63a^2b + 15ab^2 - 8b^3$
34. $36a^3 - 72a^2b + 74ab^2 - 28b^3$
35. $42u^3 - 32u^2v - 36uv^2 + 14v^3$
36. $4x^3 - 2xy^2 - 2y^3$
37. $35u^3 + 2u^2v + 9uv^2 + 2v^3$
38. $24x^3 + 43x^2y - 8xy^2 - 42y^3$
39. $m^3 - m^2n - 4mn^2 - 32n^3$
40. $4a^3 + 38a^2b + 36ab^2 - 18b^3$
41. $16x^3 - 20x^2y + 24xy^2 + 36y^3$
42. $30x^3 + 18x^2y - 13xy^2 + 56y^3$
43. $40m^3 + 17m^2n - 10mn^2 + n^3$
44. $5x^3 - 41x^2y + 17xy^2 + 30y^3$
45. $32x^3 - 24x^2y + 12xy^2 - 40y^3$
46. $42x^3 - 48x^2y + 36xy^2 - 30y^3$
47. $6u^3 - 31u^2v + 50uv^2 - 25v^3$
48. $21a^3 - 14a^2b + 5ab^2 + 4b^3$
49. $49x^3 - 49x^2y + 61xy^2 - 21y^3$
50. $12x^3 + 25x^2y + 16xy^2 + 3y^3$
51. $24m^3 + 2m^2n - 8mn^2 - 2n^3$
52. $8x^3 - 26x^2y + 8xy^2 - 6y^3$
53. $7x^3 + 22x^2y + 18xy^2 + 4y^3$
54. $35m^3 - 44m^2n - 23mn^2 + 14n^3$
55. $20x^3 - 5x^2y - 25xy^2 + 10y^3$
56. $10x^3 - x^2y - 13xy^2 - 12y^3$
57. $2x^3 - 7x^2y - 20xy^2 - 8y^3$
58. $20a^3 - 42a^2b + 22ab^2 - 6b^3$
59. $42a^3 + 78a^2b - 13ab^2 - 42b^3$
60. $16x^3 + 16x^2y - 16xy^2 - 6y^3$
61. $56x^4 + 96x^3y + 5x^2y^2 - 41xy^3 - 21y^4$
62. $24x^4 - 6x^3y - 88x^2y^2 - 42xy^3 + 16y^4$
63. $24a^4 + 58a^3b + 67a^2b^2 + 47ab^3 + 14b^4$
64. $6x^4 - 35x^3y + 51x^2y^2 + 14xy^3 - 48y^4$
65. $42u^4 - 13u^3v - 57u^2v^2 - 28uv^3 - 4v^4$
66. $6u^4 + 8u^3v + 11u^2v^2 + 25uv^3 + 25v^4$
67. $21a^4 - 35a^3b - 100a^2b^2 - 88ab^3 - 32b^4$
68. $14m^4 + 9m^3n - 17m^2n^2 - 7mn^3 + n^4$

69. $35m^4 + 8m^3n - 73m^2n^2 + 12mn^3 + 18n^4$

70. $24x^4 - 16x^3y - 63x^2y^2 + 35xy^3 + 25y^4$

71. $25u^4 - 5u^3v - 40u^2v^2 - 76uv^3 - 48v^4$

72. $4u^4 - 18u^3v - 2u^2v^2 - 2uv^3 - 6v^4$

73. $12x^4 + 11x^2y^2 - 23xy^3 - 40y^4$

74. $12x^4 + 46x^3y - 28x^2y^2 - 30xy^3 + 8y^4$

75. $6x^4 - 38x^3y - 48x^2y^2 + 2xy^3 + 6y^4$

76. $36x^4 - 24x^3y + 7x^2y^2 - 16xy^3 - 3y^4$

77. $3x^4 - 19x^3y + 3x^2y^2 - 16xy^3 - 6y^4$

78. $15x^4 + 46x^2y^2 - 19xy^3 + 56y^4$

79. $12u^4 - 37u^3v + 35u^2v^2 - 21uv^3 - 49v^4$

80. $21x^4 + 29x^3y + 23x^2y^2 - 27xy^3 - 18y^4$

81. $6x^4 - 25x^3y - 32x^2y^2 - 17xy^3 - 42y^4$

82. $8a^4 - 6a^2b^2 - 18ab^3 - 10b^4$

83. $5a^4 - 27a^3b - 19ab^3 - 15b^4$

84. $8m^4 - 10m^3n + m^2n^2 - 5mn^3 + 2n^4$

85. $30x^4 + 26x^3y + 17x^2y^2 + 44xy^3 - 7y^4$

86. $56m^4 - 14m^3n - 154m^2n^2 + 14mn^3 + 56n^4$

87. $2x^4 - 10x^3y + 9x^2y^2 + 4xy^3 - 5y^4$

88. $64x^4 - 72x^3y + 80x^2y^2 - 58xy^3 + 14y^4$

Page 192: Quadratic Equations

1. (-3.269, 1.469)
2. (-4, 3)
3. (5, -4.6)
4. (1.24, -5.24)
5. (3, 2)
6. (-5.5, 5.5)
7. (-0.628, -6.372)
8. (1.361, -2.694)
9. (2, 0.25)
10. (4, -6.75)
11. (2.291, -2.291)
12. (3.2, -3)
13. (-1.307, 0.085)
14. (3.308, -1.058)
15. (0.392, -1.392)
16. (-8, -3)
17. (-0.849, 1.766)
18. (1.313, -1.741)
19. (3, -3.75)
20. (1.69, -1.69)
21. No real solution.
22. (-1, 1)
23. (-15, 5)
24. (0.837, -0.837)
25. (1.913, 0.087)
26. No real solution.
27. (0.952, -2.452)
28. (2.253, -0.824)
29. (-5, 5)
30. (0.904, -0.737)
31. (-2, 2)
32. (-2, 0.6)
33. No real solution.
34. (3, -4)
35. (2, -2)
36. (-6, 6)
37. (1.5, -2.5)
38. (7, -4.25)
39. (1.861, -1.194)
40. (8, -8)
41. (-2.23, 0.897)
42. (-4, 4)
43. (9.772, 1.228)
44. No real solution.
45. No real solution.
46. (-3, 3)
47. (4, -4)
48. (-0.359, 8.359)
49. (1.173, -1.173)
50. (5, -5.5)
51. (-2.866, 1.466)
52. (-0.782, 0.532)
53. (-4.309, 0.309)
54. (9, -9)
55. (0.333, -1.5)
56. (6, -5)
57. (2, -2.5)
58. (4.766, 0.734)
59. (-0.87, 2.299)
60. (0.926, -0.926)
61. (1)
62. (1.564, -1.439)
63. (1, -0.4)
64. No real solution.
65. (-3.333, 2)
66. (-0.544, 1.378)
67. (1, -1)
68. (1.565, -1.065)
69. (-0.667, -2)
70. No real solution.
71. (2.168, -0.968)
72. (4.123, -4.123)
73. No real solution.
74. (6, -6)
75. (1.42, -3.17)
76. (-3.414, -0.586)
77. No real solution.
78. (-6, 6)
79. (2.325, -1.075)
80. (2, -3.667)
81. (-17, 7)
82. (-2.186, 0.686)
83. (-2.828, 2.828)
84. (-5, 5)
85. (-1)
86. (-6, 1.5)
87. No real solution.

88. (0.255, -1.683) 91. (-1.095, 1.095) 94. (2.38, -2.38)
89. (-1.747, 1.947) 92. (4, -4) 95. (-8, 8)
90. (9.09, -2.09) 93. (1.368, -0.94) 96. (0.956, -1.831)

Page 204: Exponents

1. 4,096
2. 1/36
3. 2,401
4. 1/25
5. 324
6. 1/16
7. 160,000
8. 1/196
9. 10,000
10. 1/5832
11. 49
12. 343
13. 144
14. 1
15. 1/729
16. 1/4096
17. 1/343
18. 1/1000
19. 125
20. 50,625
21. 121
22. 1/256
23. 1/6859
24. 1/125
25. 6,859
26. 27
27. 196
28. 1/121
29. 1/3375
30. 1/1728
31. 100
32. 1/144
33. 1/361
34. 169
35. 20,736
36. 64
37. 256
38. 5,832
39. 1/324
40. 1/64
41. 1/400
42. 8
43. 1
44. 1
45. 9
46. 3,375
47. 28,561
48. 4
49. 289
50. 1
51. 1/49
52. 4,096
53. 1/8
54. 1/169
55. 1/512
56. 1/27
57. 1/8000
58. 2,197
59. 16
60. 400
61. 64
62. 1/4913
63. 1,000
64. 81
65. 8,000
66. 130,321
67. 65,536
68. 1/216
69. 1/2197
70. 1/100
71. 36
72. 1/64
73. 361
74. 1
75. 83,521
76. 1,728
77. 1/9
78. 729
79. 1,296
80. 1/289
81. 225
82. 256
83. 81
84. 216

Page 211: Scientific Notations

1. 2.41×10^5
2. 60,000
3. 3,300
4. 5.6×10^4

5. 87,000

6. 8.7×10^1

7. 150

8. 2,500

9. 270,000

10. 1,938,000

11. 1.1×10^3

12. 5.8×10^1

13. 2.274×10^6

14. 3,000,000

15. 77

16. 5.8×10^5

17. 8.9×10^1

18. 760

19. 340

20. 7.9×10^5

21. 4.6×10^3

22. 2.4×10^3

23. 48

24. 2.3×10^4

25. 3.9×10^3

26. 350,000

27. 1.22×10^6

28. 910

29. 2.5×10^5

30. 9.5×10^6

31. 2.67×10^6

32. 6.4×10^4

33. 7.8×10^2

34. 6.6×10^5

35. 4,489,000

36. 7,800

37. 5.5×10^4

38. 90,000

39. 1.8×10^5

40. 6,183,000

41. 2.8×10^2

42. 73

43. 9,000

44. 5.5×10^1

45. 2.53×10^6

46. 5×10^4

47. 4,000

48. 4.46×10^6

49. 430

50. 8.2×10^4

51. 3×10^2

52. 52,000

53. 201,000

54. 5.56×10^5

55. 7.6×10^3

56. 5,000,000

57. 44,000

58. 760,000

59. 710

60. 3,100

61. 9.17×10^6

62. 7,400,000

63. 8,500

64. 3.3×10^4

65. 4,128,000

66. 1.2×10^6

67. 1.8×10^3

68. 5.54×10^5

69. 1.9×10^5

70. 4.6×10^1

71. 2,301,000

72. 1.2×10^1

73. 6,307,000

74. 2×10^5

75. 41,000

76. 5.4×10^4

77. 7,830,000

78. 7.4×10^1

79. 5.6×10^1

80. 8.9×10^3

81. 9.2×10^1

82. 7,000,000

83. 6.6×10^1

84. 4×10^6